The Rise and Fall of SPLM/SPLA Leadership

The Rise and Fall of SPLM/SPLA Leadership

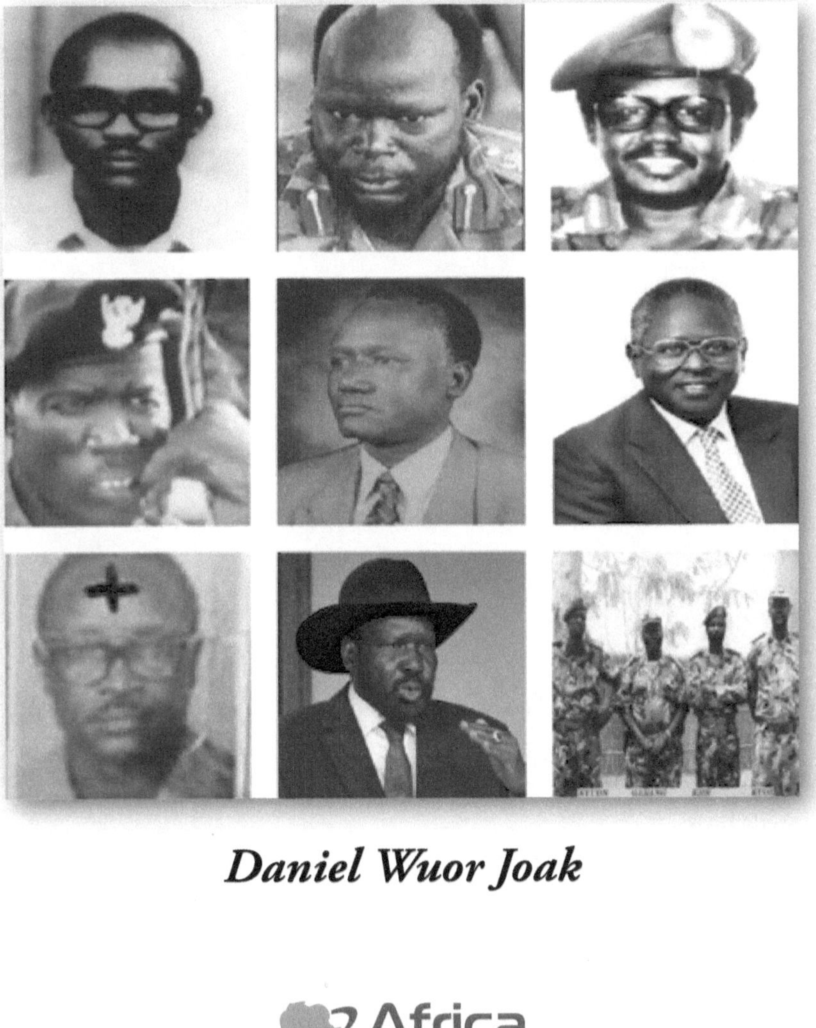

Daniel Wuor Joak

Copyright © 2015 Daniel Wuor Joak
All rights reserved.

ISBN 978-0-6482591-5-2
Africa World Books
Library of Congress Control Number: 2015919224
CreateSpace Independent Publishing Platform
North Charleston, South Carolina

Author: Daniel Wuor Joak

THE HONORABLE DANIEL WUOR JOAK is a highly influential politician in South Sudanese politics. *The Rise and Fall of SPLM/SPLA Leadership* examines South Sudan in the wider context of Sudanese history. Hon. Daniel shows that the South Sudanese have not only shaped their own destiny but have also played a people central role in a number of reforms in Sudan. In doing so, the book encourages readers to reconsider many misrepresented facts about some leaders of South Sudan within the context of the liberation struggle and independent South Sudan. It also explores many issues, controversies, and debates about the roles of some revolutionary leaders of South Sudan in relation to the secession of South Sudan from the Sudan. *The Rise and Fall of SPLM/SPLA Leadership* offers several insights that other South Sudanese books do not: a South Sudan historical perspective, lively and descriptive narratives of key leaders of South Sudan revolutions, and special attention to the debates and issues that make South Sudan history relevant to contemporary South Sudanese. It is an educational document relevant to all ages and all sociopolitical, social, and economic levels, not only in South Sudan, but also worldwide. I consider it to be a general book on Sudan. Though it is a challenge condensing the whole of Sudanese history and its actors into one container, given the diversity of the country, the multiplicity of peoples and regions, and the tribal rivalries, Hon. Daniel has done an excellent job in his research, so I endorse this book with no reservation

John Chuol Kuek, PhD, MFTI
Marriage and Family Therapist Intern
La Maestra Community Health Centers

It is my sincerest compliments to Hon. Daniel Wuor Joak on writing an extraordinary book on historical significances of social, political, and economic problems of South Sudan. *The Rise and Fall of SPLM/SPLA Leadership* tells the historical facts of how a man of peace was forced into a tragic civil war at a very young age and witnessed painful events that have consumed the country for a number of years. It is a remarkable story, compelling and descriptively written from the historical background of a knowledgeable man who has overcome difficulties but strives to establish peace of mind to support his oppressed people throughout their national struggles for peace, justice, accountability, and independence. It is an important and rich story to be shared with a wider audience to recognize the contributions of founding fathers and mothers of South Sudan.

Gatluak Ter Thach, PhD
President/ CEO of Nashville International Center for Empowerment

Dedication

This book is explicitly dedicated to the Honorable Samuel Gai Tut, the leader of the South Sudan Liberation Movement Anya Nya II. The late Honorable Samuel Gai Tut was born in the 1940s, at Kurmayom village, Waat Payam, Nyirol county, in south Sudan. He began primary school at Wanglel and later attended Atar Intermediate School in Jonglei state. In 1961 the late Samuel Gai entered Rumbek Secondary School, where he completed first and second year. In 1963, before beginning his third year at Rumbek Secondary School, Samuel Gai quit school and joined the South Sudan Liberation Movement (SSLM), better known as Anya Nya. While in the Anya Nya movement, he rose to the rank of commander and conducted most of his operations, like other Anya Nya field commanders, in the Upper Nile province of present-day South Sudan.

Acknowledgments

I WOULD LIKE TO EXPRESS my profound gratitude and appreciation to all those who have contributed to making my dream of writing a book a reality. Words are not enough to express my thankfulness for the enormous help each of you have accorded me during the editing stage and the kind words of encouragement you have all offered. I would like to thank Ms. Margaret Akulia of Millennium Global Associated Services for her tireless efforts in editing the manuscript from page to page and for her unreserved encouragement to me to publish this book as soon as possible. I would sincerely like to thank Dr. John Chuol Kuek and Dr. Gatluak Ter Thach for helping me in the selection process and for helping with financial contributions enabling me to publish this book. Without your combined efforts, this book would never have found its way to the web and to so many people who know little about the Sudan and South Sudan conflicts. My special thanks go to Sammy Arap Korir for having assisted me during my early days in the 1990s, when I was pursuing my political activism in Norway for advice and connections. My appreciation also goes to my younger brothers Gatkuoth Joak and Mabek Nyang Deng for their immense financial contributions to the publication of this book.

I would, however, like to especially thank my beloved son, Deng Wuor Joak, and the rest of my family who supported and encouraged me in spite of all the time I was away from them. It was a long and difficult journey for them, as I was always away and spent most of my time participating in the cause of the South Sudan's struggle while leaving them behind in Norway for about thirteen years. My thanks also go to my late father, John Jock *(Joak)*

Koang Deng, for encouraging me right from the inception of the SPLM/SPLA in 1983 to join the South Sudan liberation movement, as he was also a veteran Anya Nya freedom fighter who was involved in the struggle from 1963 to 1972 along with Samuel Gai Tut and several others. His rich knowledge about the history of South Sudan motivated me to write this book. Furthermore, a significant financial contribution by my South Sudanese loving brothers and sisters to publish this book will not go unnoticed. These caring siblings are Dr. George Imuro, William Pay Tuoy-Giel, Gatbel Nyak Chamjock, Kueth Yul Dieu, Nyakade Tot Rualmim, Nyakuiy Ruach Chan, Dr. Isaac Kueth Gang, John Kun Lam, Koang Bakual Chol, Ustaz Yahannes Jock Dup, John Koang Tut, Ustaz Gai Wuol and Samuel Mayian Pan.

I want to thank Colonel William Deng Monga, Moses Malek Chol, Bol Kiir Diew, Duoth Khon, William Reath Gai, Stephen Duol Chol, Paulino Matip Nhial, Hoth Guor Luak, Chuol Wan Luot, Goot Leer, and several Anya Nya II veterans for narrating to me fully the root causes of the conflict between the SPLM/SPLA and Anya Nya II movement from 1983 to 1988.

I also want to thank Professor Gabriel Giet Jal of Kenyatta University, Professor Lual Chany Chol of Juba University, Dr. John Gai Yoh of the University of South Africa, and Dr. James Mabor Gatkuoth and Professor Sharon Hutchison of Wisconsin State University for their immense contribution in proofreading the manuscript from the preliminary stage. I want to thank Honorable Bol Gatkuoth Kol, Dr. John Yien Tut, Rev. James Duol Kwek, ACHA staff, and several others for their unwavering words of encouragement during the writing of this book.

Last but not least, I thank many other people too numerous to list and beg for forgiveness from the ones who have not been with me over the years and whose names I have failed to mention.

Contents

Acknowledgments ... ix
Premise ... 1
Liberation Struggle Ignited in Torit on August 18, 1955 ... 7
Sudan's Independence ... 17
The Formal Launching of Anya Nya in 1963 and a Split in 1964 ... 23
The Fall of General Abboud's Government in October 1964 ... 27
The Round Table Conference of March 1965 ... 30
The Addis Ababa Agreement of 1972 ... 34
Formation of The Anya Nya II Movement ... 41
The Beginning of the Fall of President Nimeiri ... 47
The Formation of the SPLA and Its Hostility Toward Anya Nya II ... 55
SPLA Military Operations and Continuing Hostilities ... 60
The Fall of Nimeiri, More Hostilities, and an Effort For Peace ... 66
SPLA and Anya Nya II Reunification in a Shaky Alliance ... 72
Peace Initiatives and the Church ... 75
Progress and Sabotage Within the SPLM/SPLA ... 78
Breeding Tribal Tension in Refugee Camps and Mengistu's Fall ... 80
SPLM/SPLA Splits in August 1991 ... 82
More Peace Initiatives and Continuing Hostilities ... 95
Nuer Peace Initiatives ... 98
Other Activities, Peace Initiatives, and the Death of Joseph Oduho ... 100
The SPLA/NDA Asmara Declaration of June 12, 1995, and Another Nuer Peace Initiative ... 104

More Peace Initiatives and Attempts to Oust Riek Machar From The SSIM/A Leadership And Other Leadership Roles········106
The Redefection of Dr. Riek Machar To the Southern Sudan Bush·····111
The South-South Peace Initiative, The Role of the Church, and Peace Prospects in the Sudan········113
The African Centre For Human Advocacy (ACHA)········122
A Narrative of Human Rights Violations in the Sudan From 1821······124
Sudan's Relations With Its Neighboring Countries········128
The Role of International NGOs in the Sudan········132
The Civil Wars in Darfur and Eastern Sudan········136
The Comprehensive Peace Agreement (CPA)········139
The Inauguration of Dr. John Garang········145
The Death of Dr. John Garang and Ascension of General Salva Kiir····146
Formation of Goss and Its Subsequent Bad Governance········150
Institutionalized Corruption in South Sudan········152
Independence of South Sudan········161
SPLM Internal Crisis········165
The Defection of the SPLA Forces in Greater Upper Nile········180
Conclusion········191
Appendix I: Participants in Addis Ababa Peace Talks of 1972········201
Appendix II: List of SPLM/SPLA Political Detainees and Those Executed········203
Appendix III: List of SSDF Commanders That Remained With SAF and Later Rejoined the SPLA········205
Appendix IV: Press Statement Made by Dr. Riek Machar on December 6, 2013········207
Glossary········211
A Select Bibliography········231
About the Author········233

Premise

THE PEOPLE OF SOUTH SUDAN suffered from wars for quite a long time before they gained independence on July 9, 2011. The first Sudanese civil war, which started on August 18, 1955, and ended on February 27, 1972, with the signing of the first Addis Ababa Peace Agreement, cost more than a million lives. But the war that began with the formation of Anya Nya II on March 5, 1975, and continued with the inception of the SPLM/SPLA in July 1983—both of which were South Sudanese liberation movements—caused enormous and incomparable damage in terms of human and material losses. During this second liberation war, which lasted for thirty years, about three million lives were lost. Despite popularly held beliefs, the thirty-year war did not start with Colonel John Garang and his associates as some historians and the leadership of the SPLM/SPLA have claimed. It started seven years before the SPLM/SPLA came into existence in 1983, and many more lives were lost as well.

The few South Sudanese who dedicated their lives to the cause of liberation during that time deserve a million congratulations and sincere appreciation. Places like Bonga Training Centre and Bilpam were not created by the SPLA in 1983, as widely believed, but by Anya Nya II beginning in 1975, when the second liberation struggle was launched.

The later history of the South Sudan liberation struggles was entirely dominated by the SPLA simply because its leadership openly stole the show from the real founders of the liberation struggle that led to the independence of South Sudan and distorted the history of South Sudan for their self-gains. Most of the atrocities committed during the war waged on the government of Sudan by the SPLA were directed against southern separatists who wanted an independent South Sudan and vehemently rejected the objectives of the SPLA, which were associated with maintaining a united Sudan. This resulted in the violent death, at the hands of the SPLA, of prominent South Sudanese politicians and student activists who joined the movement in good faith to liberate their oppressed people by bringing about an independent South Sudan. The title of this book—*The Rise and Fall of SPLM/SPLA Leadership*—basically refers to the old SPLM/SPLA leadership, or, most importantly, the nine founding members of the SPLM/SPLA, many of whom were murdered by their colleagues in the SPLM/SPLA in cold blood for their fight for an independent South Sudan instead of a united Sudan. The names of the founding members of the SPLM/SPLA are as follows:

1. Akuot Atem de Mayen
2. Samuel Gai Tut
3. Colonel John Garang de Mabior
4. Major Kerubino Kuanyin Bol
5. Major William Nyuon Bany
6. Captain Salva Kiir Mayardit
7. Joseph Oduho
8. Martin Majier Gai
9. William Chuol Deng

Indeed, many of the nine founding members of the SPLM/SPLA were murdered or died in tragic accidents; this is what I refer to as the fall of the SPLM/SPLA leadership. I have no ill intentions toward any of the nine founding members of the SPLM/SPLA, whether alive or dead, but I am furious about many of their misdeeds, which actually derailed the progress of the South Sudan struggle for independence and created a strong hatred among our people in general, which will take a long time to conciliate.

This book series should be taken as a reminder of the shortcomings of our previous leaders who embarked on creating disharmony in our struggle from the onset, which eventually divided our people along tribal lines. Incorrect policies and social injustices within our movement intentionally deprived large numbers of southern Sudanese communities of opportunities to participate in the liberation war that eventually led to the independence of South Sudan. Minority communities such as the Mundari, Acholi, Madi, Murle, Fertit, Taposa, Didinga, Buya, and many others would have had no good reasons to side with the enemy from the initial stage of the struggle if the movement had treated them fairly. The case of the Nuer, the second largest tribe in South Sudan, is elaborated upon in this book

The enemy still has a strong ambition to reconquer the Republic of South Sudan if we fail to manage our own affairs responsibly. That is the reason why issues that have damaged the SPLM/SPLA and by extension the liberation struggles for the independence of South Sudan right from their inception need to be understood and resolved to prevent South Sudan from reverting back to an oppressed southern Sudan. This book series aims to do just that, as all the sixty-four nationalities in the Republic of South Sudan are equally important and should be treated fairly with all the respect they deserve as citizens of the South Sudan nation.

During the Regional Government of 1973, representatives from small tribes were respectably included as ministers in both the governments of Abel Alier and that of General Joseph Lagu. For example, Dr. Pacisico Lado Lolik and his colleague Simon Mori Dedimo were appointed ministers of health and social welfare and of culture and information, respectively, under General Lagu. Dr. Lolik hailed from one of the smallest tribes in the south—the Lokoya—while Simon Mori Dedimo came from the Anyuak tribe. During Abel Alier's government, he appointed Oliver Batali, who hailed from the smallest tribe in the South—the Makaraka—as a minister in his cabinet.

Most of the minority communities are not represented in our government today despite the fact that many of them have highly educated and qualified personalities. To make the unity of South Sudan attractive, each community must be reflected in our setup with great confidence, to show that they are truly part of the country. Things should not be manipulated continually by the majority at the expense of the minority in our newly born nation. Grooming only one community to stay at the top of the system, or appointing weak and irresponsible characters who cannot deliver the services desired by the people, actually encourages corruption.

Billions of dollars have been squandered and hidden in foreign banks, and nobody is ready to retrieve those amounts or apprehend the culprits and try them in courts of law. Our economy is completely in ruins either because our government did not have a sound financial-management policy to manage our resources diligently or because the wrong people were unwittingly put in the right places.

With respect to human rights violations, it is a high time all governments in South Sudan stop condoning the infringement of rights; they must prosecute perpetrators to the fullest extent, because allowing them to go free not only gives our country a bad image at home and abroad but also defeats the purpose of the liberation struggles that cost so many lives. The government must thoroughly deal with people who are still committing human rights violations and take responsibility for its own role in violating the human rights of South Sudanese citizens and foreigners alike.

It was a rare and honorable move that the former vice president of the Republic of South Sudan, Dr. Riek Machar, took by coming out publicly and apologizing to the Bor community for atrocities committed by his SPLA Nasir Faction during the SPLA split of 1991, which is elaborated upon in this book series. Although he did not specifically order his soldiers to kill the civilians, he took the responsibility as a leader. The SPLM/SPLA leadership must also apologize to the people of South Sudan, especially the communities they sadly humiliated and annihilated during the war they waged against the government of Sudan, particularly the Murle, Mundari, Gajaak Nuer, Lou Nuer and Gawar Nuer, Taposa, Didinga, Buya, Fertit, Anyuak, Acholi, Madi, and Latuka. They should also apologize to the relatives of South Sudanese nationalists the SPLM/SPLA leadership liquidated privately and publicly for voicing their concerns for the liberation of South Sudan instead of the so-called "United New Sudan," which was the slogan of the SPLM/SPLA.

South Sudan needs leaders who will immediately accept any mistakes made and atrocities perpetrated by their followers in the past or the present, as the former vice president of the Republic of South Sudan Dr. Riek Machar did. The independence of South Sudan from Sudan, which occurred on July 9, 2011, did not come out of the blue. All the Southern Sudanese participated in it, and the credit must be given to all of them whether they are majority or minority. Their equal participation from battlefields, negotiations, and the referendum should be acknowledged, as all those phases were necessary in bringing about an independent South Sudan nation. A South Africa–like Truth and Reconciliation Commission needs to be established in South Sudan under the direct supervision of the South Sudan Council of Churches, which is a neutral and respected body, to bring those who committed crimes during the war waged by the SPLA on the government of Sudan to trial. Our unity as a people is a must, and it should be embraced by all South Sudanese without any exception. Let us put South Sudan above our tribal affiliations by loving and building a country that respects and embraces all the sixty four tribes. In conclusion, the name SPLM/SPLA has, since its inception in July 1983, been the source of all conflicts among various communities, divisions, hatreds, discriminations, massacres, wanton killings, destructions of property, massive displacements of civil population, political blackmailings, distortions, manipulations, corruption, tribalism, nepotism, and other ills. And as long as this party, which is still associated with the name "Sudan," remains politically dominant in the Republic of South Sudan, our unity in diversity, peace, and harmony will never be enjoyed. The country may end up divided into mini-states or, in the worst-case scenario, become ungovernable—as with Somalia, Afghanistan, Iraq, Libya, and Syria—if the SPLM party and its military wing, SPLA, are not completely abolished and new parties created with new spirits that will embrace national aspirations of the people of South Sudan without any forms of discrimination and subordination among its sixtyfour nationalities.

Liberation Struggle Ignited in Torit on August 18, 1955

THE TORIT MUTINY, WHICH OCCURRED in southern Sudan on August 18, 1955, was the culmination of dissent that had been building in southern Sudan for over a century because of exploitation by a predominantly Arab northern Sudan throughout a number of colonial periods in the Sudan, namely the Turko-Egyptian period, the Mahdist era, and the Condominium under Anglo-Egyptian rule. The Arabs entered southern Sudan during the 1840s as soldiers and slave traders during the Turko-Egyptian period in the Sudan, which began in 1821 when Mohammed Ali Pasha, the ruler of Egypt, conquered the northern part of the Sudan and ushered in the Turko-Egyptian period in the country.

In 1839, he opened up regular trade routes to southern Sudan in search of ivory and slaves. This development accelerated the movement of northern Sudanese Arabs to southern Sudan in order to extend their commercial dealings in gum and cattle with Egyptian and European traders. Commercial dealings by northern Sudanese Arabs also included the export of ivory and black African slaves from southern Sudan.

After Mohammed Ali Pasha, the ruler of Egypt, opened up regular routes to southern Sudan as a conqueror of the northern part of Sudan, the expeditions to southern Sudan were directly financed from Egypt under its flag. At later stages Egypt increasingly involved the British as partners in administering the Sudan. The British sought an economic foothold in central Africa, and Sudan became a conduit. From 1863 to 1879 Britain's colonial strategy in Egypt was to encourage British mercenaries to serve under the Khedive

Ismael, Egypt's ruler. Consequently, Major General Charles Gordon, the British chief administrator of the southern region of the Sudan, was appointed as the overall governor general of the Sudan in 1877.

The Turko-Egyptian colonial period in the Sudan was followed by the Mahdia period, during which Muslims and northern Arab Sudanese, particularly the Mahdist Ansars, rejected the appointment of Major General Charles Gordon as British chief administrator of the Southern region of the Sudan. They did not want the British-Egyptian influence, particularly after the abolition of the slave trade in the Sudan by the British, who had championed abolition globally. General Gordon was also tasked with negotiating and implementing the British policy of separating the Sudan from Egypt, with the possibility of transferring the administration of southern Sudan to the British East Africa Federation, a move that the Mahdist Ansars strongly opposed. The plan failed to take off, but it did provoke the Mahdists to stage an uprising in Khartoum against the British-Egyptian rule in the Sudan.

The followers of Mohammed Ahmed the Mahdi, which literally means "savior" in Arabic, killed General Charles Gordon, along with many of his forces. Mohammed Ahmed then proceeded to establish a theocratic Islamic state that lasted for thirteen years. He advocated an Islamic state based on the Koran and proclaimed jihad (holy war) in defense of Islam in the Sudan. Throughout their thirteen-year reign in northern Sudan, the Ansars terrorized northern Sudan and took to raiding southern Sudanese communities for slaves and livestock despite the abolition of the slave trade. While the Mahdist state was still flourishing in northern Sudan under Mohammed Ahmed, who continued as the Mahdi of the time, French and Belgian troops had already penetrated deeply into the Sudan through the provinces of Equatoria and the Upper Nile. Their objective was to divide the administration of southern Sudan among themselves.

At the Battle of Omdurman, which occurred on September 2, 1898, the Anglo-Egyptian troops under Lord Kitchener defeated the Mahdists, who were now under the command of Khalifa Abdullah, the successor of the Mahdi known as Mohammed Ahmed the Savior. To prevent France and Belgium from making possible claims to the Sudan, as they had already encroached into southern Sudan, the British signed the Condominium Agreement with Egypt in 1899, which accorded Britain political domination over Sudan. Hence began the history of Anglo-Egyptian Sudan, which lasted until 1955, the year of the Torit Mutiny.

In January 1899 the Condominium Agreement between the British and Egypt restored Egyptian rule over Sudan. However, the rule was part of a joint authority exercised by both Britain and Egypt, and it designated the territory to the south as the Anglo-Egyptian Sudan. Although the agreement emphasized Egypt's indebtedness to Britain for its participation in the reconquest of Sudan from the Mahdist Ansars, the agreement failed to clarify the juridical relationship between the two countries. Furthermore, it did not provide a legal basis for the British to continue governing the territory on behalf of the Khedive, the ruler of Egypt at the time.

Article II of the Anglo-Egyptian Agreement vested the military and civil command in the Sudan in the governor general of Sudan and stipulated that he was to be appointed by Khedival Decree on the recommendation of Her Britannic Majesty's government. It also stipulated that he could be removed only by Khedival Decree with the consent of Her Britannic Majesty's government. In 1899 Sir Reginald Wingate succeeded Lord Kitchener as governor general of Sudan, and in each province, the British governor, known as *mudir* in Arabic, was aided by two inspectors and several district commissioners.

At the onset, nearly all administrative personnel were British army officers affiliated with the Egyptian army. However, in 1901 civilian administrators started arriving in Sudan from Britain and formed the core of the Sudan Political Service. Egyptians filled middle-level posts while Sudanese acquired lower-level positions in small stages.

According to Oliver Batali Albino, the author of *The Sudan: A Southern Viewpoint*, the early years of the Anglo-Egyptian Condominium rule in Sudan were marked by the return of missionaries to southern Sudan. According to him, Roman Catholics entered the Shilluk areas in 1901, American Presbyterians went to the Sobat River in 1902 and Nasir in 1904, and the Church Missionary Society (CMS) went to Malek, Bor district, in 1905.

The governor general and provincial governors exercised great liberty in governing Sudan during the early years of the joint authority exercised by Britain and Egypt over Sudan, known as the Condominium Period. However, after 1910 an executive council, whose approval was required for all legislation and for budgetary matters, assisted the governor general. The governor general presided over this council, which included the inspector general; the civil, legal, and financial secretaries; the general officer commanding the troops, known as the kaid; and two to four other British officials appointed by the governor general.

After restoring order and the government's authority, the British dedicated themselves to creating a modern government in Sudan jointly administered by Britain and Egypt. Jurists adopted penal and criminal procedural codes similar to those in force in India, a colony of Britain at the time. Commissions established land tenure rules, and taxes on land remained the basic form of taxation.

It is important to note that there was little resistance to the Anglo-Egyptian condominium in the Sudan, and breaches of the peace only took the form of intertribal conflict, banditry, or revolts of brief duration. The biggest problem facing the condominium was undefined borders. However, a 1902 treaty with Ethiopia fixed the southeastern boundary with Sudan. Seven years later, an Anglo-Belgian treaty determined the status of the "Lado Enclave" in the south by establishing a border with the Belgian Congo (present-day Democratic Republic of the Congo).

Because of the Condominium Agreement between Britain and Egypt, France had to pull out from southern Sudan in 1899 and hand over its portion to British authorities. Based on an agreement of 1896 respecting the "Lado Enclave," the Belgians withdrew from the enclave in 1910 following the death of King Leopold of Belgium. The 1896 agreement had stipulated that Lado Enclave would be handed over to the Sudan government upon the death of King Leopold.

British policy in the Sudan in 1910 was to cut off southern Sudan from northern Sudanese influence. To accomplish that, Britain encouraged Christian missionaries to work in southern Sudan. They discouraged Arab traders from trading in southern Sudan and withdrew northern Sudanese Arab troops from southern Sudan. This plan was aimed at dividing the Sudan into two countries: the southern part was to be incorporated into a Federation of East Africa States as a buffer zone against the spread of Islam. To that effect, the British colonial authorities in 1920 introduced an "indirect rule," or "closed district ordinance" policy in southern Sudan that involved "native administration." This policy recognized and established, under British juridical authority, certain tribal chiefs and tribal courts. This policy actually confirmed the gap between southern Sudan and northern Sudan and widened the difference between the two parts of Sudan.

Although it was the richest part of the Sudan, southern Sudan was virtually neglected economically from developmental benefits. Meanwhile, northern Sudan enjoyed all the benefits meant for the whole country. The south relied educationally on the literacy system of missionaries aimed at teaching pupils to read the Bible.

Sudan was relatively quiet in the late 1920s and the 1930s, and during this period the Anglo-Egyptian colonial government continued favoring indirect rule, which continued to allow the British to govern through indigenous leaders. In northern Sudan, the traditional leaders were the village, tribal, and district shaykhs, and in southern Sudan the traditional leaders were the tribal chiefs.

Despite efforts to modernize Sudan during the Anglo-Egyptian Condominium and with the exception of efforts to suppress tribal warfare and the slave trade, southern Sudan's remote and undeveloped provinces of Equatoria, Bahr El Ghazal, and Upper Nile received little official attention until after World War I. The British justified this policy by claiming that southern Sudan was not ready for exposure to the modern world. To allow it to develop along indigenous lines, the British closed the region to outsiders. As a result, southern Sudan remained isolated. A few Arab merchants controlled the region's limited commercial activities while Arab bureaucrats administered whatever laws existed. Christian missionaries, who operated schools and medical clinics, provided limited social services in southern Sudan at the time.

The first Christian missionaries in southern Sudan were the Roman Catholic Verona Fathers, who built churches and schools throughout southern Sudan. Other Christian missionaries included Presbyterians from the United States and the Anglican Church Missionary Society of England. These Christian groups established mission schools to educate southern Sudanese, and the schools were eventually subsidized by the government. Because mission graduates usually succeeded in gaining posts in the provincial civil service, many northern Sudanese regarded them as tools of British imperialism. The few southern Sudanese who received higher training attended schools in British East Africa (present-day Kenya, Uganda, and Tanzania) rather than in Khartoum, an occurrence that continued to intensify the division between northern and southern Sudan.

British authorities treated the three southern provinces of Equatoria, Bahr El Ghazal, and Upper Nile as a separate region, and as the colonial administration amalgamated its southern position in the 1920s, it separated southern Sudan from the rest of Sudan for all practical purposes. During this period, "closed door" statutes continued to block northern Sudanese from entering or working in southern Sudan. These statutes strengthened the separate development policy for the two regions of the Sudan, and the British gradually substituted Arab administrators. They also dismissed Arab merchants and consequently cut southern Sudan's last economic contacts with northern Sudan. The colonial administration discouraged the spread of Islam, the practice of Arab customs, and the wearing of Arab dress, and at that time, the British made efforts to revitalize the African customs and tribal life that the slave trade in southern Sudan had disrupted.

In 1930 the colonial administration issued a directive stating that black Africans in the southern provinces of Equatoria, Bahr El Ghazal, and Upper Nile were to be considered a people distinct from northern Sudanese Muslims and that the region should be prepared for eventual integration with British East Africa (present-day Kenya, Uganda, and Tanzania).

From 1944 to 1948 there also existed an Advisory Council for the Northern Sudan whose functions were advice and consultation. This advisory council had eighteen members representing province councils, ten members nominated by the governor general, and two honorary members. The executive council retained legislative authority until 1948. However, a year earlier the British authorities had forced the unification of southern and northern Sudan at the Juba Conference of June 1947, which was convened purposely to inform the tribal chiefs that represented southern Sudan of the reversal of the 1930 policy. Recall that the policy stated that black Africans in the southern provinces of Equatoria, Bahr El Ghazal, and Upper Nile were to be considered a people distinct from northern Sudanese Muslims and that the region should be prepared for eventual integration with British East Africa.

The southern conferees at the Juba Conference of 1947 had been informed about the new decision to hand over the administration of southern Sudan to the new rulers, the Arabs in northern Sudan. A Sudan Legislative Assembly was formed by the British administration, which handpicked thirteen delegates from southern Sudan to represent southern Sudan in that assembly. This was the start of the self-determination process for Sudan's independence, but the southern Sudanese were effectively excluded from the decision-making process. Consequently, the fate of the southern Sudanese people was effectively handed to the northern Sudanese.

Following a July 1952 revolution in Egypt, the British speeded up the northern Sudanese demand for the country's independence. Accordingly, they drafted plans with the Umma Party of the Ansars for the formation of a transitional government. On February 12, 1953, the Egyptian government and the northern Sudanese sectarian political parties met without the southern Sudanese political groups and made the Cairo Agreement, which initiated the process of independence for Sudan.

In 1954, on the eve of independence—which occurred two years later on January 1, 1956—there were over eight hundred positions that the British colonial administration left for Sudanese to occupy. However, only four junior posts were allocated to southern Sudanese. The southern Sudanese people were dissatisfied with such an unfair allocation of positions, and they sensed this exercise as another type of discrimination and colonization of southern Sudan by northern Sudanese Arabs.

The Torit Mutiny on August 18, 1955, which led to the eventual formation of the Anya Nya movement, occurred a few months before Sudan declared its independence from Great Britain even though the immediate causes of the mutiny were attributed to a trial of a southern Sudanese member of the National Assembly and a telegram alleged to have falsely urged northern Sudanese administrators in the south to oppress southerners. The main cause of the uprising in Torit on August 18, 1955, was the total rejection by southern Sudanese in the Sudanese army under the British rule to incorporate southern part of Sudan into northern Sudan. Thus, the British colonial authority wanted the whole country to remain under northern Sudan Arab rule. Whereas this notion of forced unity between the two parts of Sudan was totally rejected by all southern Sudanese from all spectrums who viewed this imposed unity with great suspecion due to the past human rights violations during the Turko-Egyptian rule and that of the El Mahdists rule before the British fully conquered Sudan in 1898. However, the fews southern Sudanese politicians mostly the chiefs who were representing their constituencies at the national parliament in Khartoum before the declaration of Sudan's independence in 1956, had requested the British authority to let southern Sudan remain a separate entity under their protection or merge it with the British East Africa colonies of Kenya, Tanzania and Uganda and obtain its independence at a later date. But the British and northern Sudanese sectarian political parties of UMMA, NUP and National Charter Front <u>outrightly</u> rejected this motion raised by the southern Sudanese block to the British colonial authority and this later provoked the Torit uprising in 1955.

Exclusion by the northern Sudanese sectarian parties in independence discussions and rejection of their demand for a federal association with or secession from northern Sudan that they had made led to disappointment, and the explosive mutiny by members of the British-administered Sudan Defence Force Equatorial Corps in Torit on August 18, 1955.

Having entered the Sudan during the 1840s as soldiers and slave traders under the Turko-Egyptian period in the Sudan, the southern Sudanese considered the northern Sudanese Arabs and their rule over the whole of Sudan a history of economic exploitation, social degradation, and political subjugation. Moreover, the situation was exacerbated when the British handed over political power in the entire country of Sudan to the northern Sudanese. This resulted in the emergence of new social forces and a new political leadership that worked to create a unique sense of unity among the southern Sudanese people. The developments were what eventually provoked the Torit Mutiny on August 18, 1955.

Noting that the Arabs had accompanied British and Egyptian forces as traders, soldiers, police, and civil servants in the 1900s as the Anglo-Egyptian Condominium period in Sudan and Arab conquest of southern Sudan went through numerous phases, social reformers in southern Sudan had decided by the time of the Torit Mutiny that the status quo of political subjugation, consistent economic exploitation, and social degradation needed to be deposed or changed.

Northern Sudanese had continued to exploit the suffering southern Sudanese people and had gradually extended their political domain to southern Sudan until the British forcibly united the whole country under their leadership in 1947. The British handing over political power in Sudan to the northern Sudanese Arabs was an awakening that compelled southern Sudanese to come together for the mutual purpose of fighting for the rights of all the people of southern Sudan. The Torit Mutiny on August 18, 1955, would eventually lead to the formation of the Anya Nya movement and the independence of South Sudan after decades of relentless wars waged by southern Sudanese against the government of Sudan.

The Torit Mutiny was followed by similar mutinies in Juba, Yei, and Maridi and although these mutinies were suppressed, the survivors fled the towns and began an uncoordinated insurrection in the rural areas. These events would progress to the formal launching and establishment of the Anya Nya guerrilla movement in the south in the early 1960s. It was a movement that aimed to establish an independent South Sudan.

MAP OF THE REPUBLIC OF SUDAN IN 1956

Sudan's Independence

Sudan's flag being raised at the independence ceremony on January 1, 1956, by Prime Minister Ismail El Azhari in the presence of opposition leader Mohamed Ahmed Mahjoub

THE FIFTY-SIX YEARS OF ANGLO-EGYPTIAN rule in the Sudan came to an end when Sudan declared its independence on January 1, 1956. As a result,

Anglo-Egyptian Sudan became the Independent Republic of the Sudan. On December 19, 1955, the Sudanese parliament, under Ismail al-Azhari had unanimously adopted a declaration of independence that became effective on January 1, 1956. At independence, Mr. Ismail El Azhari was elected prime minister of the newly proclaimed Sudan, having served in that role from 1954.

Although it achieved independence without conflict, Sudan inherited many problems from the Anglo-Egyptian Condominium. One notable issue was the fact that southern Sudanese begrudged the replacement of British administrators in southern Sudan with northern Sudanese.

Although Sudanese nationalism had developed by the time Sudan attained independence from the British, it was an Arab and Muslim phenomenon with minimal to no involvement by southern Sudanese. Consequently, such nationalism had its support base in northern Sudan and not the whole country. Sudanese nationalists opposed the indirect rule that had been introduced during the Anglo-Egyptian Condominium and advocated for a centralized national government in Khartoum that would be responsible for both southern and northern Sudan. Sudanese nationalists at the time also perceived Britain's southern policy as artificially dividing Sudan and preventing its unification under an arabized and Islamic ruling class. Notwithstanding that, however, Sudan's first modern nationalist movement was led by a Muslim Dinka named Ali Abd al Latif. A former army officer, Ali Abd al Latif founded the United Tribes Society in 1921, which called for an independent Sudan in which power would be shared by tribal and religious leaders. Three years later, Ali Abd al Latif's movement reorganized as the White Flag League. However, he was arrested and subsequently exiled to Egypt following demonstrations organized by his nationalist movement in Khartoum. His arrest and exile triggered a mutiny by a Sudanese army battalion, but that insurrection was suppressed and temporarily halted the Sudanese nationalist movement based in northern Sudan.

In the 1930s, nationalism reemerged in Sudan, but nationalists and religious leaders differed on whether Sudan should be independent or part of a union with Egypt. Various parties surfaced and made a case for both positions. However, the moderates who favored Sudanese independence in cooperation with Britain emerged victorious, and, together with the Ansar, established the Umma Party. In 1942 the Graduates' General Conference, a quasi-nationalist movement formed by educated Sudanese, petitioned the government for self-determination after World War II. They demanded that self-determination be preceded by abolition of the "closed door" ordinances respecting southern Sudan, an end to the separate curriculum in southern Sudan, and an increase in the number of Sudanese in the civil service. A government-supervised transformation of indirect rule into a modernized system of local government was eventually implemented, and northern and southern Sudan were unified. The southern Sudanese were informed about the unification process at the Juba Conference of 1947.

During World War II, some British colonial officers questioned the economic and political viability of the southern provinces as separate from northern Sudan. Furthermore, Britain had also become more receptive to Arab criticism of the southern policy. In 1946 the Sudan Administrative Conference determined that Sudan should be administered as one country. Moreover, the conference delegates agreed to readmit northern administrators to southern posts, abolish the trade restrictions imposed under the "closed door" ordinances, and allow southerners to seek employment in northern Sudan. Khartoum also nullified the prohibition against Muslim proselytizing in southern Sudan and introduced Arabic in the south as the official administration language.

Some southern Sudan British colonial officials responded to the Sudan Administrative Conference by charging that northern Sudanese agitation had influenced the conferees and that no voice had been heard at the conference in support of retaining the separate development policy. These British officers argued that northern Sudanese domination of southern Sudan would result in a rebellion against the government by southern Sudanese. Khartoum therefore convened the conference at Juba, commonly known as the Juba Conference of 1947, to quiet the fears of southern Sudanese leaders and British officials in southern Sudan and to assure them that a postindependence government would safeguard the political and cultural rights of southern Sudanese.

Despite these promises, however, an increasing number of southern Sudanese expressed concern that northern Sudanese would overwhelm them. In particular, they took exception to the imposition of Arabic as the official language of government, which would deprive most of the few educated English-speaking southern Sudanese of the opportunity to enter public service. They also felt threatened by the replacement of trusted British District

Commissioners with northern Sudanese, whom they perceived as unsympathetic. After the government replaced several hundred British colonial officials with Sudanese, only four of whom were southern Sudanese, the southern elite abandoned any hope of attaining a peaceful, unified, and independent Sudan.

In 1948, despite objections by Egypt as a partner in the Anglo-Egyptian Condominium respecting Sudan, Britain approved a partially elected consultative Legislative Assembly representing both southern and northern Sudan. This body was to replace the Advisory Executive Council.

In 1952 leaders of the Umma-dominated Sudanese legislature negotiated the Self-Determination Agreement with Britain. The legislators then enacted a constitution that provided for a prime minister and Council of Ministers responsible to a bicameral parliament. The new Sudanese government would have responsibility in all areas except the military and foreign affairs, which remained in the British governor general's hands. Egypt, which demanded recognition of Egyptian sovereignty over Sudan, renounced the Anglo-Egyptian Condominium Agreement in protest and declared its reigning monarch, Faruk, king of Sudan. After taking control of power in Egypt and ousting the Faruk monarchy in late 1952, Colonel Muhammad Naguib broke the impasse on the problem of Egyptian sovereignty over Sudan. Egypt had previously linked discussions on Sudan's status to an agreement on the evacuation of British troops from the Suez Canal, but Colonel Naguib separated the two issues and accepted the right of Sudanese to self-determination. In February 1953, Britain and Egypt signed an Anglo-Egyptian agreement that allowed for a three-year transition period from Anglo-Egyptian Condominium rule to self-government in Sudan. During the transition phase, British and Egyptian troops would withdraw from Sudan. At the end of this period, the Sudanese would decide their future status in a referendum conducted under international supervision. This agreement successfully led to the independence of Sudan on January 1, 1956.

In spite of Sudan's independence on January 1, 1956, hostility from southern Sudanese toward predominantly Arab northern Sudanese had already emerged forcefully when southern Sudanese army units mutinied in Torit on August 18, 1955. Although the Torit Mutiny involved confrontation by only a few southern Sudanese soldiers who defied a transfer order to garrisons under northern Sudanese officers, it was the foundation for the drawn-out wars that eventually led to the independence of South Sudan. In Torit mutinous soldiers killed several hundred northern Sudanese, including government officials, army officers, and merchants. The government of Sudan quickly subdued the rebellious soldiers from the British-administered Sudan Defence Force Equatorial Corps and eventually executed seventy of them for subversion. However, this severe response failed to bring an end to the frustration that had already taken root and morphed into determination to found a Southern Sudan free of Arab oppression. As a result, some mutineers escaped to remote areas and began an organized resistance to the Arab-dominated government of Sudan.

On July 5, 1956, Sayed Abdallah Bey Khalil began serving as the second prime minister of Sudan, but his elected civilian government had to grapple with rising economic and political stagnation. This situation eventually provoked the army, led by General Ibrahim Abboud, to stage a military coup on November 17, 1958. However, many observers believed that the November 17, 1958, coup was indeed a prearranged move—a conspiracy by Prime Minister Abdalla Khalil to hand over the government of Sudan to the military. On the other hand, General Ibrahim Abboud's intention of seizing power was to end the rebellion in southern Sudan. It had built up since the Torit Mutiny on August 18, 1955 and taken deep roots. v

Military chief General Ibrahim Abboud ruled until a popular uprising in 1964. During his six-year rule of the Sudan, General Abboud's military regime waged a holy war (jihad) against Anya Nya freedom fighters who had persisted in their insurrection. They were led by the group of southern Sudanese officers within the colonial army in the Equatoria Corps who had staged the Torit Mutiny on August 18, 1955. General Abboud's policy was to forcibly establish Islamic institutions in southern Sudan in direct opposition to the original plan by the British, during the Anglo-Egyptian Condominium, to divide the Sudan into two countries. You will recall that the plan was for the southern part of Sudan to be incorporated into a Federation of East Africa States as a buffer zone against the spread of Islam through the "Indirect Rule," or "Closed District Ordinance," policy in southern Sudan that involved "Native Administration" in 1920.

In 1962 the government of Sudan enacted the Missionary Societies Act to regulate missionary activities. The act stipulated that no missionary society or any member of such a society could do missionary work in the Sudan outside the provisions of a permit granted by the council of ministers. However, such a permit could arbitrarily enforce any conditions the council of ministers deemed fit, including refusing to grant or renew a permit and rescinding one at its sole discretion. Such permits imposed limitations on space and outlawed a missionary society from doing "any missionary act toward any person or persons professing any religion or sect or belief thereof other than that specified in its license."

At that time, missionaries were not allowed to "practice any social activities except within the limits and in the manner laid down from time to time by regulations." The 1962 Missionary Law Act also stated that "No missionary society shall bring up in any religion or admit to any religious order, any person under the age of eighteen years without the consent of his lawful guardian." Furthermore, "No missionary society shall adopt, protect, or maintain an abandoned child without the consent of the Province Authority." The formation of clubs, establishment of societies, organization of social activities, collection of money, famine and flood relief, the holding of land, and the publication and distribution of papers, pamphlets, or books were subject to ministerial regulations.

In the process of General Abboud's determination to wage a holy Muslim war against predominantly Christian southern Sudanese, his regime committed enormous human rights abuses in southern Sudan. The Christian Sunday worship was banned throughout southern Sudan, and Friday was declared a holiday for both Muslims and Christians in the whole country. Security organs in southern Sudan were instructed to round up and force all male adults in the different towns of southern Sudan to attend Friday worship in mosques. Islamization and Arabization were strongly imposed on all non-Muslims, especially Christians. All the schools in southern Sudan were either closed down or moved to northern Sudan. All the mission schools were nationalized or closed down. The missionaries who worked in southern Sudan were expelled and denied entry visas into Sudan. Hundreds of thousands of civilians were restricted to concentration camps, and southern Sudan experienced a rigorous and repressive army occupation leading to intensified insurgency by the Anya-Nya revolutionary movement.

The Formal Launching of Anya Nya in 1963 and a Split in 1964

IN THE EARLY 1960S THE Sudan African National Union (SANU), the first southern Sudanese party, was formed in exile by students and junior administrators who fled to neighboring countries after the Torit Mutiny on August 18, 1955. The founders of SANU also organized a guerrilla army from the remnants of the 1955 Torit mutineers, and student recruits and called it Anya Nya, which means a poisonous snake in the Madi language. This movement became known as Anya Nya I, and a future regrouping in 1974 was named Anya Nya II. Having started its first military operations in the Equatoria province of southern Sudan in 1963, the Anya Nya guerrilla movement soon spread to the other two southern provinces of Upper Nile and Bahr El Ghazal. The main objective of the movement was to fight for the right of self-determination for the oppressed people of southern Sudan. That goal was intended to lead to the ultimate independence of southern Sudan. SANU, the first southern Sudanese party, was the political wing of the Anya Nya movement.

Anya Nya freedom fighters

From its inception, the Anya Nya guerrilla movement was a southern movement with individuals from all the corners of southern Sudan participating. For example, in early 1963, many students dropped out from different levels of education to form Anya Nya combat units in the eastern, central and northern Upper Nile province. Since this region was predominantly inhabited by the Nuer, Dinka, Shilluk, Anyuak, Maban, and Murle, such prominent figures as Paul Ruot Wichluoth, Paul Awel, Paul Adung, Paul Nyigore, Philip Pedak Lieth, Daniel Yiech Diew, Chuol Chagor, David Dak Gai, Nguot Diet, Samuel Gai Tut, David Koak Guok, Nyang Rundial, Mabil Ariak, Joseph Akon (Otew), Daniel Koat Duoth Lual (Matthews), and Daniel Choki became the movement's first leaders in the region. They were also joined by some policemen and prison warders who were already effectively trained. However, the Anya Nya freedom fighters in the Upper Nile province faced difficulties in acquiring adequate military hardware and in convincing the masses to rally behind them. The civilian population was reluctant to cooperate with (and rather skeptical about) the rebels in the early days of the Anya Nya movement for some of the following reasons:

1. The civilians were afraid of consistent government reprisals that often led to destruction and loss of their lives and property.
2. The suspicious government army constantly accused the civilians of collaborating with and harboring the guerrilla forces.
3. Lack of political consciousness made the civil population reject the presence of the rebels in their homesteads and villages.
4. The newly organized Anya Nya fighters had acute logistic problems, particularly the scarcity of military hardware with which to defend themselves and the civil population against regular raids by Sudanese government troops on their bases and civilian settlements.

Moreover, the Anya Nya forces operating in the areas bordering Ethiopia had communication and coordination problems with their comrades in other parts of southern Sudan. Because they needed to be seen as an effective force in order to be reckoned with, these forces equipped themselves militarily by bartering elephant tusks, oxen, and bulls for guns and ammunition from Ethiopian merchants who mainly comprised Oromo tribesmen. To acquire guns, others had to carry elephant tusks on foot from the Ethiopian border to the Congo, where they exchanged these commodities for modern rifles from the remnants of the Simba rebels of the Katanga region of Congo, who had fled to southern Sudan after the execution on January 17, 1961, of Patrice Lumumba, the founder of the Congolese National Movement and the first prime minister of Congo (Zaire) after its independence from Belgium in June 1960.

To gain the confidence of the local population in their areas, the Anya Nya undertook their first effective surprise attack against the Sudanese government forces stationed at Pochalla. They successfully overran that post as their initial military achievement in 1963. Between 1955 and 1963, the Anya Nya insurgency had been poorly armed and organized by the mutineers of August 18, 1955, who were a minimal threat to the outgoing Anglo-Egyptian colonial power or the newly formed Sudanese government. During that period, the movement was mostly characterized by guerrilla warfare. However, by 1963 the Anya Nya revolution had developed into a secessionist movement composed of the mutineers of August 1955 and southern students who felt compelled to join the guerrilla movement and form the Anya Nya guerrilla army. However, before the Anya Nya separatist movement could take off as a unified front, internal ethnic divisions arose. As a result, the movement was weakened. There was a split within the leadership of the Sudan African National Union (SANU), the political wing of the Anya Nya guerrilla movement, leading to a change in the name from SANU to South Sudan Liberation Movement (SSLM). Following the disagreement within the Anya Nya leadership, SANU continued under William Deng, and it moved inside Sudan in late 1964. It operated as a political party advocating for federation for southern Sudan.

The Fall of General Abboud's Government in October 1964

As GENERAL IBRAHIM ABBOUD'S GOVERNMENT continued its repressive policies toward southern Sudan beginning from the time he took over the government in a military coup on November 17, 1958, the Anya Nya movement intensified its insurgency. In the early 1960s the south Sudanese church leaders and the missionary societies working in southern Sudan suffered intensely from the repressive regime of General Abboud. From 1962 to 1964, General Abboud ordered the immediate closure of all missionary schools and mission centers. Abboud's regime nationalized some of the missionary schools, and all the missionaries that were operating in different parts of southern Sudan were expelled from the country. This policy, carried out during the implementation of the 1962 Missionary Law Act, was to deny the people of southern Sudan the opportunity provided by these missionaries in the field of education. You will recall that this 1962 act regulated and restricted missionary activities. The same act empowered the council of ministers, which was the body mandated to grant permits to refuse or repeal permits to missionary organizations without giving any explanation.

In March 1964 the government of Sudan expelled all foreign missionaries from southern Sudan, claiming that missionary organizations that had provided services to southern Sudanese in areas such as education had exceeded the limits of their missions. At that time the government of Sudan contended that the missionaries had exploited religion to communicate hatred and instill fear and hostility in the minds of southern Sudanese against their fellow countrymen in northern Sudan. The government further alleged that the missionaries had a premeditated plan to separate southern Sudan from northern Sudan, thus jeopardizing the integrity and unity of the country.

Following the expulsion of all expatriate missionaries from the Sudan from 1962 to 1964, the Abboud government began persecuting the indigenous clergymen on the pretext that they were Anya Nya collaborators. Many of them eventually escaped and went either to neighboring countries for their own safety or to the rebel-held areas in southern Sudan.

The intensity of the government's repressive policies eventually led students, political parties, trade unions, and other syndicated organizations in the north to demonstrate en masse, and they actually brought down General Ibrahim Abboud's regime on October 21, 1964.

The downfall of Abboud's government was attributed to the southern Sudan problem and with its demise, a nonpartisan interim government was immediately installed under Sirr Al-Khatim Al-Khalifa Al-Hassan, the former director of education in southern Sudan. However, before the interim government had lasted three months, it experienced a most brutal conflict on Sunday, December 6, 1964, which became known as the Black Sunday incident in Khartoum. A Sunday that had begun as a normal day of worship turned out to be one of the worst Sundays in history. On that day church congregations throughout the capital composed mostly of southern Sudanese were exhorted to assemble at the airport to meet one of their respected leaders, Minister of Interior Clement Mboro, who was returning from a trip to southern Sudan. Because the plane transporting Mboro did not arrive on time, southern Sudanese became suspicious and concluded that their leader had been murdered by the government soldiers who continued to terrorize the entire population in southern Sudan. Southern Sudanese took to the streets of Khartoum, smashing and burning cars and attacking passersby in the process. At the end of the day, several people were reported dead and many more injured.

After 1964 the situation in the Sudan fluctuated from moments of progress to a return to conflict between northern and southern Sudanese. There was also an unrelenting dedication by northern Sudanese to forcibly spread

Islam throughout Sudan. After the overthrow of General Ibrahim Abboud's repressive regime on October 21, 1964, and the assumption of power by a temporary government under Sirr Al-Khatim Al-Khalifa Al-Hassan as prime minister, there was shared hope to return the country back to democracy within a year. Because he was an educator with considerable experience in southern Sudan and sympathy for the southern cause, southern Sudanese had faith in Sirr Al-Khatim Al-Khalifa Al-Hassan's ability to prepare the country for and return it to democracy within a year. They were hopeful that he would resolve the conflict in southern Sudan because his government included respected southern Sudanese. This hope came to fruition with the convention of a conference in 1965 that laid a firm foundation for southern autonomy.

The Round Table Conference of March 1965

IN AN ATTEMPT TO END the civil disturbances in southern Sudan, the Round Table Conference was held in Khartoum in March 1965. This conference was attended by all the opposition parties inside and outside the Sudan, including the Sudan African National Union (SANU), the political wing of the Anya Nya movement at the time, now headed by Aggrey Jaden and William Deng Nhial. Seven African countries—Ghana, Nigeria, Algeria, Uganda, Kenya, Tanzania, and Egypt—participated in the conference as observers. At the conference, the southern delegates introduced a motion for self-determination for the people of southern Sudan, to be exercised through an internationally supervised referendum with the options of federation, unity with the north, or separation for the south to become an independent state. However, the north offered a vague autonomous status to southern Sudan. The conference finally agreed to establish a Twelve-Man Committee to recommend a solution to the conflict in the Sudan, and although the committee gave its report to the parties concerned three months later, none of its recommendations were implemented, thus leading to more insurrection by the Anya Nya freedom fighters. The southern delegates said that their proposed plebiscite should satisfy the wishes of everybody—namely unionists, separatists, and federalists—but that plebiscite never occurred.

The Observer Corps was suggested as a body that would supervise the plebiscite, while SANU and the Southern Front would appeal to the southern Sudanese freedom fighters for calm. It was therefore suggested that the southern Sudanese army stationed in the south be withdrawn to their barracks in the north. However, to the disappointment of the southern delegates, the Round Table Conference produced no concrete results at all. Both the Islamist and the Arabist groups in the north were against the granting of any sort of autonomy to the south. Consequently, progress in resolving the ongoing conflict between southern and northern Sudan was impeded, and the country was plunged back into intensified conflict, with the Anya Nya freedom fighters continuing their revolution. This led to intensification of the rebellion led by the Anya Nya freedom movement and the beginning of the unprecedented massacre of innocent south Sudanese civilians in Juba, Wau, and other towns by northern Sudanese.

In a continuing attempt to bring stability to Sudan, a government of national unity was formed in 1965, but it was unsuccessful in fixing the strife between southern and northern Sudan, which continued unabated. Also in 1965 all the churches in the Sudan became united under the umbrella of the Sudan Council of Churches (SCC), a body formed by Sudanese churches. In spite of all the attempts for pacification and development, a sequence of changes and unstable regimes in this period were unable to unite northern and southern Sudan, and the fighting between the two distinctive parts of Sudan continued after the Round Table Conference of March 1965. The Anya Nya freedom movement thus embarked on accumulating more powerful weapons.

During the Arab-Israeli war of June 1967, the Anya Nya movement acquired some sophisticated weapons from Israel. This acquisition equipped the movement to become a formidable force capable of effectively resisting the Sudan government troops stationed at different garrisons in southern Sudan. Hostilities escalated and continued unabated.

On May 5, 1968, William Deng Nhial, the leader of SANU, was murdered by Sudan government troops while on an election campaign mission to his home area in Tonj, Bahr El Ghazal province. He was a Dinka who believed in democratic socialism and the solidarity of Sudanese of African descent in resisting Arab colonialism. He had aimed for political partnership between southern Sudanese and the indigenous African Sudanese people of Nuba, Fur, Beja,

Nubia, Ingesenia, and other parts of northern Sudan. His death dealt a devastating blow to the Anya Nya freedom movement. By the time of this demise, other prominent northern Sudanese had grown weary of the conflict between northern and southern Sudan, leading to a revolution on May 25, 1969.

The May 25, 1969, revolution, spearheaded by Colonel Jaafar Mohammed Nimeiri, was a bloodless coup that overthrew the Umma civilian government of Prime Minister Muhammad Ahmad Mahgoub, who was Sudan's foreign minister between 1956 and 1958 and then again between 1964 and 1965. Mohammed Ahmed Mahgoub was elected prime minister in 1965, but he was subsequently forced to resign during the continuing tumultuous times in the Sudan. He was elected prime minister for the second time in 1967 and served in that position until 1969, when he was overthrown on May 25. It is reported that Mohammed Ahmed Mahgoub was the first Sudanese to say a word in the White House.

Sudan's Nimeiri, Egypt's Nasser, and Libya's Gaddafi in Tripoli, Libya, in 1969

The army, under the chairmanship of Colonel Nimeiri, seemed to have come to power through the support of the Sudanese Communist Party. It immediately formed the Revolutionary Command Council (RCC), which proceeded to ban all sectarian political parties and establish its own political organization, the Sudan Socialist Union (SSU). On June 9, 1969, Nimeiri's regime made a declaration to recognize the political, historical, and economic differences between southern and northern Sudan, which appeared to appease the southern Sudanese, especially the Anya Nya freedom fighters. He offered southern Sudan regional autonomy, which later brought an end to the seventeen-year-old civil strife.

The Addis Ababa Agreement of 1972

Abel Alier Kuai—vice president of Sudan from 1971 to 1983

THROUGH THE GOOD OFFICES OF the World Council of Churches, northern and southern Sudanese delegations started secret negotiations in May 1971, two years after Colonel Jaafar Mohammed Nimeiri took over power in a bloodless coup on May 25, 1969. The Sudan government representatives led by Ambassador Abdin Ismail, Professor Mohammed Omar Bashir, and Barbara Haq met the southern Sudanese members of the movement based in Britain. The Sudan government representatives informed the members of the South Sudan Liberation Movement (SSLM), the political wing of the Anya Nya movement, of their government's intention to grant local autonomy to the people of southern Sudan. In the meantime, the conflict continued unceasingly. In mid-1971 a fierce one-month battle took place in the Jonglei Canal–Sobat Mouth between government forces and the Anya Nya freedom fighters under Commander Joseph Akuon, leading to his death. It was unfortunate that Commander Joseph Akuon died a few months before the 1972 Addis Ababa Accord was signed. Joseph Akuon's death was regarded by his comrades in arms and the civil population as a great setback for the advancement of the Anya Nya movement. He was a tough and skillful guerrilla fighter trained by Israeli Intelligence along with his colleagues John Garang de Mabior, Vincent Kuany Latjor, and Corporal Bol Kur Alongjok.

The Addis Ababa Agreement, also known as the Addis Ababa Accord, came about after an insurgency and vicious armed struggle carried on tirelessly by the Anya Nya freedom fighters against successive governments in Khartoum. As mentioned earlier, the insurgency started on August 18, 1955, with a mutiny in Torit and lasted for seventeen years. More than one million southern Sudanese people died as a result of the conflict. As mentioned previously, at the time of the agreement, the Anya Nya had just acquired some sophisticated weapons from Israel during the Arab-Israeli war of June 1967. This had prepared the Anya Nya to become a formidable force capable of effectively resisting the Sudan government troops stationed at different garrisons in southern Sudan. Representatives of the political wing of the Anya Nya movement, the South Sudan Liberation Movement (SSLM), and Sudan government representatives signed the accord in Addis Ababa on February 27, 1972, under the auspices of the Ethiopian Emperor Haile Selassie.

Emperor Haile Selassie of Ethiopia

Many parties played a crucial role in bringing together the northern and southern Sudanese parties, including Reverend Canon Burges Carr on behalf of All Africa Conference of Churches (AACC), the secretary general, and Dr. Gaafer Bakheit of the Sudan government. This effort ended with the signing of the peace agreement in Addis Ababa on February 27, 1972. The church therefore played a leading role in ending the seventeen-year civil war, and the war came to a peaceful end officially on February 27, 1972. After the agreement, the church continued its spiritual and social activities in southern Sudan as it had done since Christianity entered Southern Sudan from the time when Great Britain conquered Sudan in 1898. You will recall that the first Christian missionaries in southern Sudan were the Roman Catholic Verona Fathers, who built churches and schools throughout southern Sudan. Other Christian missionaries to follow included Presbyterians from the United States and the Anglican Church Missionary Society of England.

At the time of the Addis Ababa Agreement of 1972, all the churches in the Sudan were united under the umbrella of the Sudan Council of Churches (SCC), a body that had been formed by the Sudanese churches in 1965 following intense persecution during the repressive rule of General Ibrahim Abboud from November 17, 1958, to October 21, 1964, when he waged a holy war against Anya Nya freedom fighters, who had persisted in their insurrection.

The provisions of the Addis Ababa Agreement of 1972 included the following:

(a) Upon ratification of the agreement by President Jaafar Nimeiri and General Joseph Lagu, which was to take place in Addis Ababa on March 2, 1972, a cease-fire would come into force throughout southern Sudan.
(b) The cease-fire would be followed by the gradual establishment of regional autonomy, under which the three southern provinces of Bahr El Ghazal, Upper Nile, and Equatoria would be united into a Southern Region under its own regional president.
(c) The regional president would be chosen by an executive council, whose members would be appointed by the Sudanese head council upon recommendation by a regional assembly. This council would control all aspects of Southern Region policy except defense, foreign affairs, currency and finance, and economic and social planning, which would remain under the control of the central government in Khartoum. However, southern Sudan would be represented in the central government.
(d) The executive council would be responsible to the regional assembly, which would be elected by universal adult suffrage within eighteen months of the ratification of the agreement.
(e) For a transitional period, the Anya Nya military forces of about twelve thousand men would be incorporated into the Sudanese Army's Southern Command and placed under the command of a commission of southern and northern officers in equal numbers. These officers would be responsible to the central government. The army would

gradually be reduced to twelve thousand men, half of whom would be northerners and half southerners until the south set up its own machinery for maintaining law and order. It would have its own armed police force and two to three thousand frontier guards.

(f) While the official language would be Arabic, English would be the common language, and it would be taught in schools in the south.

The Addis Ababa Accord thus granted the three southern provinces of Upper Nile, Bahr El Ghazal, and Equatoria a self-governing region within the framework of a united socialist Sudan with Juba as its principal capital. In the agreement, the Southern Region would have its own People's Regional Assembly and the High Executive Council. It gave the regional government in the south control over education, health, agriculture and forests, the police, among other things. But the control of defense, foreign affairs, communications, and national economic planning were left to the central government in Khartoum. After being assured of his own safety by the Ethiopian Emperor Haile Selassie, the leader of the political wing of the Anya Nya movement the South Sudan Liberation Movement (SSLM), Joseph Lagu, left for Khartoum to make the final arrangements with the president of the Democratic Republic of the Sudan General Jaafar Mohammed Nimeiri. Upon his arrival in Khartoum, Lagu was promoted to the rank of major general.

It was expected that Joseph Lagu would head the regional government in the South as its first president. However, Nimeiri appointed one of his close associates, Abel Alier Kuai, to head the newly established local autonomous government in the South instead. This was interpreted to mean that President Nimeiri still mistrusted southern Sudanese, especially the Anya Nya freedom fighters, or that he lacked a serious intent to implement the Addis Ababa Accord regarding the interests of southern Sudanese freedom fighters. General Lagu was absorbed into the Sudanese Armed Forces along with his six thousand former Anya Nya fighters. They were stationed in the three southern provinces alongside the six thousand northern Sudanese troops already in the south. This put the total number of the Sudanese armed forces in the south to twelve thousand.

General Joseph Lagu, leader of Southern Sudan Liberation Movement (SSLM) Anya Nya I

The Addis Ababa Agreement itself had supporters and opponents on both sides in the Sudan. Many southern Sudanese politicians and some Anya Nya fighters did not agree with the outcome of the accord. Some radical southern Sudanese politicians who were living outside Sudan denounced the accord, calling it a sellout. The same stand was taken by some northern Sudanese politicians of the sectarian and Islamist groups, who accused President Nimeiri of betraying the Islamic and Arab interests in the whole Sudan by offering local autonomy to the southern Sudanese Christians and animists. Many southern Sudanese politicians in neighboring countries and abroad boycotted and refused any contact with the parties participating in the negotiations. Among them were Philip Pedak Lieth, Aggrey Jaden, Gordon Mourtat Mayen, Stephen Chich Lam, Daniel Koat (Matthews), David Koak Guok, Agolong Chol, and Eliah Aduang. Following the implementation of the accord, the countries that hosted southern Sudanese refugees, in cooperation with the United Nations High Commissioner for Refugees (UNHCR), forcefully repatriated them to Southern Sudan. This move was against the will of many refugees. A sizable number of southern Sudanese people believed that the death of Commander Joseph Akuon (Otew), the first deputy of the Anya Nya leader, and the hostility of the neighboring countries (especially Uganda and Ethiopia)—the main backers of the Anya Nya movement—paved the way for the Addis Ababa Accord. Commander Joseph Akuon (Otew) had been killed in a fierce battle between governmnent forces and the Anya Nya freedom fighters a few months before the 1972 Addis Ababa Accord was signed. His death had been regarded by his comrades in arms and the civil population as a great setback for the advancement of the Anya Nya movement.

As mentioned earlier, only six thousand ex-Anya Nya fighters were incorporated into the Sudanese National Armed Forces. Another three thousand were absorbed into the police force, prison warders, and game rangers. However, a year after the agreement was signed, most of the twenty thousand former Anya Nya fighters absorbed into the civil service were laid off and left jobless. Most of them either went back to their villages, searched for menial jobs in big towns, or returned to neighboring countries, where they settled as refugees without the support of the UNHCR.

Formation of The Anya Nya II Movement

THE SOUTHERN ELEMENTS THAT REFUSED the Addis Ababa Accord remained at Itang Refugee Camp in Ethiopia. Among them were the following: Elija Yong Kiir, William Deng Monga, Peter Gatkuoth Wakoa, Top Yangdow, Jieng Jany, Kuol Nyadew, Stephen Wei Dup, Isaiah Tut Garpan, Bor Juong, Reath Chol, Domach Ruai, Andrew Mawei Ruai, James Ruon Yoy, Both Nyador, Duoth Khon, Gatchany Nuar, Rev. Moses Hoth Goy, Peter Riek Bayiek, Michael Thichuong Duol, Puol Cheng Leiy, Leo Thoc, Enoch Mayomdit, Moses Malek Chol, John Jak Deang, Elija Adwong, Johnny Jock Reth, Hoth Guor Luak, Bol Kiir Diew, Paleak Lual, Tut Bok Joak, Mabor Chol, Abraham Wal Jal (Nyamak), Paulino Matip Nhial, Gabriel Gatwech Chan (Tanginya), Gordon Koang Chol, Pathot Dup, William Yiec Riek, John Dewit Yiec, Moses Mading Kueth, Stephen Duol Chol, Ruach Nyadeng, Michael Majok Yai, Peter Ruot Chol, Gatluak Domach, Peter Par Golong, Tito Biel Chor, Ter Lor Guandong, Jikmir Puok, Biel Nguot, Biel Yuol Nyuot, and Makuach Wiu, Pon Liem (Chotjiok).

These officers formed the Anya Nya Patriotic Front (APF) in August 1974 under the overall command of veteran politician Mr. Gordon Mortat Mayen. This movement became known as Anya Nya II after the first movement named Anya Nya I. It was a regrouping of Anya Nya I by disgruntled freedom fighters from the first insurgency launched in 1963. This second liberation movement was formed in August 1974, but it was not formally launched until 1975. Born amid ideological uncertainties, Anya Nya II was launched with a mutiny in the military garrison of Akobo. In 1975, three years after the Addis Ababa Agreement, a group of Anya Nya fighters who were absorbed into the

Sudanese National Armed Forces stationed in Akobo district staged a mutiny upon receiving orders of a transfer to northern Sudan. The leaders of the mutiny were First Lieutenant Vincent Kuany Latjor, Staff Sergeant Peter Tap Liey, Private Michael Waat Latjor, and Corporal Bol Kur Alongjok. However, in the process of the mutiny, their commanding officer, Lieutenant Colonel Abel Kol Ater, lost his life and several northern soldiers in the garrison were also killed.

General Vincent Kuany Latjor was the leader of the Akobo Uprising of March 1975 (in this picture he had been promoted to the rank of general)

The mutiny in Akobo, which indeed sparked off the second rebellion in southern Sudan, took place as a result of dissatisfaction among the former Anya Nya soldiers absorbed into the Sudanese Armed Forces. The ex-Anya Nya soldiers were treated differently compared to their Northern colleagues stationed in southern Sudan. For one, they were poorly paid and they lacked most of their basic requirements. Some were transferred to parts of northern Sudan, and they interpreted such transfers without prior consultation as a conspiracy by their northern Sudanese Arab colleagues in the army. Accordingly, the mutineers of Akobo decided to return to the bush and continue the struggle against the Khartoum regime with the ultimate goal of liberating southern Sudan as an independent country this time. They crossed the border to Ethiopia and joined the other southern Sudanese refugees who refused to support the Addis Ababa Accord in 1972 and opted to remain at Itang Refugee Camp. The mutineers from Akobo found these refugees organized, and after the formation of the Anya Nya Patriotic Front, the founders remained there until they were officially recognized by the Ethiopian Marxist regime of Colonel Mengistu Haile Mariam in 1976.

It is worth mentioning that some of the ex-Anya Nya soldiers who refused to support the mutinying soldiers and chose to remain in Akobo were later court-martialed and executed by firing squad. Eight of them were summarily executed by firing squad in Malakal. Those executed by firing squad included Sergeant Major Andrew Pakon, Sergeant Reath Gatloach, and six others. Others were sentenced to life imprisonment.

Thereafter, some middle-ranking officers who hailed from Akobo district were also implicated in the conspiracy and sentenced to long periods of imprisonment. Among those officers arrested were Major Peter Tot Bangoang, Second Lieutenant Isaac Gatluok Riek, Major James Gatwech Kuany, Captain Peter Reath Koda, First Lieutenant James Tut Bachuch, Paul Gatnor Gew, Ustaz Adiang (Jal pony Adiang), and several NCOs and enlisted men. Most of them were held in Swakin, a notorious state prison in Port Sudan.

Following in the footsteps of the 1975 mutineers of Akobo, the ex-Anya Nya soldiers in the government garrisons of Juba and Wau also staged mutinies the following year. Staff Sergeant Paul Puok Reat led the mutiny in Juba, and he and his colleagues almost took over Juba, but they ran out of ammunition. After they exhausted all their efforts and ran short of ammunition, they retreated to Jammeza, some one hundred kilometers from Juba, where they were quickly overrun and immediately arrested by the government troops. The mutineers in Wau attempted to overrun Wau town but failed. However, they managed to find their way to the Central African Republic. Their ringleader was Captain Alfred Aguet, who ordered the execution of his superior officer in charge of the Grinti Garrison, Brigadier Emmanuel Abur Nhial. Captain Alfred and his company were later apprehended by Central African Republic security and handed over to the Sudanese security agents, who summarily executed Captain Alfred Aguet and arrested the rest.

Anya Nya II, consisting of the former ex-Anya Nya fighters who had rejected the Addis Ababa Accord and had remained in Ethiopia, started their military activities after they had officially been recognized by the Marxist regime of Colonel Mengistu Haile Mariam in 1976. The Ethiopian government allowed them to retain their military bases inside Ethiopian territory. It provided them with three locations to establish their bases: Bilpam as their operational headquarters, Bonga Training Centre, and Kongdekuach. At that initial stage, the Anya Nya II force was very small in number, consisting of between approximately three hundred and five hundred well-organized, highly trained, and battle-hardened soldiers.

The Ethiopian military ruler Colonel Mengistu Haile Mariam, who ruled Ethiopia from 1974 to 1991

In the meantime, the 1975 and 1976 mutineers of Akobo, Juba, and Wau who were arrested and jailed continued to languish in prison, most of them having been held in Swakin, the notorious state prison in Port Sudan. There was no indication that the former Anya Nya fighters who were absorbed into the Sudanese National Armed Forces following the Addis Ababa Accord in 1972, but became disgruntled and staged mutinies in Akobo, Juba, and Wau, were of any relevance to the politics of the day. As a result, the mutinous soldiers were eventually released. In June 1977 President Nimeiri signed a Memorandum of Understanding with the leaders of the three northern sectarian political parties: Sadiq El Mahdi, leader of the Umma Party; Mohammed Osman El Mirghani, leader of the Democratic Unionist Party; and Dr. Hassan Abdalla Turabi, leader of the Moslem Brotherhood. Following their release, the mutineers were barred from serving in their previous positions in the army. Instead, they were incorporated into the wildlife department at their old military ranks.

In the meantime, the Anya Nya II had continued recruiting and training fighters with the blessing of the Ethiopian Marxist regime of Colonel Mengistu Haile Mariam. These fighters began their military campaigns in 1979 by disrupting communication links in eastern and western Upper Nile province as well as northern Bahr El Ghazal province, with the purpose of paralyzing state economic power. They used mostly guerrilla tactics—hit and run methods—in order to avoid overusing their meager supply of ammunition. Anya Nya II managed to overrun the government garrisons of Kutkea in 1979, and some influential southern Sudanese politicians such as Gordon Mourtat Mayen, Elija Adwang, Agolong Chol, David Dak Gai, Johnny Jock Reth, William Deng, Philip Pedak Lieth, David Dogok Puoch, Leo Thuoc, Hoth Guor Luak, John Jack Deang, Moses Malek Chol, and Bol Kiir Diew represented the Anya Nya II political wing, the South Sudan Liberation Movement (SSLM).

Although officially recognized by the Ethiopian regime in 1976, the Anya Nya II fighters had some difficulty in freely conducting their military operations against Sudanese government troops based in southern Sudan because the Ethiopian government did not want them to intensify the war. Colonel

Mengistu was not fully committed to allowing Libyan agents who were cooperating with Anya Nya II to give them adequate military assistance. Indeed, Addis Ababa was just using them to pressure the Sudanese government into not intensifying its support to the Ethiopian opposition forces already operating on Sudanese soil, including the Eritrean People's Liberation Front (EPLF), Oromo Liberation Front (OLF), and Tigre People's Liberation Front (TPLF). This policy prevented the Anya Nya II forces from conducting full-scale war in southern Sudan and denied them fresh recruits. Many students, youth, and government officials living in different towns in Upper Nile province were willing to join the Anya Nya II rebellion, but, unfortunately, they were discouraged by the Ethiopian Marxists' lack of interest in fully assisting Anya Nya II.

Regardless of discouragement by the Ethiopian government, Anya Nya II forces continued their military operations and managed to overrun the government garrisons of Akoka in June 1982. During the same year, 1982, a large group of university and high school students escaped from Malakal, the capital of Upper Nile, and joined the Anya Nya II rank and file at Bilpam in Ethiopia. Their ringleaders were Lakurnyang Lado, Pagan Amum Okiech , Yien Thong Riang, Nyachigak Nyachuluk, Nyatipling, Oyai Deng Ajak, James Hoth Mai, just to mention a few. They remained at Anya Nya II bases in Ethiopia until another rebellion took place on May 16, 1983, in Bor, Pibor, and Pochalla respectively. Another rebellion was also staged in Ayod by Major William Nyuon Bany on 6 June 1983. In future years, some of the abovementioned individuals would become the leaders of the SPLM/SPLA in the Government of Southern Sudan (GOSS).

In 1982 the regional autonomy that had been granted to southern Sudan at the Addis Ababa Peace Agreement of 1972 had lasted for a decade. However, the self-government had been shaky from the onset because Colonel Jaafar Mohammed Nimeiri, who came to power in 1969 and facilitated the agreement, had slowly chipped away at its terms. Although he had granted southern Sudan regional autonomy and ensured precarious peace in that part of the country for a decade, unilateral decisions made by him led to the resumption of hostilities between southern and northern Sudan as well as his gradual fall from the presidency.

The Beginning of the Fall of President Nimeiri

TOWARD THE BEGINNING OF THE 1980s, President Jafaar Nimeiri introduced certain policies that provoked the people of southern Sudan and eventually resulted in a full-scale resumption of the second civil war in the Sudan. The main causes of the ongoing civil war were:

1. The digging of the Jonglei Canal in Upper Nile province, a project that would result in draining the water-rich central parts of southern Sudan for the benefit of irrigating agricultural projects in northern Sudan and Egypt.
2. The construction of pipelines to carry crude oil from Bentiu in southern Sudan to Port Sudan in northern Sudan as a way of exploiting the natural resources in the south for the benefit of northern Sudan.
3. The attempted annexation of the rich agricultural lands in the southern districts of Renk, Abyei, Bentiu, and Kofia Kingi.
4. The introduction of a South Africa apartheid-like discriminatory policy known as Kasha, which was introduced in 1980 against peoples from southern, central, western, and eastern Sudan, by which police and other security forces forcibly rounded up people from these mentioned areas during working hours, mostly in Khartoum and other big towns in the north, and either jailed them or sent them back to their places of origin.

It was an open secret that some Equatorian intellectuals, reportedly out of fear of domination by their Dinka and other Nilotic allies, encouraged the redivision of southern Sudan into three mini regions. They wanted all non-Equatorians, particularly Dinka, Nuer, and Shilluk, to leave Juba and return to their places of origin. They were advocating for separate development as a way of denying all non-Equatorians from Upper Nile and Bahr El Ghazal political domination in the southern Region. Retired General Joseph Lagu, former president of the High Executive Council in the Southern Region from 1978 to 1979, was the one who masterminded all these divisive ideas in collaboration with President Nimeiri. He did so, indeed, because of his opposition to his erstwhile enemy Abel Alier, who had previously hijacked the leadership of southern Sudan from him after the Addis Ababa Accord in 1972.

You will recall that after Ethiopia's Emperor Haile Selassie guaranteed his safety on the signing of the Addis Ababa Accord, Joseph Lagu as the leader of the political wing of the Anya Nya movement—the South Sudan Liberation Movement (SSLM)—had landed in Khartoum and immediately been promoted to the rank of major general. He had expected that President Nimeiri would appoint him to head the government of southern Sudan, but Nimeiri appointed Abel Alier Kuai instead, which led to an ongoing acrimony.

As a longtime friend and close associate of Nimeiri, Abel Alier had served as the second vice president of Sudan from September 1971, so he was a natural choice for Nimeiri. The bitterness experienced by Joseph Lagu continued until he was himself elected president of the High Executive Council following regional elections in 1978, during which his supporters became the majority group in southern Sudan's People's Regional Assembly. However, in 1979, Joseph Lagu was removed by the opposition group under his rival Abel Alier after they accused him and his associates of corruption. It was an accusation that brought down his government and led to its fall.

As a result, both the High Executive Council and the People's Regional Assembly under Joseph Lagu were dissolved. President Nimeiri eventually appointed Mr. Peter Gatkuoth Gual as a caretaker president of a reconstituted High Executive Council of the Southern Region in Juba. After that, a new election was conducted throughout the Southern Region that brought Abel Alier back to power in May 1980. However, in 1981, President Nimeiri dissolved his government because of a disagreement between Abel Alier and his longtime friend Peter Gatkuoth Gual. Their disagreement was over Peter Gatkuoth Gual's appointment of Manasseh Abraham Yar to the post of director at the Ministry of Wildlife Conservation and Tourism.

Peter Gatkuoth Gual—caretaker president of the High Executive Council from 1979 to 1980

The disagreement occurred when Abel Alier was on a private visit to the United Kingdom and Peter Gatkuoth Gual became acting president. Peter Gatkuoth Gual, as acting president of the High Executive Council, endorsed the appointment of Manasseh Abraham Yar, an economist and a qualified candidate for the post of director at the Ministry of Wildlife Conservation and Tourism. Manasseh Abraham Yar had previously worked at the Ministry of Commerce and Supply as a deputy director.

When Abel Alier returned from London, he summoned Peter Gatkuoth and asked him to immediately withdraw the appointment of Manasseh Abraham Yar, but the vice president refused to do so. Eventually, the Manasseh Abraham Yar affair was referred to President Nimeiri because Abel Alier and Peter Gatkuoth Gual failed to reach a compromise over the issue. At that point, President Nimeiri decided to dissolve the High Executive Council and the People's Regional Assembly and appoint an interim government headed by an army officer, Major General Gasimallah Abdalla Rasas, a southern Sudanese Muslim from Bahr El Ghazal province. General Rasas led the Southern Region until new elections were conducted in 1982. Following the elections, Joseph James Tombura was elected as the president of the High Executive Council. He was the last president of the High Executive Council before the Southern Region was redivided into three regions by Colonel Jaafar Mohammed Nimeiri.

Fully convinced that he would now easily get rid of whoever might oppose his policies in southern Sudan, President Nimeiri, at the beginning of 1983, ordered one of his generals, Sadiq El Bana, then the overall commander of the Sudanese Armed Forces in the Southern Regional Headquarters in Juba, to transfer all the southern Sudanese soldiers in different garrisons in the south to the north. They were to be replaced with their northern Sudanese colleagues in the army. The actual motive behind the transfer was to send the southern soldiers to Iraq. By then, Sudan was sending its soldiers to fight alongside Iraq in its war with Iran.

Apparently, the president's secret plan had already been discovered by the soldiers themselves following the action taken earlier the same year when he ordered the transfer of southern Sudanese soldiers stationed at Aweil District in Bahr El Ghazal province under the command of Colonel Alfred Deng Aluk. When the southern Sudanese soldiers within the Sudanese Armed Forced were informed that they would be transferred to the north, they disobeyed the orders and remained on full alert until President Nimeiri was compelled to order his aides to send more northern Sudanese soldiers to the south to suppress the discontent within the army.

Major General Sadiq El Bana planned to attack the mutinying soldiers in the three garrisons of Bor, Pochalla, and Pibor, but this did not take place until May 16, 1983, when he ordered his forces from Juba to attack. Major Kerubino Kuanyin Bol led the mutinous soldiers at Bor. Whereas, Captain David Riek Machuoc led the soldiers at Pibor and Pochalla, where the two rebel commanders coordinated their rebellion simultaneously. Both leaders were veteran and battle-hardened Anya Nya freedom fighters who had participated in the seventeen-year war between southern and northern Sudan. That particular war had begun with the Torit Mutiny on August 18, 1955, and ended with the signing of the Addis Ababa Agreement on February 27, 1972.

On May 16, 1983, the mutinous soldiers in Battalion 105, stationed at Bor and composed mostly of ex-Anya Nya troops, were attacked by government troops after continuing to refuse to be transferred to northern Sudan. The government soldiers were deliberately sent from Juba in order to put down the rebellion at their garrison at Malek, outside Bor town.

Around this time, Colonel John Garang, a senior officer in the Sudanese army, supposedly went to Bor to placate the five hundred southern Sudan government soldiers in Battalion 105 who were resisting relocation to northern Sudan. However, Garang was reportedly already part of a conspiracy to arrange for the defection of Battalion 105 to the antigovernment rebels, who were predominantly Anya Nya II freedom fighters. Consequently, when the fighting in Bor took place, Colonel John Garang was already in the area, so the only option left for him was to join the mutinying soldiers who were heading toward the Ethiopian border. He took a different route to join them at the rebel stronghold in Ethiopia. Colonel Garang's wife, Rebecca Nyandeng de Mabior, their two sons Mabior and Chol, Maker Deng Malou, and Chigai Atem accompanied him. The group used a small Land Rover owned by CCI Company and traveled along the road linking Bor, Kongor, Duk Padiet, Yuai, Waat, and Khor Nyanding up to Nyangore on the western bank of the Sobat River. However, their car broke down at Nyangore village, and they left it on the bank of the Sobat River (Wei Dengnyang), which is opposite Ulang.

The car was later recovered and taken to Ulang by the Sudanese Armed Forces stationed at the garrison. Because the Sudanese government was worried about John Garang's defection, they urgently dispatched a helicopter to search all the routes Colonel Garang and his associates could have used. The local Nuer did their level best to hide the Garang party throughout their journey to Marol, a small village located on Ethiopian territory. On their arrival at Marol, they met Samuel Gai Tut and Akuot Atem de Mayan at the Anya Nya II mobile station. After that, they made contact with the Ethiopian authorities, who flew them by helicopter to Addis Ababa.

The large groups of university and high school students that escaped from Malakal, the capital of Upper Nile province, in 1982 and joined the Anya Nya II rank and file at Bilpam in Ethiopia were still in Ethiopia when John Garang arrived. You will recall that their ringleaders were Lakurnyang Lado, Pagan Amum Okiech, Yien Thong Riang, Nyachigak Nyachuluk, Nyatipling, Oyai Deng Ajak, James Hoth Mai, and others. They had remained at the Anya Nya II bases in Ethiopia until this rebellion at Bor, Pibor, Ayod, and Pochalla took place on May 16 1983. As stated previously, some of the above-mentioned names would become the leaders of the SPLM/SPLA in the Government of Southern Sudan (GOSS).

Less than a month later, on June 5, 1983, Major William Nyuon Bany and his supporters at Ayod mounted another mutiny. President Nimeiri had attempted the same deceptive technique he tried on the mutineers at Bor. He secretly ordered the northern Sudanese soldiers in Malakal to arrest Major William Nyuon Bany and his supporters because his loyalty was doubted. However, before they could execute their orders from President Nimeiri, the government soldiers from northern Sudan were killed in large numbers by Major William Nyuon's forces at Ayod. There was only one survivor to report the events of the mutiny at Ayod to the army headquarters in Malakal. Major William Nyuon Bany then made his way to Ethiopia to join the other southern Sudanese groups that were now stationed there.

Upon arrival, he met some prominent future southern Sudanese politicians and senior army officers who were already at Itang Refugee Camp. Among them were Akuot Atem de Mayan, Samuel Gai Tut, Joseph Oduho, Martin Majier Gai, Colonel John Garang de Mabior, William Chuol Deng, Lieutenant Colonel Francis Ngor Machiek, Major Arok Thon Arok, Major Kerubino Kuanyin Bol, Captain Salva Kiir Mayardit, Captain David Riek Machuoc, Gabriel Gany Juoch, Captain David Bediet Deng, Moses Malek Chol, Gatjiek Wei, and Elijah Yong Kier. All these prominent southern Sudanese figures came together and formed the Sudan People's Liberation Movement and Sudan People's Liberation Army (SPLM/SPLA).

As the mutinying soldiers of Bor, Pochalla, and Pibor began regrouping with other disgruntled southern Sudanese who had joined forces in Ethiopia, President Nimeiri continued implementing policies that went against the Addis Ababa Peace Agreement of 1972. In June 1983 he unconstitutionally declared and implemented the redivision of southern Sudan into three mini regions. In doing so, he abrogated the Addis Ababa Accord of 1972, which he personally signed in order to bring the war in southern Sudan to an end. Within the same period, Nimeiri appointed Joseph Lagu as his second vice president, having dismissed his longtime friend and close associate, Abel Alier, who held that position from September 1971 to 1983. At that time, President Nimeiri dissolved the People's Regional Assembly and the High Executive Council and then appointed new governors for the newly created three southern regions of Equatoria, Upper Nile, and Bahr El Ghazal. The three appointed governors were Joseph James Tombura, the last president of the High Executive Council of the Southern Region, who was appointed governor of Equatoria; Daniel Koat Matthews, who was appointed governor of Upper Nile; and Dr. Lawrence Wol Wol, who was appointed governor of Bahr El Ghazal. Meanwhile, President Nimeiri specifically ordered the detention of some prominent southern Sudanese politicians who opposed the redivision of southern Sudan into three regions. Because of their opposition to the redivision, he accused them of collaborating with the Anya Nya II rebels, who had intensified their military operations in various parts of Upper

Nile province. Among those detained were Matthew Obur Ayang, Speaker of the People's Regional Assembly, and Dhol Acuil Aleu, vice president of the High Executive Council to Joseph James Tombura. Matthew Obur, a former Minister of Education and Guidance, was also the last speaker of the People's Regional Assembly in Juba in 1983. The redivision of the southern Sudan into three fragile regions as a result of the presidential decree of June 1983 was intended by President Nimeiri to weaken southern Sudanese unity, trust, and confidence among themselves, and it appears to have succeeded.

The Formation of the SPLA and Its Hostility Toward Anya Nya II

IT IS AN OPEN SECRET that the Sudan People's Liberation Movement/Sudan People's Liberation Army (SPLM/SPLA) was a direct product of the Anya Nya II movement. Established in an area controlled by Anya Nya II, the SPLA drew its first recruits from former members of Anya Nya II. Consequently, the first three SPLA battalions of Tiger, Crocodile, and Buffalo were predominantly former Anya Nya II members, and the other two battalions (104 and 105) composed of former government soldiers who mutinied in Bor, Pibor, Ayod, Pochalla, and Wangkei districts in southern Sudan. It is also to be recalled that between 1983 and 1985, about 80 percent of the SPLA combat units were mainly from the Nuer ethnic group. Consequently, the fact that the majority of SPLA combatants came from the Nuer tribe indicated that the split that took place in subsequent years within the SPLM/SPLA was political rather than ethnic rivalry between the Nuer and the Dinka tribes. It was a struggle for power by opposing groups in the movement.

During the process of forming the SPLM/SPLA, Anya Nya II leader Commander Vincent Kuany Latjor and Deputy Commander Gordon Koang Chol were invited to take part in the meeting. At the end of the meeting, the leaders overwhelmingly elected Mr. Akuot Atem, a former minister of public service and manpower in the Southern Region government, as the chairman of the newly established movement. The other important positions were to be occupied as follows: Samuel Gai Tut was to head Defence; Joseph Oduho was elected to head Foreign Affairs; Martin Majier Gai was elected to head Legal

Affairs; Colonel John Garang was elected as the chief of staff; and William Chuol Deng was elected as his deputy. However, Colonel Garang objected that a politician should not head the SPLM/SPLA and thus rejected the outcome of these elections. Joseph Oduho, Martin Majier, William Nyuon, Kerubino Kuanyin, Arok Thon, Francis Ngor, and Salva Kiir supported Colonel Garang's position.

The reasons why Colonel Garang and his group rejected the election of Akuot Atem, who hailed from the same ethnic group as he, were the same differences that the southern Sudanese people had experienced in the past under Abel Alier and Joseph Lagu in the Southern Sudan Regional government. These differences also surfaced in the bush during the formation of the SPLM/SPLA. Colonel Garang did not want to be led by Akuot Atem and Gai Tut simply because they belonged to a different political grouping. Gai Tut, Akuot Atem, and William Chuol Deng were always ardent supporters of Joseph Lagu, while Colonel Garang and his supporters were known to be Abel Alier's supporters when they were still inside Sudan. Despite the fact that the southern Sudanese founders of the SPLM/SPLA popularly elected Akuot Atem to lead the new movement, the Ethiopian government under the leadership of Colonel Mengistu Haile Mariam decided to back Colonel Garang. President Mengistu had many reasons for supporting Garang. For one, Colonel Garang's aim and objective was to create a secular system based on equality for all Sudanese. He wanted a united Sudan and not an independent South Sudan. Another factor was that Colonel Garang was a soldier who embraced Marxist ideology as the basic principle of his movement. On the other hand, Akuot and Gai's group wanted total independence for South Sudan.

If they were to achieve their goal, they would have to seek and win support from the OAU (Organization of African Unity) member states. This was a difficult task because of the fact that the OAU did not encourage secessionist movements on the continent. It has been speculated that Colonel Mengistu's support for Colonel Garang might also have been due to the fact that both were military men. It is important to note that while supporting Colonel Garang, Colonel Mengistu had his own problems to sort out at home. For example, the Eritrea separatist movement in northern Ethiopia was fighting for its people's inalienable right for self-determination. Of interest was also the fact that while Ethiopia under Colonel Mengistu was supporting the SPLA of Colonel John Garang to achieve its goal in Sudan, the Sudanese government was aiding the Eritrea People's Liberation Front (EPLF), the Ethiopia People's Revolutionary Democratic Front (EPRDF), and the Oromo Liberation Front (OLF). All of these movements were opposing Colonel Mengistu's leadership in Ethiopia.

As the SPLM/SPLA began building its structures and operations under the leadership of Colonel John Garang, Anya Nya II forces continued their military operations in southern Sudan. They managed to overrun the government garrisons of Wangkei in August 1983. In the meantime, the relationship between the SPLM/SPLA, now under Colonel Garang, and the Anya Nya II movement disintegrated, leading to a schism that would be characterized by unprecedented treachery and bloodshed among southern Sudanese fighting forces. For example, upon request from Colonel Garang, the Ethiopian security organs attempted to arrest Akuot Atem, whom John Garang forcibly replaced as the leader of the SPLM/SPLA, Samuel Gai Tut, William Chuol Deng, Moses Malek Chol, Gabriel Gany Juoch, Bol Kiir Diew, Gatjiek Wei, and many others at Itang Refugee Camp, where many southern Sudanese forces were stationed. In order to avoid the arrest, Akuot and Gai Tut with their supporters escaped and went back to Sudan in early August 1983. They did not want to confront either the Ethiopian security personnel or Colonel Garang's supporters. When the Ethiopian security failed to arrest Akuot and Gai Tut, Colonel Garang asked them to attack the Anya Nya II headquarters at Bilpam again. In the meantime, President Nimeiri continued with policies that completely went against the Addis Ababa Agreement of 1972.

On September 24, 1983, President Nimeiri introduced Islamic sharia law, or the September Laws. By doing this, the secular laws that had governed Sudan since her independence from Britain under the Anglo-Egyptian Condominium were abrogated. For the first time, Sudan became an Islamic state being governed under sharia penal code. Nimeiri's new laws completely ignored the fact that Sudan is a multireligious and multicultural society. Meanwhile, there were more forced transfers of southern Sudanese soldiers stationed in different garrisons in southern Sudan to northern Sudan and later to fight alongside Iraq against Iran, which continued to cause dissent in addition to the schism between the SPLM/SPLA and the Anya Nya II forces.

In the middle of October 1983, Ethiopian troops and Colonel Garang's supporters, led by Lieutenant Colonel William Nyuon Bany, mounted a joint attack against Anya Nya II forces. As a result, several Anya Nya II soldiers were killed in action at Bilpam, which is about forty kilometers from Itang Refugee Camp. Commander Duac Taytay, a senior commander of Anya Nya II, was gunned down and captured alive by Colonel Garang's supporters. He was later executed by firing squad. This is how the differences between the southern Sudanese fighting groups of the SPLA and Anya Nya II emerged. After that battle Anya Nya II lost Bilpam to Colonel Garang's loyalists and decided to go back to Sudan, where they joined Akuot and Gai Tut's group. However, after Anya Nya II left Ethiopia, Colonel Garang and his group began accusing one of their supporters, Second Lieutenant Joseph Kiir Tang, of collaborating with Anya Nya II forces. His only crime was that when he left Bor for Ethiopia together with other mutinying soldiers at Bor, he was the one in charge of administration. On arriving in Ethiopia, the mutinying soldiers from Bor, Pibor, and Pochalla had handed over all their military hardware to the Anya Nya II headquarters at Bilpam because they were not allowed to take them into the refugee camp at Itang.

As mentioned earlier, soon afterward, Colonel Garang's supporters mounted an attack on the Anya Nya II headquarters at Bilpam but failed to obtain the military hardware stored there. They eventually executed Joseph Kiir Tang by firing squad despite the fact that he was not acting in isolation. He was carrying out his duties in consultation with his superior officers, including Kerubino Kuanyin, William Nyuon, and Colonel John Garang himself, but they executed him nonetheless. From its very inception, and ideologically speaking, the SPLM/SPLA basically adopted a Soviet-style model of dictatorial leadership similar in structure to that of Colonel

Mengistu Haile Mariam. Colonel Garang and his associates were running the movement in an authoritarian way that victimized and suppressed anyone suspected as an opponent within and outside the movement, including innocent civilians.

SPLA Military Operations and Continuing Hostilities

SPLA soldiers – Juba 2011

Toward the end of 1983, the SPLA acquired sufficient military weaponry from Libya through Ethiopia. It then stepped up a military campaign against both the Sudanese government and the Anya Nya II forces. The SPLA began attacking the government garrisons at Malual Gahoth and Nasir. In November 1983 it attempted to capture Malual Gahoth garrison from the

Sudanese government forces but failed. Malual Gahoth was a small outpost of 150 Sudanese troops on the Ethiopian border. For reasons best known to them, they blamed a Nuer government soldier stationed at Malual Gahoth garrison named Tongyik Gil for their failure. They held Tongyik Gil responsible for the death of SPLA fighters who perished during their attempt to capture the town. Infuriated by their loss, the SPLA dispatched a platoon of thirty soldiers to seize cattle from the cattle byre of Tongyik Gil's brother, Bol Gil, after they returned to their bases inside Ethiopia. Bol Gil was just a civilian living in an area controlled by the SPLA, and he had nothing to do with the activities of his brother Tongyik Gil, but the SPLM/SPLA implicated him anyway. Upon learning about the intention of the SPLA soldiers to punish Bol Gil for the alleged actions of his brother Tongyik Gil, the Gajaak Nuer civilians refused to hand over Bol Gil's cattle to the SPLA soldiers.

Fighting erupted between the SPLA soldiers and the Gajaak Nuer, during which several people were killed on both sides. When the SPLA soldiers returned to their general headquarters at Bilpam and reported these events to their superior officers, a large force was dispatched to punish Gajaak Nuer in general. Fighting went on between the Gajaak Nuer and the SPLA soldiers for several months. Because the SPLA was undoubtedly a strong movement with formidable and powerful military hardware, it inflicted enormous casualties on Gajaak Nuer. During those times, hundreds of innocent civilians, mostly children, women, and old people, were killed. Several hundred civilians were also massacred in cold blood at Manjangdit village by SPLA soldiers under the command of Lieutenant Colonel Francis Ngor Machiek. During these operations, the SPLA forces burned down civilian homes and looted cattle, sheep, goats, and food. Several women and young girls were raped and sexually abused.

Before the SPLA forces attacked the town of Nasir in their military campaign against both the Sudanese government and the Anya Nya II forces, the SPLA leader Colonel John Garang sent a message to the Anya Nya II leaders asking them to go to Ethiopia in order to reunite the two groups under one leadership. When the Anya Nya II leaders Akuot Atem de Mayen and Samuel Gai Tut received Garang's message, they thought it was a genuine move to close the ranks of the southern Sudan armed struggle. They immediately ordered their supporters to march toward Ethiopia in order to finalize the reunification process with the SPLA leadership. In turn, SPLA Chief of Staff William Nyuon Bany was already at Tierguol in Ethiopian territory waiting for the arrival of the Anya Nya II soldiers. As soon as they arrived in the SPLA camp, they were ordered by Commander William Nyuon to lay down their arms and surrender or else be disarmed by force.

When the Anya Nya II soldiers defied the order, Commander William Nyuon immediately ordered his troops to fire at them. In the fight that ensued in Kuratong village in early December 1983, many Anya Nya II soldiers and officers, including their senior commanding officer Deng Majok Chamcar, were killed instantly. The Anya Nya II leadership then decided to return to Sudan and camped at Man-reth homestead in Nyangore area. When the civilians heard of the return of the Anya Nya II forces, the head chiefs from the different homesteads convened an emergency meeting at which they decided to collect food for the freedom fighters. The Anya Nya II leadership met the chiefs and called for a general gathering of the people to explain to the civilians the reasons behind their return from Ethiopia within such a short time compared to the projected length of their mission to reunite the two factions. The Anya Nya II leadership told the civilians that the SPLA of Colonel John Garang under the command of Lieutenant Colonel William Nyuon Bany attacked them. The entire civil population in the area was extremely disappointed to see their sons killing themselves while they had a common enemy awaiting all of them, namely the predominantly Arab northern Sudan.

Undeterred by the trickery they experienced from the SPLM/SPLA that had led to the cold blooded murder of their colleagues, the Anya Nya II forces continued their military operations and eventually closed down the oil fields in Bentiu at the beginning of 1984. They also made numerous successful raids at Nasir and Ulang towns. The Anya Nya II forces spent nearly three months at Nyangore area before they finally returned to Ethiopia in March 1984. On their arrival, the SPLA leader Colonel John Garang and all his commanders refused to meet the Anya Nya II leadership. Instead they were mobilizing their forces stationed in different camps inside Ethiopia with the intention of disarming and capturing all the Anya Nya II leaders. The Anya Nya II forces spent three days without food or water at Itang while the SPLA was planning to mount a joint attack with the Ethiopian security forces that were already at Itang. When Anya Nya II sympathizers attempted to relieve them with food and water, the SPLA denied them access. The Ethiopian chief of security in Gambella, however, did not want the two factions to fight at the refugee camp. Moreover, he was against the SPLA conspiracy, so he informed the Anya Nya II forces. Mr. Thowath Pal, a Nuer from Ethiopia, warned Samuel Gai Tut and the rest secretly that they would be captured and killed if they did not evacuate Itang immediately. Then at midnight Gai and Kuot ordered their soldiers to leave Ethiopia for Sudan. Unfortunately, Samuel Gai Tut was eventually killed by the SPLA forces on March 28, 1984.

Death of Samuel Gai Tut—Leader of Anya Nya II Movement

After the SPLA and Ethiopian security discovered that the Anya Nya II forces were no longer at Itang Refugee Camp, they followed them in helicopters but did not attack them until they reached Liet-nyaruach village, which was close to Adura. It was in this village on March 28, 1984, that the first severe fighting took place between the SPLA and Anya Nya II forces before it escalated to Adura. Following the death of Samuel Gai Tut on March 28, 1984, at the hands of SPLA forces, the Anya Nya II forces went back to Sudan and remained as an opposition force to the SPLA under the leadership of Akuot Atem and William Chuol Deng. The Anya Nya II movement then moved its forces deep into the central Nuer area of Pangak district in order to avoid further military confrontations with the SPLA forces that were occupying the Ethiopia/Sudan frontiers under the continuing leadership of Colonel John Garang.

Meanwhile, the UNHCR was searching for countries to resettle the southern Sudanese refugees. As that was occurring, Bol Kur Alongjok, Bernard Pakam Chap, Opat Opiew, Doluoth Kuoth, Gabriel Aluong, and many others escaped from Gambella to Southern Blue Nile region inside Sudan, which is located along the Sudan-Ethiopia border. They attempted to establish a military camp that was separate from both the SPLA and the Anya Nya II movements. They did this in collaboration with Matthew Obur Ayang, a southern Sudanese politician who was now living in Addis Ababa. Matthew Obur Ayang went to Ethiopia in July 1984 with the intention of joining the SPLM/SPLA, but he was quickly at loggerheads with its leader, Colonel John Garang, when he criticized the Colonel for inciting divisions among southern Sudanese people. You will recall that Matthew Obur was a minister of Education and Guidance and also the last speaker of the People's Regional Assembly in Juba in 1983, before southern Sudan was redivided into the three mini regions of Equatoria, Upper Nile, and Bahr El Ghazal. While in Ethiopia, he stayed at Harambee Hotel in Addis Ababa with the assistance of Libyan agents who rendered him some financial support.

Matthew Obur Ayang

Matthew Obur Ayang wanted to form his own faction under the direct command of Commander Bol Kur Alongjok, a fellow tribesman from his own ethnic Shilluk tribe. Bol Kur, Bernard Pakam, and Opat Opiew were former Anya Nya II commanders who remained in Ethiopia when the joint SPLA and Ethiopian army at Itang and Bilpam expelled their forces to Sudan. Before they escaped to Southern Blue Nile in September 1984, Bol Kur stayed with me (Daniel Wuor Joak) inside the UNHCR campus in Gambella. Under UNHCR protection in Gambella, Bol Kur and other former Anya Nya II commanders secretly decided to escape to the bush inside the Sudan. They were aware of the UNHCR plan to take them out of Ethiopia for resettlement and were opposed to the plan. After they escaped from Gambella, they were attacked by the Oromo Liberation Front (OLF) in their hideout in Southern Blue Nile. One of their associates, Gabriel Aluong, a trained theologian, was killed instantly during the attack. After they escaped the OLF onslaught, they moved to another destination, but they were eventually rounded up again and captured by the Ethiopian security agents pursuing them. Bol Kur, Opat Opiew, Bernard Pakam, and Doluoth Kuoth were arrested and detained for more than a year.

The Fall of Nimeiri, More Hostilities, and an Effort For Peace

MAHMOUD MOHAMMED TAHA, ALSO KNOWN as Ustaz Mahmoud Mohammed Taha, was a Sudanese religious thinker, leader, and trained engineer. He developed what he called the Second Message of Islam, which postulated that the verses of the Qur'an revealed in Medina were appropriate in their time as the basis of sharia (Islamic law) but that the verses revealed in Mecca that represented the ideal religion would be revived when humanity had reached a stage of development capable of accepting them, ushering in a renewed Islam based on freedom and equality. Because of his views, he was executed for apostasy on January 18, 1985, during the height of sharia (Islamic law) in Sudan under President Nimeiri. As Sharia law became entrenched in Sudan, so did the war in southern Sudan. The Anya Nya II freedom movement continued its operations, and at the beginning of 1985, William Chuol Deng emerged as the new leader after the death of Akuot Atem.

During the same year, the fighting between the SPLA and Anya Nya II also intensified vigorously while the SPLA continued to target Gajaak Nuer. At this time, the SPLA also diverted its military offensives against the Gajaak Nuer civilians of Ethiopia on suspicion that they supported the Anya Nya II movement. Because the SPLA soldiers began to routinely loot their cattle and rape their women, the Gajaak Nuer of Ethiopia fought against SPLA forces in self-defense during early 1985. Thus the hostility that began in November 1983 between the SPLA and Gajaak Nuer continued. For example, in March 1985, the Gajaak Nuer civilians fought the SPLA forces and in the process captured and executed Lieutenant Colonel Francis Ngor, the SPLA operation commanding officer, along with ten of his personal bodyguards. He was captured when his car ran out of fuel at Marial village near Jakou. In this fierce fighting, hundreds of civilians and SPLA soldiers were killed, forcing the SPLA forces to retreat to its general headquarters at Bilpam. It is important to note that the Gajaak Nuer civilians of Ethiopia were victimized by the SPLA for no other reason than their sympathy toward the Anya Nya II movement. After this episode, the Anya Nya II forces felt obliged to move to the Ethiopian border in order to protect the Nuer civilians from the constant onslaughts of the SPLA. Because of the constant fights between Anya Nya II combat forces and the SPLA, by early 1985 the whole Upper Nile and some parts of Bahr El Ghazal regions were in a completely chaotic condition. It even became difficult for southern Sudanese living in government-held towns to escape to the rebel-controlled areas. Unfortunately, the conditions of the civilians were just the same in the rebel-controlled areas, as they were in government-controlled areas because the SPLA was also fighting the Anya Nya II rebels who had previously evacuated their military camps inside Ethiopia. The SPLA wanted to destroy Anya Nya II while fighting their common northern Sudanese enemy at the same time—an objective that was practically impossible. It should have concentrated its efforts on Sudanese government troops in southern garrisons instead of fighting both.

As the hostility between the SPLA and Anya Nya II continued, the fall of President Nimeiri became imminent. He was finally overthrown on April 6, 1985, and his fall came as a result of mass demonstrations organized by doctors, lawyers, engineers, students, bankers, and railway workers on the streets of Khartoum. With the airport closed, telephone links cut, and Radio Omdurman off the air, a group of Sudanese professional leaders formed a People's Alliance to coordinate the protests, which the army refused to quash. On April 6, 1985, the army stepped in and declared that Jaafar Nimeiri, who had ruled Sudan from May 25, 1969, was overthrown.

Nimeiri's Defence Minister General Abdulrahman Sawar el Dahab took over, declared emergency law, and suspended the constitution. To Nimeiri's embarrassment, he came to know of his overthrow while boarding a plane in Cairo on his way home from the United States. Egyptian President Hosni Mubarak immediately offered him asylum in the country.

The causes of Nimeiri's downfall include economic stagnation, the civil war that escalated throughout southern Sudan, and the execution of the spiritual leader of the Muslim Brotherhood, Mohammed Mohamud Taha, for apostasy on January 18, 1985. His overthrow brought traditional sectarian interests back to power, and the war continued unabated. Before his overthrow, President Nimeiri in 1983 had undermined and unilaterally abrogated the 1972 Addis Ababa Peace Agreement between southern and northern Sudan.

On April 9, 1985, General Sawar el Dahab formed the Transitional Military Council (TMC) comprising of fifteen senior army officers to act as collective heads of state. He promised a hand-over to civilian rulers as quickly as possible. After President Nimeiri's overthrow, the SPLA immediately declared a cease-fire, demanding that Sawar el Dahab hand over power to civilians within one week. The SPLA's call for transfer of power to civilians within one week was completely rejected by the junta. Consequently, the SPLA withdrew its support for the new government after its demand was turned down. The Transitional Military Council promised that general elections for a civilian government would be held within one year. An election committee was formed to prepare for new elections and a fifteen-member council of ministers was formed to rule the country during the interim period under the premiership of Dr. Gizouli Dafallah, who had been the head of the doctor's association that led the protest against Nimeiri. Samuel Aru Bol, a prominent southern Sudanese politician, was chosen as the deputy to Dr. Gizouli Dafallah. The new government retained the Islamic law (sharia) that was introduced by Nimeiri on September 24, 1983, and had already haphazardly claimed more than three hundred victims of amputation.

Following the fall of President Nimeiri on April 6, 1985, the TMC, headed by General Abdulrahman Sawar el Dahab, initiated contact with the Anya Nya II leadership through an intermediary, Daniel Koat Matthews, the governor of Upper Nile region. Governor Daniel Koat Matthews requested the Anya Nya II movement to send a delegation to Malakal to meet and present its demands to the concerned authorities in Khartoum. As requested, the Anya Nya II leadership indeed sent a delegation to Khartoum in order to negotiate with the government. Commander Gabriel Gany Juoch, a former Commissioner of Jonglei Province led the Anya Nya II delegation.

Daniel Koat (Duoth) Matthews, former governor of Upper Nile state

The crippled Anya Nya II leadership then intensified fights and denied SPLA control in eastern Upper Nile. They made a deal with the new government of Sudan, ostensibly to buy more time in order to consolidate their military strength for possible resumption of full-scale war in the near future.

This deal came to light on July 5, 1985, before the assassination of William Chuol Deng, the Anya Nya II leader. William Chuol Deng was killed by SPLA forces under the Command of Major John Kulang Puot, who was operating in Pangak area. Actually the Anya Nya II forces had known that they could not achieve any durable peace in the south while their brothers were still fighting the Sudanese government. However, they struck that deal with the new government of Sudan in order to temporarily survive the SPLA onslaughts that had continued just as vigorously as before. Khartoum was ready to provide them with military hardware if they agreed to fight the SPLA alongside the government soldiers. As the death of any leader is a setback, so was that of William Chuol Deng. Following William Chuol Deng's death, Commander Gordon Koang Chol took the Anya Nya II leadership. By this time, the SPLA had almost lost control of eastern Upper Nile province because of Anya Nya II hostility toward them. The two factions were fighting almost daily for control of the eastern Upper Nile area. During that fighting, several hundred Nuer civilians got killed, either deliberately by SPLA forces or accidentally in cross fire. The Anya Nya II forces blocked all the routes to Ethiopia and thus denied the SPLA access to fresh recruits and supporters.

In November 1985, the Transitional Military Council officially endorsed the Election Act. During this time, forty-seven parties began preparations for contention. The biggest parties were the Umma Party, led by Sadiq El Mahdi, the Democratic Unionist Party of Mohammed Osman El Mirghani, and the Fundamentalist National Islamic Front (NIF), led by Hassan Abdallah El Turabi. Following the elections, the Umma Party gained the majority in parliament with ninety-seven seats compared with sixty-four for the Democratic Unionist Party of Mohammed Osman El Mirghani. There was no election conducted in southern Sudan because of the ongoing civil war. As the majority leader in the Parliament, Sadiq El Mahdi was elected the prime minister. In the meantime, the SPLA had continued its assaults on the Sudanese government. In late 1985 it was forced to open new routes through the Boma Hills in Pibor County for their forces to reach Jonglei and eastern Equatoria provinces. In spite of the fighting, both sides of the war in the Sudan continued to work for a peaceful resolution of the southern problem. Consequently, in March 1986 the Sudanese government and the SPLM produced the Koka Dam Declaration, which called for a Sudan "free from racism, tribalism, sectarianism and all causes of discrimination and disparity." The declaration also demanded the repeal of the sharia and the opening of a constitutional conference, but the government also wished to avoid a confrontation with the Democratic Unionist Party (DUP) and the National Islamic Front Party (NIF) because they opposed the Koka Dam Declaration. So Nimeiri's former defense minister, General Abdulrahman Sawar el Dahab, who took over from him in preparation for democratic elections, decided to leave the sharia question to the new civilian government.

Following the fall of President Nimeiri, two prominent southern Sudanese politicians were released from Kobar Prison in Khartoum. They were Daniel Koat Matthews, former governor of Upper Nile region who facilitated a meeting between the new government and the leadership of the Anya Nya II movement, and David Dak Gai, former diplomat in the Sudan embassy in Tanzania. They left Sudan for Ethiopia in June 1986 with the intention of joining the SPLA. Three days after Nimeiri's downfall, General Abdulrahman Sawar el Dahab authorized the creation of a fifteen-man Transitional Military Council (TMC) to rule Sudan.

During its first few weeks in power, the TMC had suspended the constitution, dissolved Nimeiri's Sudan Socialist Union (SSU), the secret police, and the parliament and regional assemblies. It had also dismissed regional governors and their ministers and released hundreds of political detainees from Kobar Prison. General Abdulrahman Sawar el Dahab had also promised to negotiate an end to the civil war raging on in southern Sudan and to relinquish power to a civilian government in twelve months. The general populace welcomed and supported the new regime; however, despite the Transitional Military Council's energetic beginning, it soon became evident that General Abdulrahman Sawar el Dahab lacked the skills to resolve Sudan's economic problems, restore peace to southern Sudan, and establish national unity.

SPLA and Anya Nya II Reunification in a Shaky Alliance

THE REUNIFICATION PROCESS OF THE two movements came about in late 1987 through the efforts of Daniel Koat Matthews, former governor of Upper Nile region, and David Dak Gai, former diplomat in the Sudan embassy in Tanzania. They had been released from Kobar Prison in Khartoum following the fall of President Nimeiri. These two politicians left Sudan for Ethiopia in June 1986 with the intention of joining the SPLA. They also had a plan to initiate the reconciliation of the two warring southern Sudan groups that had been battling each other for almost five years for control of the Nasir and Akobo areas. The aim of the SPLA was to eliminate Anya Nya II in order to get fresh recruits from these areas, and the Anya Nya II leadership was on its part fully aware that giving the SPLA access to these areas would undermine their support from the local population.

It took mediators Daniel Koat Matthews and David Dak Gai almost seven months at the border of Sudan and Ethiopia to convince the two rival groups to reconcile their differences. The SPLA Chief of Staff Commander William Nyuon Bany led the SPLA delegation, and the Anya Nya II delegation was headed by the Chief of Staff Commander David Bidiet Deng. The negotiations were conducted at the Ethiopian village of Kuanylou, which was also used by the SPLA as its operational base. After the two groups stopped their hostilities, the Anya Nya II delegation and that of the SPLA went to Addis Ababa and held talks with President Mengistu Haile Mariam and other Ethiopian senior government officials.

The Anya Nya II delegation informed President Mengistu Haile Mariam that it wanted to maintain its status as a separate movement. On the other hand, the SPLA movement, which had an upper hand through the support rendered to them by Mengistu Haile Mariam's regime, wanted to incorporate the Anya Nya forces under their leadership. The Anya Nya II movement split into two groups over this issue. One group, led by the overall leader Gordon Koang Chol, accepted the reunification with the SPLA. However, five other commanders—namely Paulino Matib Nhial, William Reath Gai, Gordon Koang Banypiny, John Both Teny, and Gabriel (Gatwech Chan) Tang Ginya—led the opposing group. The latter commanders categorically refused to work jointly under Colonel John Garang de Mabior, whom they vehemently accused of inciting tribalism and divisive attitudes through his deceptive policies against the people of southern Sudan. They remained at their operational headquarters at Doleib Hill near Malakal and continued to be supported by Khartoum with military supplies against the SPLA.

In the meantime, the Anya Nya II faction led by Gordon Koang Chol was finally incorporated into the SPLA toward the beginning of 1988, and the position reserved for his group in the SPLA hierarchy was called the Politico-Military High Command (PMHC). Commander Gordon Koang himself occupied that position, and the rest of his senior commanders were demoted to lower military ranks. These were Stephen Duol Chol, Vincent Kuany Latjor, James Gatwech Kuany, Peter Tot Bangoang, James Gai Duach, James Yiec Biet, David Bidiet Deng, David Gok Thuok, John Duit Yiec, Riek Machuoc, John Gile Yual, Duoth Lam Juuk, James Biel Joak, Johnny Jock Reth, Hoth Guor Luak, Peter Reath Koda, Peter Bol Kong, David Riek Machuoc, Ruach Nyadeang, Gatwec Yiec Rom, James Tot Wai, Duoth Khon, and several others. There were mixed reactions from the supporters of each group, particularly among the Dinka members within the SPLA. Some Dinka members in the SPLM/SPLA reacted negatively and went so far as accusing Colonel John Garang of betraying the SPLM/SPLA principles and objectives by signing an agreement with *Nyagats*—a name that literally referred to the Anya Nya II as bandits. The SPLM/SPLA Dinka who opposed reunification considered

Anya Nya II as potential enemies, and to make this viewpoint clear, they organized a public rally at Itang Refugee Camp following the endorsement of the reunification. The rally was attended by all SPLA senior commanders, and Commander Arok Thon Arok told the Dinka community members who attended the rally that "This is Gordon Koang Chol who has been killing the Dinka and now we are making peace with him."

The elements within the SPLA who opposed the reunification of the two factions under Colonel John Garang attempted to assassinate Gordon Koang at Itang Refugee Camp. It was through the intervention of Commander William Nyuon Bany that this conspiracy was stopped. The situation was so tense that the supporters of the two groups wanted to fight at Itang Refugee Camp once again. Many people believed that Colonel Garang's detention of Commander Arok Thon in 1988 happened because Arok Thon was against the reunification of the SPLA and Anya Nya II. It was later reported by the SPLA leadership that Arok Thon had attempted to stage a military coup against the SPLA leader Colonel John Garang so that he could sign a deal with the government in his favor as the head of the SPLA movement.

After the reunification, Anya Nya II under Gordon Koang opened its controlled areas to the SPLA. The movement of goods and people was no longer restricted. Southern Sudanese who had been reluctant to join the two groups because of their differences started to join the unified SPLA by the thousands. The newly united SPLA under Colonel John Garang became one of the most powerful liberation movements in the whole continent of Africa. Before the reunification, the SPLA had difficulties in executing the war effectively because the southern Sudanese were badly divided. Despite the fact that the SPLA had been regularly getting sufficient military hardware from different countries through Ethiopia and new recruits, it was not able to capture any important garrison in southern Sudan before reunification with the Anya Nya II forces.

Peace Initiatives and the Church

As the war between the north and the south raged on, the two sides continued efforts for peace initiatives. The SPLM decided to approach the Democratic Unionist Party (DUP) to negotiate a bilateral agreement with the view of bringing them on board into the Koka Dam Agreement, as the DUP was an important junior coalition partner in Sadiq El Mahdi's government. The dialogue with the DUP led to the historic 1988 DUP/SPLM Sudan Peace Agreement, which essentially modified the Koka Dam Declaration on the September Sharia laws of Nimeiri by agreeing to freeze these laws rather than abrogating them as in the Koka Dam Declaration. However, the senior partner (UMMA) in the coalition government opposed the DUP/SPLM Sudan Peace Agreement and actually voted it down on February 21, 1988, which was an embarrassing situation for the DUP and forced them to resign and hence bring about the collapse of the Sadiq (I) government and thereafter the take over of the military junta led by General Omar Hassan Ahmed El Bashir on 30 June, 1989.

The first SPLA major offensive against the Sudanese government troops was launched during 1988–1989, when six thousand former Anya Nya II members combined with several thousand SPLA forces and marched to Equatoria in order to liberate it from the enemy. This was the time the coalition government of Prime Minister Saldiq El Mahdi had already generated an internal rift with its coalition partner, National Islamic Front (NIF) of Hassan El Turabi who instigated the Sudanese army to stage a military coup against the elected government of Prime Minister Sadiq El Mahdi under his influence. Indeed, the Sudanese army was badly demoralized to the point of losing the war in favour of SPLA forces operating in the southern Sudan and Nuba Mountains. The last option was to make a military take over which occurred on 30 June 1989 by General Omar Hassan El Bashir. However, the first major garrison ever captured by the SPLA in that region was Kapoeta in eastern Equatoria province in 1988. This success was followed by Nasir, Torit, Akobo, Bor, Mangalla, Nimule, Waat, and others, just to mention a few of the victories a united southern Sudanese movement achieved in less than six months, following the reunification of the SPLA and Anya Nya II factions. Such victories were greatly scored by the SPLA forces between 1988 to 1989 following the reunification of the two factions in 1988.

As the war continued, so did initiatives for peace. In 1989, US President Carter brokered talks in Nairobi between the various Sudanese factions, and the church continued its involvement in trying to bring about peace in Sudan. The church had continued its spiritual and social activities in southern Sudan until the second phase of the war started again in 1975 and intensified to a full-scale civil war in 1983. Before the resumption of the second civil war, all the churches in the Sudan were united under one umbrella: the Sudan Council of Churches (SCC), a body formed by the Sudanese churches in 1965. As a result of the war, the unified church leadership was divided into two bodies. One group remained in the government-controlled areas and retained the old name Sudan Council of Churches, but in 1990, the churches that were operating in the SPLA-controlled areas were organized as the New Sudan Council of Churches (NSCC). However, the objectives of the two church organizations remained the same. As spiritual leaders of the southern Sudanese Christians, they found themselves in conflict with the Sudanese opposing leaders on all sides. The successive Islamic governments in Khartoum accused the church leaders inside Sudan of being SPLA supporters. On the other hand, the church leaders in the SPLA areas were also accused of supporting different factions, which made them prime targets of their own people.

A practical example was when Bishop Paride Taban was slapped by SPLA commander Kuol Manyang Juk in the early 1990s. The cause of the dispute was that Bishop Taban refused for his car to be used for military operations by the SPLA forces under the command of Commander William Nyuon Bany. It became difficult for the church leaders in the liberated areas in southern Sudan to bring the different opposing SPLA groups together. This was true because some of these church leaders had involved themselves by openly supporting various opposing groups. However, the church leaders in the south could still play a leading role in the reconciliation because they were a part of the society and also commanded formidable respect. This respect would be possible only if they disassociated themselves from supporting either opposing group in the south and stood firmly in their neutrality. They succeeded in that regard until the split in the SPLA/SPLM movement in August 1991.

Progress and Sabotage Within the SPLM/SPLA

BY 1990 THE SPLA WAS already controlling almost 90 percent of southern Sudan territories but not the three principal towns of Wau, Juba, and Malakal. Our dreams for attaining quick and lasting peace in the Sudan regardless of our differences were certainly closer to reality. The southern Sudanese patriots were celebrating the victories scored by the SPLA both at home and abroad with great joy and happiness. Then something odious began to happen. Members of an otherwise powerful movement began to turn on each other.

While the SPLA was scoring victories on the battlefield, its leader, Colonel John Garang, and his henchmen started hunting for suspected opponents within the movement. Several high-ranking officers or prominent politicians who had joined the movement voluntarily in order to liberate their oppressed people were unjustly detained for over five years without trial. All those detainees were kept isolated in incommunicado camps in the Boma Hills, eastern and western Equatoria regions. These detention centers were not accessible to SPLA soldiers or to common people. Some of the detainees died in prison due to starvation and torture. On orders from their superior officers, their guards murdered some of them. Over forty thousand SPLA combatants were just roaming the bushes of southern Sudan for about two years from 1990 to 1991, without any effective military gains against the government of Sudan which was still controlling major towns like Juba, Malakal, Wau, Bentiu etc. The reason for their redundancy was that Colonel John Garang did not want them to attack Juba or any other principal city in the south. Colonel John

Garang's master plan was to liquidate all his opponents before capturing Juba, the future capital of South Sudan.

Around the same time, about sixteen thousand minors, mostly young boys between ages five and fifteen, were collected by the SPLA leadership from their parents on the pretext that these children would be sent to different parts of the world for studies. The majority of them were from the Dinka and Nuer nationalities. About six hundred of them were sent to Cuba for education and military training. The rest remained in the bushes of southern Sudan and were later used as child soldiers. The minors who were taken to Cuba went to various institutions and completed their studies. They were later taken to Canada for resettlement. The SPLA forces that were wandering in the bushes also played nasty roles by terrorizing the local population in different parts of southern Sudan. Between 1987 and 1991, these forces massacred the Mundari, Murle, and Taposa minority ethnic groups in the thousands. They also looted their cattle and destroyed their homes. Such human rights abuses did not end until after the 1991 split in the SPLA.

Breeding Tribal Tension in Refugee Camps and Mengistu's Fall

THE SUSPICION BETWEEN THE NUER and Dinka mounted in the refugee camps of Itang, Pinyodu, and Dimma, where the Nuer civilians were always prime targets of gross human rights abuses. Rape and sexual harassment, torture and cold blooded killings were common. In Bonga Training Centre many new recruits were murdered in cold blood, and the officers in charge of the camp did nothing about these murders other than asking the fresh recruits to bury them without identifying the victims. During this time SPLA soldiers in the refugee camps seized thousands of young boys aged ten to fifteen from the Nuer tribe without the approval of their parents.

The so-called lost boys of Sudan - 1988

Others were captured in the Gajaak area and from other parts of Nuerland during the fighting, and they were handed over to the Ethiopian government on the pretext that they were Ethiopian citizens. During Colonel Mengistu Haile Mariam's rule in Ethiopia, over five thousand of them were forcibly conscripted into the Ethiopia National Army and sent to northern Ethiopia to fight against the Eritrean People's Liberation Front (EPLF) and the Ethiopian People's Revolutionary Democratic Forces (EPRDF). Most of these boys were either killed in action or died of war-related diseases.

On May 25, 1991, Colonel Mengistu Haile Mariam was finally overthrown. Following the fall of his regime on May 25, 1991, about 177 of the Nuer boys handed over to the Ethiopian government to fight in the Ethiopian wars on the pretext that they were Ethiopian citizens managed to find their way to Addis Ababa, where they were immediately handed over to the UNHCR office in order to transport them to Gambella en route to their areas of origin in southern Sudan. The UNHCR refused them on the grounds that they were Ethiopian soldiers because most of them wore ragged military clothes. The majority of them were bare-footed, and they could speak only the Nuer language, their mother tongue. One of the survivors was Kor Tut Lam, whom I left in Nyangore village in 1984 when he was only seven years old.

In May 1991 the Ethiopian People's Revolutionary Democratic Front forces advanced on Addis Ababa from all sides, forcing Mengistu to flee the country to Zimbabwe, where he was granted asylum as an official guest of Zimbabwean President Robert Mugabe.

SPLM/SPLA Splits in August 1991

Dr. Riek Machar—leader of SPLM/SPLA Nasir Faction, 1991

BEFORE THE FALL OF MENGISTU's regime in Ethiopia, discontent within the SPLA leadership grew tremendously following the detention of several SPLA senior commanders, some of whom had already languished in SPLA incommunicado centers for over five years. Many of the detained SPLA senior officers differed with Col. John Garang on how to prosecute the war for the independence of southern Sudan. All the southern Sudanese people have always regarded themselves as victims of political and social injustices being committed against them by different Islamic and Arabized regimes in Sudan. However, Colonel Garang was adamant about maintaining the SPLA objectives and principles of fighting for a "United Secular New Sudan." This kind of disagreement within the leadership of the SPLM/SPLA eventually brought further splits within the movement.

Following is some information quoted from the official document entitled "Why John Garang Must Go Now". This was a document sent out following the Nasir Declaration announced by three SPLA commanders—namely, Dr. Riek Machar, Dr. Lam Akol, and Commander Gordon Koang Chol—who broke away from Colonel John Garang on August 28, 1991. Among other things, the document stated that the causes of the split are traceable to the history of the SPLM/SPLA formation and to the brutal and dictatorial way in which Colonel John Garang fought his way to the leadership of the organization with the help of Mengistu's regime, the Ethiopian leader having been the first principal ally of the SPLM/SPLA.

1. The first issue that led to the Nasir Declaration in August 1991 was the state of human rights in the Movement especially the following:
   a) Summary execution of SPLM/SPLA members without trial. Examples of members who were executed without trial include Dr. Juac Kerjok, Bol Kur Alongjok, Lakurnyang Lado, Bejimen Bol Akok, Tokuach Bangoang, Mabil Chuol Git, Joseph Kiir Tang, Manasseh Manyang Dhieu, Paul Luth Tay, James Ruon Rut, James Gatwech and many others.
   b) Arbitrary imprisonment incommunicado of prominent South Sudanese politicians and SPLM/SPLA officers under sub-human and dreadful conditions. The "Nasir Declaration" produced a list of some SPLM/SPLA political detainees and those executed at that time. [The list is included in Appendix II.]
   c) Whole sections of tribes were massacred either just to loot their property or because they had protested the abuse of their fundamental human rights. The cases in point are the massacres committed against the Gajaak Nuer, the Murle, the Mundari and the Toposa people.

c) Forced recruitment of children into the SPLA.
2. The second issue of the split was the objective of the movement. When the SPLM/SPLA was formed in 1983, there was an immediate debate regarding the objective of the war. The issue was whether the objective was the liberation of Southern Sudan or the whole Sudan. This issue was discussed alongside the issue of leadership. The first split immediately erupted in 1983 when Colonel Garang opposed and attacked, with the help of Mengistu's forces, the elected leadership of the Movement.
3. The third reason for the split in the SPLM/SPLA was the issue of democracy. The examples cited below highlight the lack of democracy in the Movement:
   a) Prior to the split, the SPLM/SPLA Political and Military High Command never met but orders were passed down for implementation.
   b) There was a complete absence of collective leadership.
   c) The SPLM/SPLA lacked basic organizational structures and institutions.
   d) There was an absence of the rule of law which resulted in extra-judicial murder, lynching within the Movement and massacre of defenceless communities.
   e) There was alienation of the intellectuals and non-involvement in all creative activities of the Movement.
   f) There was mismanagement and lack of accountability of the Movement's financial and material resources.

It was clear why the split occurred abruptly within the SPLM/SPLA movement following the fall of Mengistu's regime in Ethiopia. Some external sympathizers with SPLA tried their best to find out the truth behind the split in the movement, and they concluded that the fall of Mengistu's regime was the main cause of the division within the southern Sudanese movement in 1991; the SPLA had lost its closest ally in Mengistu Haile Mariam. However, it was inevitable that even if the three SPLA senior commanders did not stage a coup against their leader, Colonel John Garang, other officers and men within the SPLA would have done the same thing. The discontent within the leadership of the movement became known even to the noncombatants. It started in 1987–1988 following the reunification of the SPLA and Anya Nya II factions under Colonel Garang's leadership. It started with the detention of two SPLA permanent members of the Politico-Military High Command, Commander Kerubino Kuanyin Bol and Commander Arok Thon Arok, who disagreed in principle with the SPLA leader Colonel John Garang. The two commanders accused Colonel Garang of running the movement as his own personal property. Colonel John Garang detained Kerubino Kuanyin, who was by then his deputy, in 1987. Commander Arok was the number four man in the SPLA ranks in early 1988 following this incident.

When Colonel Mengistu Haile Mariam was finally overthrown on May 25, 1991, about half a million southern Sudanese refugees fled back to the liberated areas of Akobo, Nasir, Pochalla, and Pibor in southern Sudan. Unfortunately, the National Islamic Front regime in Khartoum welcomed them back to Sudan with severe aerial bombardments using Russian-built Antonov planes. Some international news media as well as local and foreign NGOs reported that over one hundred innocent refugees died on their way as a result of the Sudanese government's action. It is no secret that the Islamic military regime in Khartoum considered all the southern Sudanese people as their potential enemies. On the other hand, the SPLA made a mistake of not taking precautionary measures since its leadership was aware of the imminent attack from the EPRDF rebels, one of whose aims was to drive SPLA forces off Ethiopian soil.

Instead of evacuating the refugees in advance to avoid enormous casualties, Colonel Garang ordered three senior SPLA commanders—namely, Commander Salva Kiir Mayardit, SPLA Deputy Chief of Staff, Commander Riek Machar, and Commander Gordon Koang—to attack the advancing EPRDF rebels. Despite the fact that the president of Ethiopia, Colonel Mengistu, had already fled the country, Colonel John Garang issued his orders right from eastern Equatoria through a long-range radio set. Fortunately, commanders Riek Machar and Gordon Koang Chol refused to execute

Colonel Garang's orders. Instead, they ordered the refugees to evacuate Itang and other refugee centers inside Ethiopia as quickly as possible. In turn, Commander Salva Kiir told the refugees at Itang not to evacuate the area. Since Commander Salva Kiir was the third person in the SPLA hierarchy, Commander Riek Machar and Commander Gordon Koang had little choice but to defy his orders. They eventually left Itang Refugee Camp for Nasir together with Commander Lam Akol and a small number of refugees who listened to their advice. The majority of the refugees were left behind inside Ethiopia along with Commander Salva Kiir. When the Oromo Liberation Front (OLF) and their Ethiopian Anyuak Militia allies entered Itang, Pinyodu, and Dimma refugee camps on May 25, 1991, they started an indiscriminate massacre in the camps, where more than five hundred thousand refugees lived. Several hundred refugees, mostly children and old people, were later reported to have drowned in the Baro River.

The southern Sudanese refugee casualties were so enormous because these attacks happened during the rainy season. It is also worth mentioning that before the evacuation of the refugees from Ethiopia, there were about two thousand war-disabled persons at Itang Refugee Camp alone. Only three hundred of them managed to find their way to the SPLA-liberated areas of Nasir and Akobo. The rest died inside Ethiopia. Commander Salva Kiir, along with ten thousand minors that the SPLA deliberately collected from their parents by force during 1988–1989, first went to Pochalla and later on to Kapoeta in eastern Equatoria region. The same minors later became known as the lost boys. After all the southern Sudanese refugees had evacuated from Ethiopian soil, Colonel John Garang sent a message to commanders Riek Machar, Lam Akol, and Gordon Koang Chol to go to Torit in eastern Equatoria in order to attend the Politico-Military High Command (PMHC) conference that was supposed to convene at the beginning of September 1991. According to some sources within the SPLA leadership, the three commanders were advised by their colleagues in Torit not to go because Colonel Garang wanted to arrest them for defying his orders while they were in Ethiopia. Commander Lam Akol had a problem of his own: the allegation of his collaboration with the enemy.

The refugees who managed to return to southern Sudan were settled in the liberated areas. There, they were assisted by different international humanitarian organizations. However, the suspicion and mistrust among the SPLA rank and file remained extremely high. On August 28, 1991, three members of the PMHC—Dr. Riek Machar Teny Dhurgon, Dr. Lam Akol Ajawin, and Commander Gordon Koang Chol—sent a radio message to all SPLA units announcing that Colonel John Garang no longer enjoyed the confidence of the rank and file and must therefore relinquish the leadership of the movement. On that same day the three commanders had an interview at Nasir with the BBC correspondent Colins Blake, who was based in Nairobi. The interview was broadcast on the BBC *Focus on Africa* on August 30, 1991. The reasons for the Nasir move were (a) to redefine the objectives of the struggle to accommodate the right of self-determination for the people of southern Sudan; (b) to democratize and institutionalize organizational structures in the movement; and (c) to respect human rights in the movement.

Colonel Garang's reaction to the announcement came in a press statement issued following a meeting attended by ten SPLA senior officers. He defied the announcement and insisted that he was still in charge. This meeting was attended by Colonel John Garang, Commander William Nyuon Bany, Commander Salva Kiir Mayardit, Commander Kuol Manyang Juk, Commander James Wani Igga, Commander Daniel Awet Akot, Commander Galerio Modi Horinyang, Commander Martin Manyiel Ayuel, Commander Lual Ding Wol, and Commander Yusuf Kowa Mekki, who sent his support through a radio message from the Nuba Mountains. The attendants were quoted as saying that "We are solidly behind Colonel John Garang's leadership and assure everybody that we would never attack the positions held by the three breakaway SPLA commanders in Upper Nile province." The government of Sudan was also cautious by not showing any sort of reaction that might be interpreted as supportive of the coup against Colonel Garang. The breakaway group from the SPLA was advocating the division of the country, which was not embraced by the NIF military regime in Khartoum.

Lam Akol (right) with Garang, William Nyuon and others

In an attempt to enlighten the neighboring countries and also to try to reconcile their differences with the SPLA Torit Faction, the SPLA Nasir Faction dispatched a delegation to Nairobi in September 1991 headed by Dr. Lam Akol, the secretary for external affairs and peace. Some of the neighboring countries (including Kenya) were pleased to see the change in the southern Sudanese movement. However, Dr. Riek Machar sent Dr. Lam Akol, who was known by Kenyan authorities to have close contacts with some Kenyan dissidents opposed to President Daniel Arap Moi's leadership. The Kenyan authorities frustrated the Nasir Faction delegation for nearly a month without meeting the concerned people in the Ministry of Foreign Affairs. At one point, I intervened by asking a close friend, Sammy Korir, to contact State House Comptroller Abraham Kiptanui so that the Nasir Faction's delegation could meet Foreign Minister and Permanent Secretary Bethwel Kiplagat in the ministry. Sammy Korir immediately contacted Dr. Lam Akol by telephone. They had a lengthy discussion in which he promised Dr. Akol that he would contact his government on behalf of the delegation.

During their telephone conversation, he also related to Dr. Akol the reasons why the Kenyan authorities were reluctant to meet his delegation. This reluctance was due to Dr. Akol's alleged collaboration with the Sudanese government as well as his contacts with some Kenyan dissidents close to veteran politician Oginga Odinga. They touched on the role of Dr. Akol's wife, who had been sent twice to Norway by SPLA leader Colonel John Garang. I was present during this conversation, and Dr. Lam Akol honestly regretted the role of his wife, for which he condemned Colonel Garang. He also accused Colonel Garang of using his wife in order to advance his political goals. Despite those difficulties, Dr. Riek Machar had no reason to deny Dr. Lam Akol the opportunity to head the delegation to Kenya: his critics could have accused him of using the same policies that brought the split within the SPLM/SPLA. If he had delegated another person to head the Nasir Faction mission to Kenya instead of Dr. Lam Akol, the Kenyan position would have been quite positive toward the group immediately.

It must be emphasized that on August 28, 1991, the Nasir Declaration was received with mixed reactions by the southern Sudanese people and their sympathizers abroad. Perhaps this was the case because most people had not forgotten the atrocities committed earlier, following the first split between the SPLA and Anya Nya II groups. That split resulted in the death of more than twenty thousand people in the Upper Nile region. Many observers also felt that Colonel Garang might not keep his promise of not attacking the breakaway faction of the SPLA. While the supporters of the SPLA Nasir Faction were stepping up their political campaign in order to explain to the international community the reasons that led to the movement's splitting into two factions, Colonel Garang and his henchmen were also busy in the field mobilizing their supporters in different parts of southern Sudan, to launch a military offensive against the Nasir Faction. Indeed, their first military offensive was launched in October 1991, when they used a five-hundred-ton barge belonging to the Norwegian People's Aid (NPA), which was operating in the

Bor area. A Norwegian company called Actros Framnæs A/S had donated this barge to the Norwegian Red Cross in 1990.

The Norwegian Red Cross handed over the same barge to the NPA so that the NPA could use it for delivering food and other items to the victims of war in southern Sudan through the River Nile. The barge was taken by the SPLA from the NPA for military operations against the SPLA Nasir Faction's forces stationed at Leer and Adok, either willingly or by force. The SPLA Torit Faction's chief of staff, Commander William Nyuon Bany, took the barge, along with fifteen hundred soldiers. They attacked the two garrisons and briefly occupied them. However, a week later, the combined forces of the Nasir Faction and remnants of the Anya Nya II forces under Commander Paulino Matip Nhial rooted them out. In the press statement issued by the Information Department of the SPLA Nasir Faction, it was reported that "The barge of the NPA, which was used by the Torit Faction for military operations against our forces at Leer and Adok, has completely been destroyed."

Following the defeat of the SPLA Torit Faction's forces at Leer and Adok in October 1991, the SPLA leader Colonel John Garang, along with his deputies William Nyuon Bany, Salva Kiir Mayardit, and Kuol Manyang Juk, mobilized their forces again from eastern Equatoria and Bahr El Ghazal regions. The aim was to recapture all the areas controlled by the breakaway SPLA Nasir Faction. They sent a large force under the command of Commander William Nyuon Bany to reclaim Ayod, Pangak, Waat, Akobo, and Nasir from the SPLA Nasir Faction. Because the SPLA Nasir Faction knew of the plan in advance, they also mobilized their forces, and they were put on maximum alert for imminent attacks by the SPLA Torit Faction. The SPLA Nasir Faction forces were attacked on November 7, 1991, at Kuac-Deng village near the town of Ayod. However, combined forces of the SPLA Nasir Faction and Anya Nya II under commanders Paulino Matip Nhial, William Reath Gai, Gabriel Tang Ginye, John Both Teny, and Gordon Koang Banypiny drove out the SPLA Torit Faction forces and proceeded to Kongor and Bor garrisons on November 18 and 22, 1991.

Several hundred civilians—mostly women and children—in Bor and Kongor towns were killed in the cross fire. After the SPLA Nasir Faction forces withdrew from Bor and Kongor towns on December 20, 1991, NPA, a Norwegian humanitarian organization, made a video showing that the fight was a deliberate massacre conducted by Nuer against Dinka civilians. In this fight, Colonel Garang had underrated the support rendered to the SPLA Nasir Faction by remnants of different Anya Nya II groups and the local population in the areas occupied by the new group. It appeared that the mistake of the first split between SPLA and Anya Nya II under the leadership of Kuot Atem de Mayen and Samuel Gai Tut was repeated.

The SPLA version of the fighting at Kongor and Bor towns was detailed by Lieutenant General James Wani Igga in his book titled *Battles Fought and the Secrecy of Diplomacy*. On page 262, he indicates that the "Bor statistic of losses relayed to my office, as PMHC Chief of Civil Administration and Political Work were 2053 persons decimated; 1328 women and children abducted; 1,070,389 livestock and 246,173 chickens looted." If the above figures are to be believed, the fighting truly devastated the Bor area. However, the statistics given by Lieutenant General James Wani Igga seem incorrect and misleading. The number of people killed could not have exceeded one thousand persons on both sides. The attackers from the SPLA Nasir Faction and their sympathizers indeed lost some of their fighters, too. Some women and children abductees were reported, but Dr. Riek Machar, the leader of the breakaway faction, collected and returned all of them to the Kongor area.

The figures presented in Lieutenant General James Wani Igga's *Battles Fought and the Secrecy of Diplomacy* related to events that occurred before the SPLA Torit Faction launched its major attack on Riek Machar's forces on March 27, 2003, at Panyagor in the Kongor area. The report that more than one million livestock and a quarter of a million chickens were looted by the White Army (Nuer) during the brief occupation of Kongor and Bor area was inaccurate and mere propaganda. It is to be noted that, in early 1993, Dr. Riek Machar and his British late wife Emma McCoy invited some international relief organizations to assist the displaced people in the Kongor area. It could not be denied that the most affected communities were those of Duk and Kongor, who lost some of their livestock during the fighting. However, taking live chickens from the Bor area to Nuer land—a seven-day walk—during floods was practically impossible. Lieutenant General James Wani Igga's sources were rather unreliable and probably misleading. Any southerner who loves all the communities in southern Sudan would fully regret the loss of lives and property. The killings in Kongor, Bor, and other parts of southern Sudan by southerners were unacceptable, but the events should not be distorted for propaganda purposes at the expense of the people.

Subsequently, a large number of Nuer civilians, whose properties had previously been stolen or forcibly taken by some Dinka SPLA soldiers to the Bor area before the split, participated in these interfactional fights alongside the SPLA Nasir Faction. They did so to recover their lost property. The local populations of Akobo, Waat, Ayod, and Fangak were particularly hostile to the SPLA commander Kuol Manyang, whom they specifically accused of being responsible for the loss of thousands of cattle and all the atrocities committed by some SPLA soldiers in the area. Before the split occurred within the SPLM/SPLA, Commander Kuol Manyang was responsible for the administration of these garrisons and their surrounding areas. Some SPLA soldiers from the Bor area raided these villages and forcibly took some young Nuer girls and cattle. It was for those actions that the local population of those areas perceived the SPLA as an occupying force and consequently received the split with joy.

In January 1992, when the forces of the SPLA Torit Faction failed to make any headway against the SPLA Nasir Faction, the SPLA Torit commanders Daniel Awet Akot and Magar Achiek, who were responsible for administration of the Bahr El Ghazal and western Equatoria regions, ordered their forces to massacre all their SPLA colleagues from the Nuer tribe in retaliation for the so-called Bor massacre. When the task was successfully accomplished, they were again mobilized and sent to the Bentiu area to kill the Nuer civilians and loot their property as well. When the combined SPLA Torit Faction and the Dinka civilians attempted to penetrate the western Nuer area in Bentiu, they were defeated and chased back to the Dinka areas, but, sadly, some senior

Dinka officers from the Torit Faction in the Equatoria region decided to murder their Nuer colleagues in retaliation.

The Nuer soldiers and officers in Equatoria were killed by the hundreds. Among those killed were Charles Kuot Chatim, former minister of administration, police and prison in the regional government; A/Commander Peter Reath Koda, former manager of Malakal Hotel; A/Commander Gatwech Kuany; A/Commander James Kaclech Toang; and Captain Johnny Jock Reth. When some SPLA Nasir Faction commanders received the information about the massacre of Nuer soldiers and officers in the Equatoria and Bahr El Ghazal regions, they planned to liquidate their few Dinka colleagues who were with them as well. The leadership of the SPLA Nasir Faction, however, was totally against any action of the sort, so it vigorously warned some of their suspected officers not to behave in the same manner as the SPLA Torit Faction. However, some commanders, without the knowledge of the SPLA Nasir Faction's leadership, committed some murders independently. The deaths of Captain Manyuon and Lamdit and Aluong Gabriel Aluong were committed by some Nasir Faction loyalists. Meanwhile, in the SPLA Torit Faction, the liquidation of Nuer colleagues had become a daily routine. Several hundred officers and men were deliberately killed in cold blood. These killings went on as each group accused the other of starting the factional fighting. Eventually, the split turned into tribal feuds between the Dinka and Nuer, the two largest ethnic groups in southern Sudan.

Several attempts were made by different Sudanese church leaders based in the liberated areas, under the umbrella of the New Sudan Council of Churches and National Council of Churches of Kenya, to reconcile the two SPLA factions. However, all efforts made by these church leaders ended up in failure, simply because the two factions could not agree in principle to resolve their outstanding differences through peaceful means. Colonel Garang wanted the three commanders who broke away from him to rejoin the SPLA mainstream under him without discussing their demands. On the other hand, the SPLA Nasir Faction did not want to rejoin the SPLA under Colonel Garang without any formal agreement between them. They wanted at least some of their demands to be fulfilled before any reunification of the movement took place, but this was totally unacceptable to Colonel John Garang. Colonel Garang believed that he would no longer be able to maintain the same level of political and military power once the two factions reunited under one leadership. So the best way for him was to frustrate all efforts toward unity of the two factions with the hope that in the long run the breakaway group would end up joining him the way Anya Nya II had in 1987. As the fighting between the two factions continued, there were more peace initiatives, such as the Frankfurt Peace Talks in Germany in 1992 and the Abuja Peace Talks I in Nigeria in 1992.

More Peace Initiatives and Continuing Hostilities

IN MAY 1992 THE TWO wings of the SPLA sent their delegations to Abuja, Nigeria, in order to meet with the Sudanese government delegation so that all parties involved could end the ongoing conflict between northern and southern Sudan. That round of the Sudanese peace talks was branded Abuja I Peace Talks. The then-chairman of the Organisation of African Unity (OAU), former Nigerian head of state General Ibrahim B. Babangida, initiated the talks. Commander William Nyuon Bany of the SPLA Torit Faction and Dr. Lam Akol Ajawin of the SPLA Nasir Faction led the two SPLA delegations. The government delegation was led by Colonel Mohammed El Amin El Khalifa, then the speaker of the (NIF) Transitional National Assembly. In its opening address to the peace conference, the Sudanese Islamic government delegation refused to discuss the right of self-determination for the oppressed people in southern Sudan with the SPLM/SPLA, saying that self-determination could be achieved only through the barrel of the gun. To counter the government delegation's position, the two SPLA factions agreed to form a united delegation as the only way to present their position more effectively, which is what they did.

The Abuja I Peace Talks lasted for several days, coming to an end on May 26, 1992, without finding any concrete solution to the Sudanese problem. The two SPLA delegations returned to Nairobi and proceeded to southern Sudan to brief their respective leaders about the outcome of the talks. However, the leader of the SPLA Torit Faction, Colonel John Garang, was not pleased with the initiative taken by his deputy William Nyuon to unite the two delegations during the Abuja I Peace Talks without consulting with him. Angered by the move, he opted to assassinate Commander William Nyuon, ordering one of his closest aides, Commander Kuol Manyang Juk, to carry out the plot.

On September 27, 1992, Kuol Manyang executed Colonel Garang's orders by attacking Commander William Nyuon and his bodyguards at the Pageri-Ame junction. In the first ambush, eighty people, mostly women and children, were killed by Colonel Garang's soldiers. Commander William Nyuon had about two hundred soldiers who managed to resist Garang's forces for several days. Some Latuka tribesmen rendered them some services until they were reinforced by forces from the SPLA Nasir Faction under the command of Commander Peter Bol Kong. The SPLA Nasir Faction's forces were specifically sent from the Upper Nile region to assist Commander William Nyuon and his followers in the eastern Equatoria region, following his defection from the SPLA mainstream. During the fighting between Garang's forces and those of Commander William Nyuon, three United Nations Children's Fund (UNICEF) expatriates or foreign relief workers operating in the SPLA Torit Faction–controlled areas in southern Sudan and a Norwegian journalist named Mr. Helge Hummelvoll, were also killed in the cross fire.

In his capacity as a deputy to Colonel Garang, Commander William Nyuon appealed to all the opposing groups, including those that were still under Colonel John Garang, to rally behind him for the unity of southern Sudanese people. He formed the SPLA Unity Forces with the support of some former SPLA political detainees and prominent southern Sudanese politicians based in the neighboring country of Kenya, including Joseph Oduho, Dr. Amon Wantuk, George Maker Benjamin, and Dr. Richard Kabi Mulla. At the time Commander William Nyuon's forces were fighting the SPLA Torit Faction for the control of the eastern Equatoria region, the SPLA Nasir Faction launched military operations against the advancing SPLA Torit forces, which aimed to reclaim all the territories they had previously lost to the SPLA Nasir group following the split.

On October 22, 1992, the SPLA Nasir forces attacked and briefly captured the town of Malakal, the provincial capital of Upper Nile region. Their forces inflicted heavy casualties on the NIF government forces: over seven hundred government troops were killed, including ten Iranian military advisors. The Nasir Faction forces then occupied the town for two days before they withdrew. The SPLA Torit Faction immediately dismissed the victory scored by the SPLA Nasir Faction, claiming that the fighting in Malakal and its subsequent occupation was actually done by Wurnyang Gatkek—a Nuer spiritual leader who mobilized the Nuer Youth (*White Army*)—and not by the Nasir Faction of SPLA as claimed. Numerous accusations and counteraccusations by both sides became a daily routine in which the truth could hardly be verified by independent sources.

Nuer Peace Initiatives

ON CHRISTMAS EVE 1992, A year after the split occurred within the SPLM/SPLA rank and file in the town of Nasir, some Ethiopian Nuer community elders from Gambella—namely Ato Mark Chol Joak, James Jock Moun, Dr. Koang Tut Lam, Ramesy Rambang Chol, Rev. Peter Pal Panom, and Rev. John Cheng Chut had just returned from Nasir to Addis Ababa with help from the Ethiopia government who transported them by helicopter to Addis Ababa.They fled there following the fall of Mengistu's regime in May 1991, to the southern Sudan town of Nasir, which was under the control of the SPLM/SPLA Nasir Faction. Their intention was to brief people on how the new Ethiopian government and their Anyuak allies had been conducting wanton and systematic killings against the Ethiopian Nuer of Gambella. The Ethiopian Revolutionary Democratic Front (EPRDF) and Gambella People's Liberation Front (GPLF) consistently accused the Nuer of being agents of Mengistu and sympathizers with the SPLA. Of course, the SPLA was operating throughout Ethiopia, but the Ethiopian Nuer had been opposed to the rebellious movements against Mengistu's regime. Ato Mark Chol was a former MP in the Ethiopian Parliament representing the Gambella constituency. The rest were government officials who formerly worked in Gambella before the fall of Mengistu's regime in May 1991. Ato Mark Chol accused the EPRDF and GPLF of being responsible for the death of hundreds of innocent Nuer of Ethiopia as well as southern Sudanese refugees with Nuer ethnicity. By doing so, he wanted the Nuer to take drastic action against the Anyuak. Because the intraclan conflicts throughout Nuerland had become obvious, a general conference was urgently needed. A Reconciliation Nuer Peace Committee was eventually formed. While in Addis Ababa, the Nuer elders came to me at Tourist Hotel where I was putting up following my brief visit from Norway in December 1992. Their mission was to inform me about their intention to travel to Gambella, where they would attend the conference between the Nuer and Anyuak of Gambella. But they also encountered some financial problems that would not enable them to go to Gambella as already proposed. In my response to their concerns, I told them that the idea of reconciling the two hostile communities was good. But this would need urgent intervention from the central government in Addis that should facilitate your movement to Gambella. In their response to my suggestion, the Nuer elders said that they had already approached the Ethiopia government over that issue but they were unable to facilitate their mission financially. However, the government in Addis was willing to provide them with their security to Gambella if they were to secure funding directly from any source. In this case, I promised the Nuer elders that I would be very willing to support them financially if their mission to Gambella would bring peace between Anyuak and Nuer of Gambella. This was because the Anyuak in Gambella were very hostile to Nuer presence in the town, where they intentionally targeted both the Nuer from Ethiopia and refugees from southern Sudan who attempted several times to return to Gambella. Ato Mark Chol assured me that he would contact the EPRDF leadership in Addis to provide for them somebody senior to accompany them to Gambella during the conference. Then, I promised to facilitate their traveling to Gambella financially, in which I pledged $ 500 USD as part of my personal contributions for this mission which I saw as very important. In turn, the Ethiopian Nuer elders became so pleased with my willingness to assist them financially with such an amount which was more than enough to cater for their air tickets and accommodationduring the conference in Gambella. Indeed, the Ethiopian Nuer delegation to the peace talks eventually went to Gambella where they successfully reconciled the two bitter rival communities of Nuer and Anyuak of Gambella. The resultant effects of their mission had later encouraged tens of thousands of southern Sudanese refugees to return to Ethiopia under UNHCR protection.

Other Activities, Peace Initiatives, and the Death of Joseph Oduho

Joseph Oduho—one of the founders of the SPLM/SPLA movement

IN EARLY 1993 DR. RIEK Machar and his British wife, Emma McCoy, invited some international relief organizations to assist the displaced people in the Kongor area. On March 27, 1993, the southern Sudanese political groups—except the SPLA Torit Faction under Colonel John Garang, who turned down the invitation—met at Kongor in southern Sudan, where they forged unity among themselves. They eventually formed the SPLA-United under the leadership of Dr. Riek Machar Teny Dhurgon. The southern leaders who attended the Kongor meeting were Dr. Riek Machar, Dr. Lam Akol Ajawin, Commander William Nyuon Bany, Commander Kerubino Kuanyin Bol, Commander Arok Thon Arok, Joseph H. Oduho, Commander Gordon Koang Chol, and several other senior officers. While they were conducting the reunification process, SPLA Torit forces, commanded by Commander Kuol Manyang Juk and Commander Bior Ajang Dut, made a surprise attack on the forces of the SPLA Nasir Faction, which controlled the area. In the course of the fighting, Colonel Garang's forces killed Joseph Oduho, Commander Kuach Kang Rial, and fourteen soldiers from the SPLA Nasir Faction. About fifty-two soldiers on both sides and a number of civilians were killed at Kongor. After they occupied the town on March 27, 1993, the SPLA Torit Faction murdered two brothers of Commander Arok Thon, whom they condemned for supporting the SPLA Nasir Faction.

Although he was not a soldier, Joseph Oduho was one of the few southern Sudanese nationalist politicians who devoted most of his life to defending the rights of his oppressed people against the Arab Muslim governments in Khartoum. He was one of the few southern Sudanese intellectuals who spearheaded the Anya Nya rebellion during the 1960s. His death and those of his colleagues, who had perished before and after him at the hands of their own brothers from southern Sudan, are unforgivable crimes. The interfactional fighting between the two SPLA rival factions escalated up to Yuai and Ayod. During this fighting, roughly three to four thousand innocent Nuer civilians, mainly children, women, and old people, were reported by some foreign observers working in the SPLA Nasir Faction liberated areas to have been deliberately massacred. The SPLA Torit Faction soldiers burned some of the victims inside the grass churches and huts in Ayod town and surrounding villages. The forces of the new SPLA-United managed to dislodge SPLA Torit forces and drove them to the Kongor area. This interfactional fighting between the two SPLA factions affected the innocent civilians of Kongor, Ayod, Yuai, and Waat areas.

As the war continued, so did the peace initiatives. These included the Washington Declaration in 1993, the Abuja Peace Talks II in Nigeria in 1994, the Nairobi Peace Talks in 1994, and the IGADD Declaration of Principles

(DOP). The SPLA Torit Faction conducted its convention in February 1994 in Chukudum, eastern Equatoria region. On September 26, 1994, the SPLA-United of Dr. Riek Machar convened a national convention in the town of Akobo in southern Sudan. More than one thousand delegates from all over southern Sudan attended the convention. During the convention, the name of the organization was changed from SPLA-United to South Sudan Independence Movement/Army (SSIM/A). Before the convention took place, a disagreement arose between Dr. Riek Machar and Dr. Lam Akol. This discord resulted in Dr. Akol's dismissal from the SPLA-United leadership. Dr. Lam Akol insisted on heading a faction within the SPLA-United, a move that forced Dr. Riek Machar to abolish the name SPLA-United because the name itself was confusing to those who aimed to fight for the total independence of southern Sudan. The resolutions of the Akobo Convention regarding political issues were as follows:

1. The fundamental objective of the SSIM is to struggle to achieve the inalienable right to self-determination for the people of the South Sudan, either through armed struggle or through peaceful negotiation with the government in Khartoum.
2. Establishment of democracy, equality, freedom, and justice in the movement.
3. Guarantee of individual freedom, as everyone is to be first governor of his own affairs.
4. Provision of security services for life and property.
5. Respect of human rights as contained in various international conventions.
6. Promotion of African heritage, languages, and spiritual values in the south.
7. Developing of a foreign policy based on mutual respect and interest.
8. Use of diplomatic means and coordinated action with the United Nations and other international forces.

Representatives of the two southern factions signed the Lafon Declaration immediately after the forces of SSIM/A successfully turned back government military convoys in the Torit area. These convoys had been sent by the Sudanese government troops from Juba in order to reinforce their Kapoeta garrison in the eastern Equatoria region, which was besieged by the SPLA Torit Faction. About seventy government troops were taken prisoner, with a large quantity of military hardware seized during the attack. The architects of the Lafon Declaration were some junior officers, led by commanders Gatdor Kiec Wuor of SSIM/A and Oyai Deng Ajak of the SPLA Torit Faction. Commanders Gatdor Kiec Wuor and Oyai Deng Ajak signed the final agreement between the two southern Sudanese factions at Chukudum in eastern Equatoria on April 27, 1995. The SPLA Torit Faction leader Colonel John Garang de Mabior and the SSIM/A chief of staff, Commander William Nyuon Bany, approved the Lafon Declaration. The two sides agreed on the following four points:

1. Cessation of hostilities and a cease-fire between the two movements.
2. Free movement of civilians in the areas controlled by the two movements.
3. Free movement of humanitarian and relief agencies and their personnel in the areas controlled by the two movements.
4. Free movement of goods and logistics to areas controlled by the two movements.

The SPLA/NDA Asmara Declaration of June 12, 1995, and Another Nuer Peace Initiative

ON JUNE 12, 1995, AN SPLA/NDA Asmara Declaration was completed. In the meantime, leaders of Nuer communities in Ethiopia and southern Sudan attempted to continue organizing peace initiatives that had begun at the end of 1992. Within the SPLA–United, or Southern Sudan Independence Movement/Army (SSIM/A) as it was renamed following the Akobo Convention of October 1994, the movement split into different groupings. Among them were the SSIM/A II, headed by Commander William Nyuon Bany and Commander John Luk Jok, and SPLA-United, headed by Dr. Lam Akol Ajawin. There were also some commanders who differed with Dr. Riek Machar, SSIM/A chairman and commander in chief, and acted independently. The NIF-led Khartoum government was deeply involved in instigating divisions within the SSIM/A leadership. Eventually, a Nuer Peace Reconciliation Committee was formed of the following members:

1. Rev. Peter Gai Lual of Presbyterian Church of Sudan—chairman
2. Pastor Peter Pal Panom of SDA-Ethiopia—deputy
3. Ato Mark Chol—member
4. Rev. Majiek Gai Teny—member
5. Daniel Wuor Joak (author of this book)—member
6. Engineer Samuel Tap Yol—member
7. Peter Nyieth Chol—member
8. Rev. John Both Reth—member

9. Nyagai Kun—member
10. Pastor John Cheng Chut—member
11. Evangelist Chan Thor—member

The aims and objectives of the Nuer Peace Reconciliation were to bring all the Nuer communities, regardless of the political and social differences from Ethiopia to Sudan, under a common social understanding. Such an approach was unanimously agreed to by both the Ethiopian and Sudanese Nuer to use as a model to bring the divided communities together. A team was sent to Gambella to preach this idea among the refugees and the Ethiopian Nuer. Unfortunately, the Anyuak-led government in Gambella objected to it. Instead, the Gambella government instigated Chuol Khor, the Ethiopian Nuer Gajaak subclan of Jikany Nuer, to fight whoever wished to implement this idea. Chuol Khor's Ethiopian Nuer militias and their Anyuak allies organized to attack a delegation of Ethiopian Nuer politicians and religious leaders. These leaders were led by Ato Mark Chol, who was on an official trip to Kuergeng village. During the first week of August 1995, a team of twenty militias that were well organized and heavily armed went to Kuergeng and arrived there at midnight. They attacked and instantly killed Pastor Peter Pal Panom and four others from the Gajaak subclan of Thieng. Among those seriously wounded were Ato Mark Chol and Ato Tethloac Domac Ruai, the two members of the Ethiopian Federal Parliament representing the Gambella Constituency. The death of Rev. Peter Pal Panoum at the hands of Chuol Khor's militias indeed caused a lot of problems among the Nuer of Gambella who accused Chuol Khor of aiding the Anyuak to deny the Ethiopian Nuer an opportunity to participate in the state's affairs.

More Peace Initiatives and Attempts to Oust Riek Machar From The SSIM/A Leadership And Other Leadership Roles

THE LAFON DECLARATION SIGNED BETWEEN the SSIM/A and SPLM/A Torit Faction at Chukudum in eastern Equatoria on April 27, 1995, collapsed. This collapse was attributed to Colonel John Garang's instigation of some SSIM/A senior commanders—namely William Nyuon Bany, John Luk Joak, Daniel Koat Matthews, Stephen Duol Chol, Dr. Peter Adwok Nyaba, and George Maker Benjamin—to oust Dr. Riek Machar from the SSIM/A leadership and unite the two factions under Col. John Garang's leadership. On August 14, 1995, those commanders announced from Nairobi that they had overthrown Commander Riek Machar "from the SSIM/A leadership and replaced him with Commander William Nyuon Bany as the new leader of the SSIM/A." Colonel John Garang quickly hired a small private plane for William Nyuon to Kongor and ordered a large number of his soldiers and local civilians from his home area Bor to recapture Ayod from Dr. Riek Machar's forces. He also did the same thing to Commander John Luk Joak with the assistance of three former SSIM/A commanders—Peter Manyiel Kueth, Gordon Koang Banypiny, and Nyang Chuol Dhuor.

In early September 1995 a joint SPLA force of Colonel John Garang and that of Commander William Nyuon attacked the town of Ayod. Commander Nyuon's forces captured Ayod from the SSIM/A and occupied it for three months before Dr. Machar's loyalists drove them out. Meanwhile, the supporters of

Commander John Luk Joak had also overrun the towns of Waat, Akobo, and Kaykuiny from Commander Riek Machar's forces. Unfortunately, this miscalculated action resulted in the deaths of Commander William Nyuon Bany in the Ayod area, Commander Peter Mayiel Kueth, and Commander Gordon Koang Banypiny. Following the deaths of their commanders, hundreds of the soldiers fled in disarray to the SPLA Torit Faction–controlled areas of Pochalla and Kongor. With the help of Ethiopian authorities, the SPLA units under Commander Stephen Duol Chol and Commander James Hoth Mai tried to occupy Pagak and Maiwut, SSIM/A garrisons bordering Ethiopia, but they suffered enormous defeat and casualties, so that most of them surrendered to the SSIM/A forces. The rationale behind this massive defection of those SSIM/A commanders was the hope that they would win the confidence of the SSIM/A fighters in the field to their favor. However, the rank and file within the SSIM/A held a different perception of the situation. They did not want to go back to serve under Colonel John Garang, whom they regarded as corrupt and dictatorial.

In the meantime, there were more peace initiatives, including the Political Charter signed on April 10, 1996, in Khartoum and the Khartoum (Sudan) Peace Agreement signed on April 21, 1997, in Khartoum, by seven southern Sudanese political and military leaders and the NIF regime in Khartoum. Some people assumed it to be a desperate attempt by the NIF to buy time. The NIF fooled the southern Sudanese into believing that the peace could yield some fruitful results in order to end the ongoing civil war in Sudan. However, this was a completely unworkable deal. General Omar El Bashir's government initiated and worked out this deal to strengthen its military positions by offering southerners false promises because it was easy for NIF rulers in Khartoum to deal with a divided south.

The United Democratic Salvation Front (UDSF) leadership seemed to have also miscalculated the whole process. Most of the UDSF leaders who signed the April 21, 1997, peace deal had put their personal interests first and neglected to look into the future consequences of their agreement with the NIF. Failing to approach the NIF leadership with one voice, they succumbed to the NIF's manipulation. Some of them were used by the NIF to destroy the southern Sudanese aspirations. This destructive motive became apparent when they all signed the peace agreement independently instead of under one unified leadership. Before the signing of the Khartoum Peace Agreement, most of these leaders were surviving under protection of the South Sudan Independence Movement/Army (SSIM/A), led by Dr. Riek Machar. Some signatories to that accord were former SPLM/A political prisoners or disgruntled southern Sudanese politicians who were redundant in east Africa without any effective supports from their grassroots.

Among the southern political and military leaders that participated in the Sudan Peace Agreement, the SSIM/A was the only formidable politico-military force that was internally and internationally recognized. Since the NIF's intention was to create a system based on weak southern leadership, it quickly supported southerners who wished to rival Dr. Riek Machar, the designated chairman of the Coordination Council for Southern States. Leaders such as late Kerubino Kuanyin Bol, the late Arok Thon Arok, Atem Gualdit, and Magar Aciek chose to be integrated into the Sudanese National Armed Force with senior ranks. They chose not to serve under the South Sudan Defence Force (SSDF), the former South Sudan Independence Army headed by Dr. Riek Machar because of their previous political differences. Dr. Lam Akol refused to cooperate with Dr. Riek Machar, and he signed the Fashoda Peace Agreement with the National Congress Party separately. The Fashoda peace agreement was negotiated separately by Dr. Lam Akol Ajawin from the Khartoum Peace Agreement which was earlier signed by Dr. Riek Machar and other southern Sudanese political leaders with the government of Sudan. Dr. Lam Akol signed the Fashoda Peace Agreement separately with the Sudan government during the same year of 1997.

When President Omar El Bashir appointed Dr. Riek Machar to head the Coordination Council for Southern States in August 1997, Major General Kerubino Kuanyin Bol objected to Dr. Riek Machar's appointment. He wanted himself to head the council or else be offered the vice presidency of the Coordinating Council. In the meantime, volatility continued in Sudan. The situation in the whole Upper Nile area was extremely volatile in September 1997, when Paulino Matip defected from UDSF and SSDF and joined the

NIF (government) side. The NIF regime had created a state of anarchy by supporting various former SSDF commanders who were operating independently. This strategy denied Dr. Riek Machar military hardware and other basic needs for full control over that region. The government caused widespread displacement and death of innocent civilians in the Bentiu oil-rich areas in western Upper Nile. This destruction was exacerbated by the skirmishes between the forces of Commander Paulino Matip Nhial and Dr. Riek Machar. The ongoing mess in Upper Nile and Bahr El Ghazal regions seemed to be the prize of the April 21, 1997, Khartoum (Sudan) Peace Agreement (KPA). Dr. Lam Akol signed the Fashoda Peace Agreement with the National Congress Party separately in September 1997, having refused to cooperate with Dr. Riek Machar to sign the two agreements jointly. There was no doubt that, if all the southern forces had worked cooperatively, their position would have been much stronger vis-à-vis the NIF government, but they did not. Eventually, President Bashir succumbed to Major General Kerubino Kuanyin Bol's demand and appointed him deputy to Dr. Riek Machar. Instead of the southern Sudanese leading figures joining their efforts and building the UDSF leadership for the benefit of all southerners, Major General Kerubino Kuanyin Bol decided to rejoin the SPLM/A of Colonel John Garang without informing his colleagues within the UDSF about his secret plan. He left Khartoum for Bahr El Ghazal, where he made secret contacts with the SPLA leadership on how to rejoin the movement. Commander Kerubino Kuanyin Bol's redefection to the SPLA on December 28, 1997, resulted in massive humanitarian crises in the whole region of Bahr El Ghazal for more than a year. With the help of SPLA fighters, he attempted to capture Wau, the regional capital of Bahr El Ghazal, as well as Aweil and Gogrial towns. The legacy of this failed attempt was the death of over seventy thousand Dinkas in the Bahr El Ghazal region alone, of starvation and war-related diseases. By triggering a premature attack on Wau, Kerubino created one of the worst disasters in that area. This action resembled the catastrophe of 1988, when a quarter of a million southerners died of starvation and war-related diseases in the same region.

The marriage of convenience and "unholy alliance" between Colonel John Garang and Major General Kerubino Kuanyin Bol did not last long.

They disagreed again in Nairobi in November 1998, and Commander Kerubino Kuanyin went back to southern Sudan, where he sought refuge in the area controlled by Dr. Riek Machar's rival, Major General Paulino Matip Nhial. Several times the NIF government attempted to convince Commander Paulino Matip to hand over Major General Kerubino Kuanyin Bol to them for court martial for the crimes he had committed when he redefected to the SPLA in 1997–1998, but Paulino turned down the extradition requests from the Sudanese authorities. Unfortunately, Commander Kerubino Kuanyin Bol would meet his untimely death almost a year later, on September 10, 1999, at the hands of the soldiers that defected from Commander Paulino Matip's group.

The Khartoum Peace Agreement was signed between the Khartoum government and various south Sudanese movements under an umbrella of United Salvation Democratic Front (UDSF). Among them were the following:

1. Dr. Riek Machar Teny, South Sudan Independent Movement/Army (SSIM/A)
2. General Kerubino Kuanyin Bol, Sudan People's Liberation Movement/Army (SPLM/A)
3. Dr. Thioplolus Ochang Loti, Equatoria Defence Force (EDF)
4. Kawach Makuei Mayar, South Sudan Independent Groups (SSIG)
5. Samuel Aru Bol, Union of Sudan African Parties (USAP)
6. Arok Thon Arok, Bor Group (BG)

The Redefection of Dr. Riek Machar To the Southern Sudan Bush

DR. MACHAR WAS INVITED BY the German Civil Society group to attend a brainstorming workshop in Bonn, Germany, on December 10, 1999. This workshop was attended by several southern Sudanese human rights activists from different parts of Europe, and I also attended that workshop. Dr. Riek Machar arrived in Bonn on December 12, 1999, the very day his boss, President Omar Hassan El Bashir, declared a state of emergency throughout Sudan, during which he dissolved the National Assembly in Khartoum and detained its speaker, Mr. Hassan El Turabi. In his capacity as an assistant to the president of the republic and the chairman of the Coordinating Council of Southern Sudan States, Dr. Machar found it difficult to return to Khartoum to work with the government of Sudan that had violated all the international norms while at the same time associating itself with international terrorists.

By the end of December 1999, Dr. Riek Machar had proceeded to Kenya and eventually announced his resignation from the government of Sudan before he rejoined his fighting force, which remained in some parts of Greater Upper Nile. He then formed the Sudan People's Democratic Front (SPDF) in January 2000. During the formation of the SPDF movement, Dr. Machar had problems with some of his field commanders, who were being incited by his former advisor and friend Dr. Wal Duany. Dr. Duany hails from Akobo county and worked to ensure that all Lou Nuer senior army officers loyal to Riek Machar would now support his own splinter faction, South Sudan Liberation Movement (SSLM). Indeed, Dr. Duany declared his movement in

January 2000 to become a potential rival to Riek Machar after he gained popular supports among his Lou Nuer clan's officers and soldiers who previously supported Dr. Riek Machar's movement. These two movements remained threats to the SPLA faction of Dr. John Garang but weakened the Nuer unity at large. The leadership of Riek Machar was being questioned by most Nuer intellectuals and other southern Sudanese. The SPDF and the SSLM operated independently for two years.

The redefection of Dr. Riek Machar, former assistant to the president of the republic of the Sudan and chairman of the South Sudan Coordinating Council, the body formed to oversee the ten states in southern Sudan following the Khartoum (Sudan) Peace Agreement (KPA), came about after the collapse of the Khartoum (Sudan) Peace Agreement. Dr. Machar was facing pressure from different directions. The NIF/NCP regime in Khartoum itself made it difficult for the peace agreement to be implemented. It took Dr. Machar three full years of waiting patiently for the rhetoric to take effect and the agreement to be implemented. The NIF/NCP government started dismantling the KPA slowly by instigating conflicts within the forces of Riek Machar who were stationed in various locations in southern Sudan. This was intended to deny Dr. Riek Machar full control of South Sudan Defence Forces (SSDF), the army he previously refused to integrate into the Sudanese national armed forces, following the agreement. Such conflicts first started in Bentiu, Unity province the very region Riek Machar hails from. The fight erupted between the supporters of Riek Machar and those of General Paulino Matip, and during the course of the fighting, several hundred innocent lives and much property were lost. Those displaced by the fighting either fled to SPLM/SPLA-controlled areas in the Bahr El Ghazal region or to the government-held areas in the northern parts of Sudan to seek sanctuary and protection there.

The South-South Peace Initiative, The Role of the Church, and Peace Prospects in the Sudan

THE SPDF REUNITED ITS RANKS with the SPLA in a merger announced in Nairobi on January 6, 2002. Dr. John Garang de Mabior of the SPLA and Dr. Riek Machar of the SPDF signed the merger. This led to the integration of political and military officers and the men of the SPDF under a single unified SPLM/SPLA leadership under Dr. John Garang. In order to speed up the merger in the interest of both parties, Dr. Garang appointed three deputies. Among them were Commander Salva Kiir Mayardit as first vice chairman, Dr. Riek Machar Teny as second vice chairman, and Commander James Wani Igga as third vice chairman. The former SPDF soldiers and its National Liberation Council members were all integrated into the main SPLM/SPLA. Commander John Kong Nyuon, who was also a member of the SPLM Leadership Council, the highest body within the movement, chaired the technical committee formed to oversee the merger, and Commander Peter Bol Kong, former SPDF chief of staff, deputized him.

In November 2002, Dr. Riek Machar briefed all his field commanders about the final integration of the two former SPLA factions in Pagak, the headquarters of the SPDF. I was also a member of the delegation that went to Pagak to finalize the merger between the two former SPLM/SPLA rival factions. Of course, the final merger between the SPDF and the SPLM/SPLA under one unified leadership of Dr. John Garang in November 2002 also had some serious challenges, particularly on the side of Dr. Riek Machar. Most of his close associates from his former SSDF, or SSIM/A, resented the merger. Those commanders opposed the merger and remained behind to operate independently under the name SSDF. These commanders are listed in Appendix III.

General Paulino Matip Nhial—leader of SSDF

They all remained under the SSDF umbrella headed by its chief of staff, Major General Paulino Matip Nhial, and they were continually supported by the government of Sudan to counter SPLM/SPLA activities in the south. Their relationship with the government of Sudan was just a marriage of convenience that could break up at any time. The SSDF, or the other "armed groups," as they were referred to during the signing of the Comprehensive Peace Agreement (CPA), represented different geographical locations and ethnicities in southern Sudan, and they could pose serious threats to the peace agreement if the parties involved in the agreement—namely the SPLM and the National Congress Party—did not adequately address their grievances. Their forces controlled different pockets in southern Sudan, including oil fields in western and eastern Upper Nile, Jonglei, Bahr El Ghazal, and Equatoria regions. As long as the majority of these groups of the SSDF were still operating independently with full support from Khartoum, southern Sudan would never enjoy relative peace. They posed both military and political threats to the existence of southern Sudan as one entity.

Several attempts were made by the Moi Foundation in Kenya to reconcile the warring parties in southern Sudan. Unfortunately, things did not work out because the SSDF of Major General Paulino Matip Nhial was not in a position to accept the demands put forward by the SPLM/SPLA leadership. As the conflict continued in the Sudan, the church intensified its activities.

The role of the church in the Sudanese conflict has always been instrumental, especially in regard to peaceful resolution of the conflict. The entire population of South Sudan considers itself as Christians or believers in African traditional religion. You will recall that Christianity entered South Sudan from the time when Great Britain conquered Sudan in 1898. According to Oliver Batali Albino, the early years of Condominium rule in Sudan were also marked by the return of missionaries to the south. Roman Catholics entered the Shilluk areas in 1901, American Presbyterians went to the Sobat River in 1902 and Nasir in 1904, and the Church Missionary Society (CMS) went to Malek, Bor district, in 1905. Without the involvement and participation of the church missionaries, there would have been no education in the south at all. However, the nature of the conflict in the country was transformed into a religious one in which the north Sudanese Arab Muslims were waging a holy war (jihad), to subjugate and convert the people of the southern Sudan to Islam. Christianity was also used during the early days by the British colonial authorities in the Sudan as a means of hindering the spread of Islam to Central Africa. This policy made southern Sudan the center for the church to become involved in important activities such as the following:

1. Provision of basic education for the people of South Sudan.
2. Preaching love, forgiveness, unity, and understanding among the people.
3. Giving humanitarian assistance to needy people.
4. Creating self-awareness and consciousness among the people.

5. Uniting the south Sudanese masses behind their just struggle against the Arabized and Islamized north.
6. Enlightening the international community about the plight of the south Sudanese people in the Sudan.

Recall also that, in the early 1960s, the south Sudanese church leaders and the missionary societies working in the south suffered terribly from the repressive regime of General Ibrahim Abboud. General Abboud ordered the immediate closure of all missionary schools and mission centers from 1962 to 1964. Abboud's regime even nationalized some of the missionary schools. All the missionaries that were operating in different parts of the south were expelled from the country. This policy was carried out during the implementation of the 1962 Missionary Law Act, the purpose of which was to deny the people of southern Sudan the opportunity provided by these missionaries in the field of education. Following the expulsion of all expatriate missionaries from the Sudan from 1962 to 1964, the Abboud government began persecution of the indigenous clergymen on the pretext that they were Anya Nya collaborators. Many of them eventually escaped and went either to the neighboring countries for their own safety or to the rebel-held areas in the south.

You will recall that in February 1972 the church played a leading role in ending the seventeen-year-old civil war, which officially came to a peaceful end on February 27, 1972, when the Addis Ababa Agreement was signed as a result of the meditation of All African Conference of Churches (AACC). After this agreement, the church continued its spiritual and social activities in southern Sudan until the second phase of the war started in 1975 and intensified to a full-scale civil war in 1983. Before the resumption of the second civil war, all the churches in the Sudan were united under one umbrella, the Sudan Council of Churches (SCC), a body formed by the Sudanese churches in 1965. As a result of the war, the unified church leadership was divided into two bodies. One group remained in the government-controlled areas and retained the old name Sudan Council of Churches, but in 1990 the churches that were operating in the SPLA-controlled areas were organized as the New Sudan Council of Churches—NSCC. However, the objectives of the two church organizations remained the same. As spiritual leaders of the southern Sudanese Christians, they found themselves in conflict with the Sudanese opposing leaders on all sides. The successive Islamic governments in Khartoum accused the church leaders inside Sudan of being SPLA supporters. On the other hand, the church leaders in the SPLA areas were also accused of supporting different factions, which made them prime targets of their own people.

A practical example occurred when Bishop Paride Taban was slapped by SPLA commander Kuol Manyang Juk in the early 1990s. The cause of the dispute was that Bishop Taban refused for his car to be used for military operations by the SPLA forces under the command of Commander William Nyuon Bany. It became difficult for the church leaders in the liberated areas in southern Sudan to bring the different opposing SPLA groups together. This was because some of these church leaders had involved themselves in openly supporting various opposing groups. However, the church leaders in the south could still play a leading role in the reconciliation because they were a part of the society and also commanded formidable respect. This respect would be possible only if they disassociated themselves from supporting either opposing group in the south and stood firmly to their neutrality before the split in the SPLM/SPLA movement in August 1991.

Since the inception of the SPLM/SPLA in 1983, the north Sudanese Arab rulers in Khartoum had been intransigent about accepting a peaceful solution to the ongoing conflict between the south and north Sudan. Their main objective had obviously been to crush the rebellion in the south militarily. You will recall that several peace initiatives and peace talks were carried out in different parts of the world. These peace initiatives included the Koka Dam Declaration in Ethiopia in March 1986, the SPLA/DUP Declaration in Ethiopia in 1988, the 1989 Carter Initiative in Nairobi, the Frankfurt Peace Talks in Germany in 1992, the Abuja Peace Talks I in Nigeria in 1992, the Washington Declaration in 1993, the Abuja Peace Talks II in Nigeria in 1994, the Nairobi Peace Talks in 1994, the IGADD Declaration of Principles (DOP), the SPLA/NDA Asmara Declaration of June 12, 1995, the April 10, 1996, Political Charter in Khartoum, the April 21, 1997, Khartoum (Sudan) Peace

Agreement in Khartoum, and the Fashoda Peace Agreement in September 1997. All these attempts aimed at finding an end to the civil war in the Sudan.

Perhaps the most serious attempts among all these peace initiatives on the Sudan were the April 10, 1996 Political Charter and the April 21, 1997, Khartoum (Sudan) Peace Agreement, signed between the Sudan government and seven south Sudanese movements led by the United Democratic Salvation Front (UDSF) for southern Sudan. The April 1997 agreement acknowledged the right of the people of southern Sudan to decide their own political destiny through an internationally supervised referendum before the end of the interim period. By signing this agreement, the parties to the conflict seemed to have fully admitted that the war in the Sudan would never be resolved through military means. Similarly, in the SPLA/NDA Asmara Declaration of June 12, 1995, the parties had also agreed on the issue of self-determination for the people of southern Sudan to be exercised through a referendum before the end of the interim period once they overthrew the NIF regime in Khartoum. The most important points that were stipulated in the April 21, 1997, Khartoum (Sudan) Peace Agreement were as follows:

1. The general principles contained in the political charter signed in Khartoum on April 10, 1996, shall be part of this agreement and shall guide and explain its provisions.
2. During a four-year interim period South Sudan shall enjoy a special status as defined in this peace agreement.
3. The interim arrangements shall be preceded by a declaration of permanent cease-fire and general amnesty proclamation.
4. The people of South Sudan shall exercise the right of self-determination through a referendum; options in the referendum shall be
   (a) Unity
   (b) Secession
3. The problem of Abyei has been discussed and a final solution is referred to a Conference on Abyei that will be convened in the area within the interim period.

Following the signing of the agreement, a coordination council that would run the administration of southern Sudan during the four-year interim period was set up under the presidency of Dr. Riek Machar Teny Dhurgon, leader of UDSF. The South Sudan Coordination Council comprised twenty-five members, ten state governors, fourteen ministers, and the president. The South Sudan Defence Force (SSDF), which was composed of different south Sudanese factions, was formed to protect that agreement from both internal and external threats. The only southern group that remained in opposition to the April 21, 1997, Khartoum (Sudan) Agreement was the SPLA faction under Colonel John Garang. Unfortunately, both the Asmara Agreement of June 1995 and Khartoum Peace Agreement of April 1997 went through difficult stages that made them unlikely to be implemented, as political alliances among Sudanese political forces shifted from time to time.

However, the attainment of a comprehensive peace in the Sudan depended on the unity of southern political forces when Colonel Garang joined the anticipated agreement. It also depended on the normalization of the relationship between Sudan and its hostile neighbors. Lasting peace could hardly be achieved as long as Egypt, Eritrea, Ethiopia, and Uganda were in bitter conflict with the Sudan. Those four countries had interests of their own to realize. However, the rift between Al-Turabi and General Al-Bashir at face value seemed to indicate that Bashir's government would abandon the policy of exporting the Sudanese brand of Islam. It was for this reason that those countries wanted to overthrow the NIF regime and install a moderate government that would closely work in cooperation with them.

The Inter-Governmental Authority on Development (IGAD) had made several attempts to reconcile the warring parties in the Sudan. Unfortunately, the Sudanese government accused some of the IGAD Mediating Committee members, especially Eritrea and Uganda, of involvement in Sudanese internal affairs. The Sudan government alleged that some IGAD member states were offering military assistance to the SPLA faction of Colonel John Garang and northern Sudanese opposition alliances that had been working to overthrow the NIF regime in Khartoum since 1996. On the other hand, it seemed that Colonel John Garang was not interested in reconciling his differences with the other southern Sudanese opposition groups. He was apparently uncertain of his status or position in a united movement in the south. However, Colonel Garang hoped that all the opposing groups would one day return to his leadership as it had happened with the Anya Nya II forces in 1987, but the following remarks deserve reflection:

- From May 1999 the Sudan government had opened discussions with countries that were in bitter conflict with it, namely Egypt, Eritrea, Ethiopia, and Uganda. It remained to be seen to what extent and for how long Colonel Garang could continue to exploit the differences between Sudan and its neighboring countries.
- The northern Sudanese opposition groups were leaning toward the Egyptian-Libyan peace initiatives of July 1999. This was likely to affect Garang's relationship with the north Sudanese opposition groups.
- Since the leadership of Colonel Garang was being questioned, it would no longer be possible for him to frustrate the efforts being exerted toward the unity of south Sudanese people.

The above points were vital to the downfall and survival of Colonel John Garang's leadership in south Sudan. If the neighboring countries succeeded in sorting out their differences with the NIF regime, Colonel Garang and his SPLA would be in big trouble. This could be the same case if the northern Sudanese opposition groups would mend their differences with General Al-Bashir's government in Khartoum. In that event the NDA could succeed in striking a deal with the NIF government, in which case the SPLA would have no choice other than to terminate its links with the NDA. The SPLA would then find it very hard to win the confidence of the southern Sudanese masses. Moreover, Colonel John Garang was accused of having surrounded himself with certain selfish and opportunistic southern politicians known for their egoistic tendencies. Most of these politicians had worked in the southern regional government in the 1970s as ministers, undersecretaries, directors, and members of the Regional Assembly. Some of them had made irritating and damaging remarks to the national unity of the south. Some provocative statements such as "the Dinka are born to rule" certainly served to promote tribalism and some form of colonization, but southern Sudan, as a nation, should be governed by any capable southerner who is able to accommodate all the requirements of the people.

The African Centre For Human Advocacy (ACHA)

Graduation of tutors at ACHA Centre, Riang in Ulang County in 2003

FOLLOWING THE ESTABLISHMENT OF ACHA offices in Nairobi, ACHA extended its humanitarian operation to Riang, Ulang county, where a training center for primary school teachers was opened. Riang is one of the remotest and most isolated villages located in Ulang county. It is situated along the swampy rivers of Juany and Tayebor, and it borders Sobat and Nasir counties. The Riang project was established in October 2002 by ACHA staff, who first took relief and construction materials by plane to the project site. The construction of ACHA Centre at Riang was completed in January 2003, and afterward the training of forty five primary school teachers was conducted successfully for a period of three months using a UNICEF curriculum during phase I. The second group of phase II, which numbered forty students, was also trained for a period of three months. A similar number was trained during phase III. The three phases were conducted over a period of nine months. Those who completed phases I, II, and III became primary school teachers, and they were deployed to various locations within Ulang county.

However, the ongoing training program was disrupted when the center was attacked twice by a group of Lou Nuer–sponsored Government of Sudan militias stationed at Dini/ Gelachel area. During that attack, ten people were killed and an equal number wounded. These two attacks were conducted in February and May 2004. As a result, ACHA's Kenyan teachers were taken back to Kenya for security reasons and the organization was left with only southern Sudanese tutors. The humanitarian activities of ACHA at Riang were eventually closed down in April 2006, but the activities of ACHA at Rupbout continued up to late 2007.

The major achievements of ACHA included construction of ACHA centers in Lokichoggio, Riang, and Rupbout. All the centers were equipped with radio communication and other facilities to coordinate the organization's activities. In 2004 a severe outbreak of Kalazaar took place at the village of Bimbim, Yomding Payam. During that time, more than four hundred cases of death were reported before ACHA intervened by inviting Medicins Sans Frontieres (MSF) Holland, which was by then operating at Langken, Nyirol county, to come and establish its operational base at Bimbim, where ACHA had a presence. The organization's activities were badly affected as a result of my engagement in the Southern Sudan Legislative Assembly (SSLA) soon after the formation of the Government of Southern Sudan (GOSS) in September 2005.

A Narrative of Human Rights Violations in the Sudan From 1821

THROUGHOUT THE SUDANESE CONFLICT AND even before, a number of Arab and Islamic countries had been deeply involved in supporting the successive Islamic governments in Khartoum. They strongly encouraged forced Islamization and Arabization, along with the slave trade against the people of southern Sudan, as the only viable way to convert and assimilate them into Islamic and Arab culture. Such a degrading and dehumanizing policy had been in operation since 1821, when a joint Egyptian and Turkish administration invaded Sudan and penetrated into southern Sudan in the 1840s in search of slaves and other valuable natural resources. Several hundreds of thousands of southern Sudanese people were forcibly taken and shipped by slave dealers into the Middle East and the Americas. It took nearly seventy years before slavery was finally brought to an end by the British colonial authorities following their defeat of the Mahdist supporters under Khalifa Abdulla at the deadly battle of Omdurman.

The battle of Omdurman ensued between the British troops under General Herbert Kitchener and those of Khalifa Abdulla on September 2, 1898. The slave trade was eventually abolished with the signing of Anglo-Egyptian Condominium on January 19, 1899, which gave the British authorities the leading role in the Sudan. A slave trade–type policy was practiced again in 1958, after the British authorities had left the country when Sudan gained its independence on January 1, 1956. When General Ibrahim Abboud took power on November 17, 1958, he introduced forced Islamization as well as imposition of Arabic language and culture to the people of southern Sudan through his soldiers stationed in the south. His army conducted full-scale massacres of civil settlements all over the south with the intention of deterring them from supporting the Anya Nya rebels. General Abboud ordered the closure of all missionary institutions in the south and expelled them from Sudan in the early 1960s. Some radical Arab countries including Egypt, Libya, Iraq, Syria, Saudi Arabia, Kuwait, and several others in that period were practically involved in supporting the successive regimes in Khartoum with military hardware and financial means in order to Islamize the southern Sudanese people. The military part of the support by the Arab states to the Khartoum governments was temporarily stopped in 1972, following the Addis Ababa agreement that brought the seventeen-year civil war between northern and southern Sudan to an end. Following the resumption of the second civil war in the south in May 1983, the underground slave trade was encouraged again by the then elected civilian government of Prime Minister Sadiq El Mahdi from 1986 until he was finally overthrown by General Omar Hassan El Bashir on June 30, 1989. Under Sadiq El Mahdi's rule, close diplomatic relations with Libya and Saudi Arabia were forged. El Mahdi's government encouraged such inhuman practices to be carried against the people of southern Sudan by the Muraleen Arab tribal militias of the Rizeigat and Misseriya nomadic groups of southern Darfur and southern Kordofan states.

His government allowed the Arab tribal militias to terrorize the southern Sudanese people of Dinka, Nuer, Shilluk, Burun, and other nationalities who border north Sudan. Several thousand children were forcibly taken from their villages after their parents were murdered. In 1987–1988, El Mahdi's Muraleen Arab militias massacred over three thousand south Sudanese at El Dhaein in western Sudan. Premier Sadiq El Mahdi's regime was also responsible for the death of about a quarter million southern Sudanese innocent civilians who died of starvation in 1988. When some of them fled to north Sudan to avert looming starvation and other war-related diseases in the south, Sadiq El Mahdi categorically denied both foreign and indigenous NGOs from relieving the south Sudanese victims. He said in an interview with the BBC's *Focus on Africa*, "I cannot allow those NGOs to feed people who are killing my soldiers." This was a direct reference to the SPLA fighters whose mothers and sisters had fled to north Sudan. His army perpetrated indiscriminate aerial bombardments and raided civilian targets, which resulted in massive displacement of millions of people from their homes.

Over three million southern Sudanese had abandoned their homes since 1988, and some of them fled to the north in search of shelters and protection there. Some of them were now living under subhuman conditions in the outskirts of Khartoum and other major cities in the north. The UN and other international bodies were denied access by the previous government of Sadiq El Mahdi, and even the NIF regime was using the same policy to prevent NGOs from relieving the south Sudanese displaced persons in north Sudan. Instead, they were using some government-affiliated Islamic NGOs that were known to have been using food as a means of converting the south Sudanese Christians to Islam.

Since assuming power through a bloodless military coup on June 30, 1989, General El Bashir adopted a vigorous and radical Islamic policy of forced Islamization and Arabization in the south. Like General Nimeiri before him, General El Bashir changed all secular laws that had been governing the Sudan since the British era, and replaced them with Islamic rules in order to promote Islamic influence in the Sudan. The architect of the June 30, 1989, military coup was Dr. Hassan Abdalla Turabi, leader of the National Islamic Front (NIF) and a one-time coalition partner of the government of Sadiq El Mahdi before it was overthrown by NIF-backed military officers. The Islamic Brotherhood's policy, as represented by the NIF since the 1960s, was to transform the Sudan into an Islamic country and to encourage the spread of Islam into other parts of the African continent. Apparently, the NIF dream had almost come into realization when it backed the military takeover in 1989. The first NIF regime move was declaring the jihad holy war in the south against the SPLA and SSIA forces. In 1989–1990, the government reorganized and united all Arab tribal militia groups under Popular Defence Forces (PDF) with the aim of defeating the south Sudanese rebel groups who had been fighting for their right to self-determination for the last forty-five years. They also encouraged political persecutions and massacres against suspected southerners in the government-controlled areas. The first NIF government massacre took place at Jebelien in 1989, where the NIF supporters randomly killed more than two thousand south Sudanese displaced persons. A similar number were also killed in Juba town in June 1992, when the SPLA faction of Colonel John Garang attempted to take over the town from NIF forces. Several thousand innocent civilians, including two USAID workers who worked in Juba, were reported to have been massacred by government soldiers and their bodies were thrown into the River Nile, after SPLA forces had evacuated the town. The NIF military-backed government's repressive policies, especially the policy of forced Islamization and Arabization of southerners was still unabated.

Sudan's Relations With Its Neighboring Countries

SINCE THE JUNE 30, 1989 military coup that brought the NIF-backed Islamic fundamentalist regime led by General Omar Hassan El Bashir to power, relations between the Sudan and its neighboring countries deteriorated sharply and rapidly. The Islamic military junta in Khartoum was accused by the Egyptian government of providing military support to its Islamic fundamentalist opposition Gamaa El Islamiya, whose aims were to overthrow the government of President Mohammed Hosni Mubarak of Egypt. On the other hand, the National Islamic Front (NIF) government in Khartoum accused the Egyptian government of supporting the National Democratic Alliance (NDA), an alliance of different opposition political parties that had been working since 1990 to overthrow the military government. The NIF regime was also accused by the Ethiopian government, following the assassination attempt against Egyptian President Hosni Mubarak in June 1995, when he was on an official visit to Ethiopia in order to attend the Organisation of African Unity (OAU) summit in Addis Ababa, of being responsible for the assassination attempt of the Egyptian president, which resulted in the expulsion of the Sudanese Embassy staff in Addis Ababa.

The Sudanese government retaliated by expelling the Ethiopian diplomatic corps based in Khartoum. The assassination attempt on President Hosni Mubarak, and other accusations against the Sudan government by the Ethiopian government of President Meles Zenawi, almost brought diplomatic crises between the two countries. The Ethiopian government had in the past accused the Sudanese government of aiding its Islamic insurgents' movements operating in the Sudan/Ethiopia eastern borders. The implications of the Sudanese government in the assassination attempt on the Egyptian President Hosni Mubarak created an enormously negative image of Sudan internationally. The NIF government in Khartoum was also accused by the Eritrean government of assisting its Islamic opposition group, the Islamic Jihad of Eritrea, which had its operational bases inside Sudanese territories. Such accusations against the Sudan ended in the breaking of diplomatic relations between the Sudan and Eritrea in early 1995. The Eritrean government expelled all Sudanese Embassy officials in Asmara and eventually handed over the Sudanese Embassy premises to the NDA opposition groups based in Eritrea. In 1996, Uganda broke off its diplomatic relations with the Sudan after they accused the Sudanese Islamic military regime in Khartoum of aiding the Lord's Resistance Army (LRA), a Christian fundamentalist movement whose aims were to overthrow the government of President Yoweri K. Museveni. A former cleric, Joseph Konyi, heads the LRA.

On several occasions, the LRA has been accused by Amnesty International (Africa Rights) and different NGOs operating in Uganda of a poor human rights record, particularly against the Acholi people in northern Uganda. The LRA has been accused by Amnesty International and other Human Rights bodies of abducting small children as young as five years old. They use these children as child soldiers. This is in addition to gross killings and torturing of innocent civilians that resulted in massive displacement of hundreds of thousands of people in the Kitgum and Gulu districts in northern Uganda. In turn, the NIF government in Khartoum accused the Ugandan government of aiding the SPLA faction of Colonel John Garang, who had been conducting some successful military victories against the Sudanese government troops in the areas bordering Uganda and Congo (formerly Zaire).

In fact, the Sudan accused Ugandan troops of having participated in the capture of the towns of Kaya, Morobo, Yei, Kajokeji, and Lanya from its forces during the early part of 1997. However, the same accusations were also mounted against the Ethiopian and Eritrean governments, who had publicly pledged their full support to the NDA opposition forces. The NIF accused them of providing military assistance to the NDA military alliance in the south and eastern Sudan. Apart from Eritrea, Uganda and Ethiopia categorically denied giving any military support to any Sudanese opposition groups. For its part, the Sudanese Islamic regime had adamantly denied assisting either the Lord's Resistance Army or West Nile Bank Front (WNBF) in Uganda, or Oromo Islamiya Movement in Ethiopia, or the Islamic Jihad of Eritrea. Before the fall of Mobutu Sese Seko of Zaire, now the Democratic Republic of Congo, on May 16, 1997, the Sudan government used to enjoy a good relationship with Zaire. The cooperation between the two countries reached the stage where the NIF forces used to attack SPLA positions in south Sudan using Zairean territories.

After the overthrow of President Mobutu Sese Seko by the rebel forces of the Democratic Alliance for the Liberation of Congo-Zaire, headed by Laurent Kabila, the NIF regime lost one of its vital allies in the region. Before 1999 the only neighboring countries that remained acceptable to the NIF government in Khartoum were Libya, Chad, the Central African Republic, and the Republic of Kenya. The rest either severed their relations with the NIF government of General Omar El Bashir or cut their diplomatic ties with it altogether. It was only at the beginning of 1999 that Egypt, Eritrea, Ethiopia, and Uganda began to mend their ties with the Khartoum government, when the latter started to change its policy of destabilizing their countries by aiding fundamentalist movements opposed to their governments.

The United States and its allies in the West and the Middle East also distanced themselves from the NIF government in Khartoum after accusing it of supporting international terrorism. It was reported, especially in the early 1990s, that the Sudan had become a sanctuary for some internationally well-known terrorists, including the Abu Nadal group and Carlo "the Jackal," who was later handed over to the French authorities in return for military hardware. The Sudan was also implicated in the bombing of the World Trade Center building in New York in 1994. The American government eventually withdrew its embassy personnel from Khartoum in 1996, citing security reasons.

The Sudan is now on the list of seven countries that were accused by the United States of sponsoring international terrorism worldwide. The seven countries include Libya, Syria, North Korea, Iran, Iraq, Cuba, and Sudan. Over the last decade, the United Nations and other international bodies have tried to impose an air and trade embargo against the NIF government in Khartoum but failed to do so, because the international public opinion was divided over the issue. Some moderate Arab and Islamic countries within the United Nations circles were against the imposition of any kind of sanctions against the Sudan. For these countries, Sudan is a starting point and center for spreading Islam to the rest of the African continent.

The Role of International NGOs in the Sudan

SINCE 1984, WHEN THE CIVIL war intensified, most of the meager civil infrastructure that used to be available in the southern part of the country has been destroyed. The international NGOs operating in the region had become the only source to provide basic needs for the war-affected population in the south. Following the creation of Operation Lifeline Sudan (OLS) in April 1989, under the umbrella of UNICEF, OLS became the leading humanitarian organization in south Sudan. There were several NGOs that were operating under OLS from the Southern Sector, based at Lokochoki, Kenya, and the Northern Sector in Khartoum, but both the SPLM/SPLA and the NIF regime in Khartoum had been manipulating the OLS activities since its creation. Indeed, there were some independent NGOs that refused to work under OLS and preferred to work with the Sudan Relief and Rehabilitation Association (SRRA), the humanitarian wing of the SPLM/SPLA movement. These organizations were based in Kenya. One of these organizations working independently from OLS was the Norwegian People's Aid (NPA). Though, NPA had done a remarkable job in assisting the people of southern Sudan from 1987 onwards, and also created awareness internationally for the cause of the people of southern Sudan against successive regimes in Khartoum. But following the splits within the SPLM/SPLA leadership in August 1991, the organization took sides in the southern Sudan internal conflicts in favour of the faction headed by Col. John Garang.

It is to be recalled that, when the split occurred within the SPLM/A movement on August 28, 1991, the Norwegian People's Aid (NPA), led a propaganda campaign against the breakaway SPLA Nasir Faction headed by Commander Riek Machar in favor of Colonel John Garang's faction. Two of its representatives based in Kenya, namely Egil Wisløff Neilsen and Dan Effie, visited Bor and Kongor areas following the interfactional fighting between the two southern groups, which erupted there in November and December 1991. The two NPA staff later made a documentary film, which they called *The Bor Massacre*. This documentary film was shown all over the world. In his comment on an article that appeared in the Norwegian newspaper *Arbeiderbladet* on December 20, 1991, Egil Wisløff wrote "a group of Nuer bandits headed by a certain Doctor Riek Machar apparently went on rampage and massacred the Dinkas of Bor and looted all their belongings."

This was the message he brought back to Norway in order to raise funds. Moreover, it was an open secret that the NPA was deeply involved in the south-south conflict by regularly providing the SPLM/SPLA faction of Colonel John Garang with transport facilities, money, medicine, and food in order to maintain its attacks on the areas controlled by the SPLM/SPLA faction of Dr. Riek Machar. For several years, the NPA sent five hundred trucks, which carried about one hundred fifty thousand megatons of food, to Kongor and Bor before the rainy season started. Since its civilian population had abandoned it following the 1991 interfactional fighting between the two SPLA factions, Kongor and Bor became SPLM/SPLA Mainstream garrisons. Whatever items were brought to Kongor and Bor by NPA were meant specifically for SPLM/SPLA soldiers. The SPLA faction of Colonel John Garang had successfully utilized that NPA material assistance to destabilize the Ayod and Waat areas, which were under the control of Dr. Riek Machar's faction during the dry and rainy season simultaneously. In turn, the SPLM/SPLA gave the NPA a leading role in manipulating the activities of the other international NGOs operating in South Sudan. The NPA became the "lord" of all NGOs that were operating outside the OLS in south Sudan with the full protection of the SPLM/SPLA leader, Colonel John Garang.

These arrogant behaviors of the NPA and some other international NGOs based in Kenya made it almost impossible for south Sudanese opposing parties to reach any compromise among themselves. Colonel John Garang felt that since the NPA and other NGOs were still backing his organization, there was no need for him to reach any peaceful settlement with other opposing groups in the south. The attitude of NGOs like NPA led to the prolonging of the south/south disunity. The NPA attitude had also shown that such humanitarian organizations were not there to help the needy people in south Sudan. Instead of the NPA and other NGOs embarking on south/south reconciliation activities, they became more destructive and dangerous, similar to none other than the NIF enemy in Khartoum. It was therefore important that the activities of such NGOS operating in south Sudan once a permanent peace was realized be carefully reviewed and monitored. They should not be allowed to divide the south Sudanese people on ethnic lines as they had been doing since the early 1990s.

It is to be recalled that on Wednesday, November 17, 1999, at 8:30 p.m., a thirty-minute documentary was shown on Norwegian Television (NRK 1). In that documentary, some former NPA relief workers in the Sudan, including one of the pilots, Svein Kristiansen and NPA's Sudan Programme officer, Arne Ørum, were interviewed and confirmed the alleged smuggling of weapons to the SPLA-controlled areas in southern Sudan and the Nuba Mountains through Lokochoki, Kenya. One of the airlines that were involved in the NPA smuggling ring was Skyways, based in Kenya. Alf R. Jakobsen of NRK 1 broadcast the program in the Norwegian language. Similar accusations were also leveled in October 1998, by the Kenyan authorities against the NPA's activities in south Sudan. They accused the organization of smuggling illegal items to south Sudan that were worth to the Kenyan Custom about twelve million Norwegian kroner—equivalent to US$1.7 million—in the form of taxation. This resulted in the NPA almost being expelled from Kenya.

The disputes between Kenyan authorities and the NPA's Sudan Programme in Kenya were resolved only when the NPA Secretary General, Halle J. Hanssen, flew personally to Kenya and had lengthy discussions with President Daniel Arap Moi over the issue. The Norwegian pilots working for the Norwegian People's Aid (NPA) had repeatedly smuggled large quantities of land mines, hand grenades, assault rifles, and ammunition to the SPLA guerrillas in the Sudan during the 1990s. The smuggling occurred with planes, which the Norwegian People's Aid (NPA) and other relief organizations used to carry relief assistance to south Sudan. According to Hanssen, "the alleged pilots who flew weapons from place to place for the guerrillas, did this after they first flew in relief assistance to its destinations." The pilots were also accused of smuggling narcotics (marijuana) to the SPLA guerrillas to be used for intoxicating them in order to fight without fear whenever attacking the enemy's forces. Halle J. Hanssen also emphasized most of the information contained in this chapter about the role of the Norwegian People's Aid in his book titled"PÅ LIVET LØS" which is written in the Norwegian language. With direct translation, it literally means "LIFE IS DEPENDENCE". Though, most of the information available in his book was mainly collected from different sources that also contradicted the reality of the situation in southern Sudan during the liberation war of struggles for independence, Halle Hanssen duals his critism very much on Dr. Riek Machar and Dr. Lam Akol whom he called "South Sudan's Pol Pot", which was truly not the case with the two SPLM/SPLA breakaway commanders of Nasir Faction. This is in reference to the former Kampuchea despotic ruler who unfortunately massacred more than one million civilians during his repressive rule of terror in the early 1970s. His book is biased and most importantly a one sided story, which favoured only the rival faction of SPLM/A Torit Faction headed by Dr. John Garang. Halle Hanssen did not go deep into South - South conflicts, in order for the readers of his book to understand fully the root causes of the South Sudanese conflicts. Accordingly, most of the information available in his book with respect to South – South conflicts, which he collected from different sources, was not creditably reliable. I would advise him to make more research on South Sudanese conflicts and add what information he may get to his second edition of the same book.

The Civil Wars in Darfur and Eastern Sudan

ALTHOUGH THE WAR IN SOUTHERN Sudan was virtually over, the other conflicts that had been engulfing Sudan for about two decades, particularly in the eastern part of Sudan and that of Darfur, were not yet over. The war in Darfur had been going on for three years since it started officially. In the past the government of Sudan had been playing it down by labeling the rebellion movement in Darfur as banditry activities, a claim made more credible by a group of bandits who were harassing the movement of goods and services in the Darfur region. In turn, the government in Khartoum retaliated by arming Arab tribal groups that settled in the Darfur region and branded them as Janjaweeds instead of accepting direct participation in the conflict. During the daylight the Janjaweeds acted as Sudanese regular troops, but at night they turned into Arab tribal militia, roaming the areas on horseback, during which time they perpetrated indiscriminate killings, raped women, abducted children, and destroyed the properties of their victims. The Janjaweeds inflicted heavy casualties on African civilians; more than two hundred thousand people were reported to have been killed, and two million others had become IDPs or fled to the neighboring Chad as refugees for protection under UNHCR. The situation in Darfur had always been volatile in all aspects of human life.

The African Union sent several thousand troops into the Darfur region in order to defuse the tensions between the Sudanese Government troops and their Arab-backed militias, known as Janjaweeds, against the African tribes of Fur and Zagawi, who led the Movements of Sudan Liberation Army (SLA) and Justice and Equality Movement (JEM). They had been resisting the Arab onslaughts in the Darfur region since the outbreak of war in that part of Sudan nearly three years back. The ongoing conflict in the Darfur region was still active, and millions of human beings were still facing the Janjaweeds' onslaughts. Massive humanitarian interventions had been carried out by different NGOs in the affected areas, but this did not stop the suffering of the people of Darfur in general. The African Union troops who were sent to Darfur in the year 2004, in order to defuse the tension between the Sudanese-backed Arab militias on one hand against the two Darfurian rebel movements, were not doing much, either. The African Union had also made several attempts in the Nigerian capital, Abuja, for over one year to mediate between the warring parties in the conflict to end the war in the Sudan, but to no avail. More efforts were still needed, especially on the part of the United Nations. A UN peacekeeping force from developed countries including the European Union, United States, Russia, China, and Japan was urgently needed to stop the atrocities being committed on a daily basis by the Sudanese armed forces and its Arab-backed militias known as Janjaweeds in the Darfur region of western Sudan.

While the ongoing conflict in the eastern Sudan region of Red Sea Hills had been an integral part of the war in the south and other marginalized areas of the Sudan for the previous twenty years, the SPLM/SPLA fueled the conflict in eastern Upper Nile in 1995, when its newly established force under the banner of New Sudan Berigate (NSB) was created and fully became operational with the formation of National Democratic Alliance, an umbrella organization formed in the same year. This umbrella organization was formed by Dr. John Garang de Mabior, leader of SPLM/SPLA; Mullanh Mohammed Osman El Mirghani, leader of Democratic Unionist Party (DUP); Sayed Sadiq Adurhaman El Mahdi, leader of Umma Party; and General Abdulaziz Khalid, leader of Sudan Alliance Forces and Beja Congress Party. The aims and objectives of NDA were to overthrow the National Islamic Front (NIF) regime in Khartoum and replace it with a government of national unity that could accommodate all the diverse nationalities in the Sudan. Dr. John Garang's move to unify all the northern Sudanese political and military groups under his leadership was to divide the power and public opinion in the north. This was a brilliant tactical move in order to divide the northern leadership in his favor: an idea no southerner had ever thought of in the past. It really worked in his favor in the north, but it was also a disaster in the south because the majority of the southerners were not in favor of this idea of uniting Sudan under one unified leadership, which John Garang and his associates were advocating for more than two decades during the war of liberation. In the process of resisting the unity of Sudan, many lives were lost between the supporters of SPLM/SPLA, who advocated the unity of the Sudan, and the Anya Nya II separatists and other successive movements in the south, who unwaveringly opposed the unity of the country under Arab rule.

The SPLM/SPLA eventually signed the CPA on January 9, 2005, without involving the other partners in it. The Umma, DUP, and other splinter groups within the NDA also signed separate peace deals with the Khartoum government, leaving only the Beja Congress Party and Lion Free Movement—the two factions of Beja people in eastern Sudan at war with the government in Khartoum. They were still active with the full support of the Eritrean government. According to the CPA, all SPLA forces that used to operate in eastern Sudan alongside the NDA forces in the past were to evacuate the area, as the government forces still operating in southern Sudan at the time would be transferred to northern Sudan. The deals of creating political alliances in the Sudan were virtually over. This would definitely expose the two Beja factions into an open war once again with the Khartoum regime, which SPLM/SPLA and other former NDA partners who were currently in the Government of National Unity would be a part of.

The Comprehensive Peace Agreement (CPA)

**Dr. John Garang and Ali Osman Taha signed the
CPA in Nairobi on 9 January 2005.**

THE COMPREHENSIVE PEACE AGREEMENT (CPA) was signed on January 9, 2005, in the Kenya capital, Nairobi, by the government of Sudan and the

Sudan People's Liberation Movement/Army to end the twenty-one-year-old civil war in the country. The negotiation process, which led to the signing of the CPA took the two warring parties over ten years to reach. It was a conclusion to the civil war in the country that had already cost more than three million lives and made nearly five million internally displaced persons.

The Comprehensive Peace Agreement (CPA) changed Sudan's image both regionally and internationally. Sudan was known outside its boundaries to be associated with internecine wars, famines, diseases, slave trade, Islamic fundamentalism, and terrorism. However, the signing of the CPA on January 9, 2005, rescued its bad image both regionally and internationally in some areas. Somehow, the CPA made Sudan regain its lost credibility in the context of the African continent as well as the world at large. It was thanks to external pressure being exerted on the warring parties by the IGAD countries and the international community, particularly the US government, the European Union, and Norway. They all played a big role and made concerted efforts in bringing the two conflicting parties to a serious negotiating table. The resultant effect was the signing of the CPA, which brought the twenty-one-year civil war in the Sudan between the north and the south of the country to an end.

The CPA was negotiated under the auspices of the IGAD leadership of President Daniel Arap Moi of Kenya and his chief mediator, Lieutenant General Lazaro K. Sumbeiywo. The IGAD mediation was fully supported financially and morally by the IGAD Partners Forum (IPF), which comprised the United States, the United Kingdom, Norway, Russia, Italy, the Netherlands, Japan, and others. The war had indeed cost more than three million lives and forced nearly five million others into internally displaced persons camps inside the country or sent them to neighboring countries and the diaspora as refugees. It was characterized as the longest civil war on the African continent. The signing of this most popular CPA accord became a very colorful ceremony at Nairobi Nyayo Stadium on January 9, 2005. It was attended by most of the world leaders or their representatives, some of whom authenticated their own signatures as witnesses. The two principle negotiators—vice president of Sudan H. E. Ali Osman Taha and Dr. John Garang de

Mabior, leader of the SPLM/A—signed on behalf of the government and the movement, respectively. The CPA came as a result of protocols signed earlier at different dates by the chief negotiators on both sides as follows:

1. The Machakos Protocol signed on July 20, 2002.
2. The Agreement on Security Arrangements, signed on September 25, 2003.
3. The Agreement on Wealth Sharing, signed on January 7, 2004.
4. The Protocol of Power Sharing signed on May 26, 2004.
5. The Protocol on the Resolution of the Conflict in Southern Kordofan and Blue Nile States, signed on May 26, 2004.
6. The Protocol on the Resolution of the Conflict in Abyei Area, signed on May 26, 2004.

A Pre-Interim Period of six months was agreed upon and incorporated into the CPA in order to prepare grounds for the SPLM/SPLA to establish GOSS institutions as well as take over from the Coordinating Council of Southern States, which was running such institutions during the war in the south. An Interim Period of six years, starting from July 9, 2005, was agreed by the two parties to administer Sudan jointly. Two separate administrations were to be set up at different levels in both the Government of National Unity (GONU) and the Government of South Sudan (GOSS), in which the SPLM/SPLA leader, Dr. John Garang, would hold both positions of first vice president of the republic and president of the government of South Sudan during the interim period. The allocation of positions to the Sudanese parties per ratios were as follows:

- At the national level, the National Congress Party (NCP) was allocated 52 percent, the SPLM 28 percent, the Sudanese parties from the north 14 percent, and south Sudanese parties 6 percent.
- In the south, the SPLM was allotted 70 percent, the NCP 15 percent, and other south Sudanese Parties 15 percent.

- In the north Sudan states, 70 percent was allocated for the NCP, 10 percent for SPLM, and 20 percent for north Sudanese parties.
- In Abyei, Southern Kordofan and Blue Nile states, 55 percent was allocated for the NCP and 45 percent for the SPLM.

The peace agreement was made with the sense that the unity of Sudan should remain an attractive option in order for the south not to secede from the union of Sudan at the end of the Interim Period. Sharia Islamic law, which was part of the conflict in Sudan, was to remain applicable only in northern states, and parts of the constitution were to be rewritten so that sharia would not apply to non-Muslims throughout the country. The GONU and that of GOSS had to be established at both the national and state level, and all parties involved were to be represented as per the ratios/percentages allotted them.

The GOSS and the ten states of south Sudan would have their own interim constitutions, which would comply with the national constitution of Sudan. In the constitutions of GONU and GOSS, a decentralized system of government that would grant each state more power to administer its affairs independently was to be enforced. Two houses at the national levels were to be established per the Comprehensive Peace Agreement, namely the National Assembly and Council of States, for the latter of which each of the twenty-six states had to nominate two representatives.

In the National Assembly, the nomination was to be done in accordance with constituent estimated quotas. After three years of the Interim Period, an election would be held concurrently at the national and GOSS levels. It was also agreed in the CPA that 2 percent of the oil revenues would be allocated to the oil-producing states in proportion to their output. The remainder of the net oil income was to be shared at 50 percent for the GOSS and 50 percent for the GONU, and the GOSS had no authority to negotiate any oil leases previously granted by the GONU. Two banking systems would be formed in the two areas, with the Bank of Southern Sudan operating as a branch of the Central Bank of Sudan.

Essentially, the dual banking system meant that banks would be commonly stationed with two different windows for service. Two separate currencies in the north and south were to be recognized until the Central Bank had designed a new currency that reflected the cultural diversity of Sudan. National and southern funds for reconstruction and development would be established along with two multidonor trust funds. The two parties agreed that, at the end of the Interim Period, south Sudanese people would choose whether to separate from Sudan in an internationally supervised referendum or remain part of the country. In the security sector, about six thousand SPLA soldiers were drawn from the main SPLA mother units and joined with six thousand SAF forces on equal numbers, to ensure security in the capital and other designated towns throughout the country.

The combined SPLA and SAF forces were to be stationed in the capital Khartoum, Southern Kordofan/Nuba Mountains, Blue Nile, Malakal, Wau, Bentiu, Torit, Juba, and other places. SPLA mother components were left to operate separately from Sudan Armed Forces during the Interim Period. They could be united if the outcome of the future referendum favored the unity of Sudan, or else the SPLA overhaul forces would form the future South Sudan army in an independent state.

Following the CPA signing ceremony, the SPLM leadership decided to convene an extraordinary conference in Rumbek in the middle of January 2005 that was to be attended by the entire SPLM Leadership Council—the highest organ in the movement, all senior SPLA officers, and prominent members of the SPLM in the liberated areas and the diaspora. In this conference, it was unanimously resolved to form four clusters that would work out the structures of the movement for the newly expected government (GOSS), ready to be installed in the interim administrative capital, Juba after the end of the Pre-Interim Period. The clusters were security, governance, SPLM organizational structures, and political affairs. The SPLM Deputy Chairman and SPLA Chief of Staff Commander Salva Kiir Mayardit was to head security; the governance cluster was to be headed by Deputy Chairman Commander Dr. Riek Machar Teny; SPLM organizational structures were to be headed by Deputy Chairman Commander James Wani Igga; and Commander Dr. Lam Akol Ajawin headed political affairs. The SPLM members who attended the conference in Rumbek were nominated by leaders of four various clusters to participate in each cluster based on their prime knowledge in the areas concerned.

The process took up the entire Pre-Interim Period, when structures of the anticipated GOSS were put in place while some SPLM/SPLA members who should participate at GONU level were nominated. In the first week of July, the chairman of the SPLM sent an advanced team of SPLM/SPLA members to Khartoum in order to prepare for his homecoming to the Sudanese capital after twenty-one years in the liberated areas of New Sudan, where he and his forces had waged a protracted war of liberation against successive Sudanese regimes. The advance team, whose numbering was estimated to be over one hundred persons, was dispatched ahead of time to prepare grounds for the coming of the SPLM chairman and commander in chief of the SPLA.

Finally, on July 8, 2005, Dr. John Garang and his accompanying team boarded a Kenyan Airways plane from Jomo Kenyatta International Airport and landed at Khartoum Airport, where he was enthusiastically welcomed by over three million Sudanese from all walks of life. At that time, he made a joyous speech in Green Square before taking the oath of service to the people of Sudan. On July 9, 2005, a huge ceremony was conducted at Republican Palace to inaugurate him as first vice president of the Republic of Sudan and president of the Government of South Sudan. Invited foreign dignitaries and senior government officials and SPLM/A members attended the ceremony, and all media houses from Sudan and abroad were invited to cover the historical event. Traditional dances from various communities from north and south Sudan were colorfully displayed in front of the invited guests. The protracted twenty-one-year war, which had already caused the loss of more than three million lives and displaced five million others, eventually ended with the marking of that ceremony in Khartoum. The war-shattered families of a divided Sudan had finally reunited, and a new chapter of peace was concluded throughout the country, or so the world.

The Inauguration of Dr. John Garang

SOON AFTER THE CEREMONY ENDED, Dr. John Garang de Mabior assumed his designated position as first vice president of the republic and president of the government of South Sudan at the Republican Palace Office in Khartoum and made new appointments for the SPLM Leadership Council and SPLA senior officers. He promoted Commander Salva Kiir Mayardit to the rank of lieutenant general and at the same time appointed him as his deputy in the GOSS. He also appointed some SPLM Leadership Council members as caretakers/governors in the ten states of south Sudan and two from the marginalized areas of the New Sudan, namely Southern Kordofan/Nuba Mountains and Blue Nile states, respectively. The assigned SPLM members were Dr. Riek Machar for Western Equatoria, Commander James Wani Igga for Upper Nile, Commander Daniel Awet Akot for Eastern Equatoria, Commander Deng Alor Kuol for Jonglei, Dr. Lam Akol Ajawin for Western Bahr El Ghazal, Commander John Kong Nyuon for Warrap, Commander Kuol Manyang Juuk for Northern Bahr El Ghazal, Commander Nhail Deng Nhail for Lakes, Major General Clement Wani Konga for Bahr El Jebel/Central Equatoria, Commander Abdulaziz Adam El Alweh for Southern Kordofan/Nuba Mountains, and Commander Malik Agar for Blue Nile State. While in the SPLA general headquarters, Dr. John Garang, who was also commander in chief of the SPLM, appointed the following senior SPLA members to various positions: Lieutenant General Oyay Deng Ajak was appointed as SPLA chief of general staff, Major General Salva Mathok Gengdit for Administration, Major General James Hoth Mai for Logistics, Major General Bior Ajang Duot for Operations, and Major General Mabuto Mamuor Metet for Morale and Orientations respectively.

The Death of Dr. John Garang and Ascension of General Salva Kiir

AFTER HE SPENT OVER TWO weeks in office, Dr. John Garang returned to his old headquarters in Rumbek while on his way to Kampala for a secret meeting with his longtime friend and supporter during the war, President Yoweri Kaguta Museveni. While in Rumbek, Dr. Garang made a lengthy speech during which he condemned the remnants of Anya Nya II under the leadership and command of Major General Paulino Matip Nhial. Dr. Garang assured his audience that once he returned from Uganda, he would crush General Matip's militia by force if they refused to surrender peacefully. Instead of using the presidential jet assigned to him from Khartoum, he took a private plane from Rumbek to his former base at New Side on his way to Kampala, where he spent two days or more with his host, President Museveni, at his retreat farmhouse. What the two leaders agreed on has remained a secret up to the time of writing this book.

Dr. Garang (left) with Yoweri Museveni of Uganda (right)

On his way back to New Side, Sudan, on Friday July 30, 2005, Dr. Garang was offered a presidential helicopter by his friend, Yoweri Museveni. Unfortunately, the helicopter suddenly crashed on the Imatong Mountains before it could land in its destination at New Side Airstrip, instantly killing Dr. John Garang and his six personal aides and the crew. The crash happened in the evening hours between 6:00 and 8:00 p.m., and it was reported that severe rains made the ground invisible for the helicopter pilot to see. Accusations were later leveled against Uganda's President Yoweri Museveni for having planned the murder of the former first vice president of Sudan and president of the government of South Sudan for fear of his popularity in the region. None of Dr. Garang's senior SPLM members or senior SPLA officers accompanied him during his secret journey to Uganda.

Dr. Garang boards a helicopter at Entebbe, Uganda on 30 July 2005

When the news of Dr. Garang's death was announced on Sunday morning through different news media outlets including the BBC, VOA, Associated Press, Radio French International, KTN SUNA, and several others, the whole country, and perhaps the rest of the world, was in a state of shock and disbelief about the sudden death that had befallen Dr. John Garang. Riots similar to the ones that erupted in Khartoum on Sunday December 6, 1964, which became known as Black Sunday, occurred in most of the towns all over Sudan. That Sunday in December 1964, church worshipers in Khartoum, who consisted of mostly southern Sudanese, were urged to assemble at the airport to meet Clement Mboro, a respected southern leader who was minister of interior at the time. He was returning from a trip to southern Sudan, but his plane was delayed and southerners assumed the worst; that their beloved leader had been murdered by the then government of General Ibrahim Abboud and went on the rampage in Khartoum, smashing and burning cars and attacking passersby. At the end of that Sunday, several people were reported dead and many more injured.

The day Dr. John Garang died in the helicopter crash; shops and business centers were targeted and set ablaze by demonstrators. Several rioters were reported to have been killed by police and other security organs, particularly in Khartoum and Juba. Most of those killed were from southern Sudan and other marginalized areas of Sudan. All businesses and government institutions were at a standstill for nearly one week. Dr. John Garang's body was laid to rest in Juba, and the location became John Garang's Mausoleum, opposite the South Sudan National Assembly. Sadly, at the time of his untimely death in a helicopter crash, Dr. John Garang had spent exactly twenty-one days in office. Following his death, the SPLM Leadership Council ostensibly nominated Dr. Garang's deputy, Lieutenant General Salva Kiir Mayardit, as his successor, and Dr. Riek Machar became his deputy. This was in accordance with SPLM/SPLA hierarchy. It was speculated by different sources later that Dr. John Garang's visits to Uganda were to negotiate arms deals in order to equip SPLA forces in the south to crush his potential opponents finally.

After Dr. Garang's burial on August 6, 2005, General Salva Kiir immediately went to Khartoum to take the oath of office as first vice president of the republic and president of the government of South Sudan before the president of the republic, Field Marshal Omar Hassan El Bashir, at Republican Palace in Khartoum.

Formation of Goss and Its Subsequent Bad Governance

AFTER LIEUTENANT GENERAL SALVA KIIR Mayardit took the oath of office, he and President Bashir worked out the coalition Government of National Unity in Khartoum, in which the SPLM had a share of 28 percent at the national level and 10 percent at the state level in the north. However, SPLM nominated members adequately represented the party in the national parliament, judiciary, and executive branches of the government in GONU during the six-year Interim Period. In the south, GOSS was also formed in September and October 2005, with one hundred seventy nominated MPs representing different political parties and constituencies in the South Sudan Legislative Assembly, as well as its judiciary and executive branches. In the executive branch, twenty-two ministerial positions were appointed in the new government under President Salva Kiir Mayardit. Following the announcements, various communities in the south were not happy at all with the outcome of the appointed government representatives in both GONU and GOSS. This is because most of the strategic positions in all governments from the GONU and the GOSS were allocated to the Dinka, a tribe from which the first vice president and president of the government of South Sudan hailed from. He rewarded the Dinka with the most lucrative positions, and this continued even after the independence of South Sudan in July 2011. The GOSS had, in fact, faced its own bundle of hurdles during the interim period and thereafter: gross human rights violations, corruption, tribalism, nepotism, dictatorship, land grabs, just to mention a few. There were violations of human rights that started with disarmaments among the pastoral communities, particularly the Murle, Nuer, Mundari, and Dinka, in which one tribe was disarmed while its rival was favored. These discriminative disarmaments had actually encouraged some communities to resist the disarmament policy, and they ended up fighting the SPLA forces who were assigned to disarm them. Several hundred civilians were sadly killed during the process by the government forces who enforced disarmaments. None of those who committed such heinous crimes have ever been apprehended and taken to courts of law for the offenses they committed. Wanton killings and human rights violations by the SPLA forces against civilians have been repeated since the formation of the GOSS in 2005. Inter and intra tribal and sectional skirmishes among different communities where thousands of civilians had been killed or displaced from their settlements were the status quo.

Institutionalized Corruption in South Sudan

CORRUPTION WAS SO RAMPANT AT the GOSS and state level, and accountability was nonexistent. Some of the noticeable corruption scandals were the well-coordinated corruption practices by GOSS and state officials including the "Dura saga," in which the minister of finance and economic planning, Mr. Kuol Athian Mawien, issued several hundreds of millions of bags of maize and sorghum to fake traders, with the order directed from the president's office. The real motive was to reduce acute shortages of food in the country by importing such foodstuffs from the neighboring countries of Sudan, Kenya, and Uganda to meet the high demands of the country's requirements. In turn, the suppliers were to sell the imported maize and sorghum to consumers at affordable rates. Unfortunately, this did not happen as planned. Some presidential advisors, ministers, undersecretaries, heads of commissions, MPs, senior SPLA, and other organized forces officers and senior civil servants were allocated quotas with fake companies disguised as suppliers. A good number of unlicensed company representatives who claimed to have delivered the foodstuffs to the states concerned were paid billions of South Sudanese pounds after some governors in the various states involved in the same unfortunate scams confirmed deliveries in form of letters to the minister of finance. The GOSS lost, not less than four billion SSP, in these scam deals initiated through the office of the president. The four Greater Bahr El Ghazal states of Lakes, Western Bahr El Ghazal, Warrap, and Northern Bahr El Ghazal, Central Equatoria, and Unity states were the main beneficiaries in these fraudulent dealings.

Another corruption scandal was that of the Eyat Group, which had close links with the NSS in Khartoum. The company was awarded the Aweil-Meriam Road network that the former minister Arthur Akuen Chol and his undersecretary Isaac Makur Ater granted to them. That irregular dealing, worth an amount of US$288 million, was for the construction of that road network connecting Northern Bahr El Ghazal state with Darfur region, Sudan. The then GOSS ministries of Roads and Bridges, Legal Affairs, and Constitutional Development, and the SSLA, were not directly involved in such contractual agreements at all. Normally, all GOSS contractual agreements were always signed through the Ministry of Legal Affairs and the investors concerned negotiated directly with the line ministries before taking the agreement to the council of ministers or SSLA for approval. This time around, it was strictly and secretly done through the Office of the President, and the payments to Eyat Group were also processed directly from Khartoum, where about eight to ten million US dollars were deducted on a monthly basis from the 50 percent of the GOSS oil share.

The most unfortunate corruption saga was the GOSS car deals with Al-Cardinal, a company owned by a well-known corrupt Sudanese national of Lebanese origin close to Sudan National Security (NSS) who also owned Sara Hotel in Juba and other businesses in South Sudan. Indeed, Al-Cardinal Company was subcontracted by the GOSS ministry of finance in 2006, to purchase over sixteen hundred GXR Land Cruisers and Toyota Double Cabins of various types at the rates of US$96,000 per GXR Land Cruiser and US$45,000 for Toyota Double Cabins, but 243 of them did not arrive at their destination in Juba. The lost cars could not be traced, and no one was ever held responsible for the losses. The GOSS spent more than US$150 million for the purchase and shipment of those cars from Khartoum to Juba, including air transports. The minister of finance and Al-Cardinal Chairman and CEO Mr. Asheraf Sayed Ahmed intentionally inflated the prices of the cars in order for the big "McCoys" to get their lion's shares from such fraudulent deals. The prices included the hiring of cargo planes to transport all the cars purchased by Al-Cardinal to the GOSS and the ten states from Khartoum to Juba, instead of using the most cheaply available means of river transport by vessels from Kosti to Juba, which would take only two weeks. Both the South Sudan Anti-Corruption Commission under Chairperson Dr. Pauline Riak and the Public Accounts Committee at South Sudan Legislative Assembly chaired by Hon. Dr. Jimmy Wongo, with myself as a member, launched joint investigations to find out exactly how several hundred millions of US dollars were spent unaccounted for by the GOSS. The findings were referred to the ministry of legal affairs, which was also the attorney general of the GOSS, to investigate both the Ministry of Finance and the Al-Cardinal boss over the disappearance of 243 cars, and thereafter refer the matter to the office of the president for action. This was according to South Sudan Auditor General Stephen Wondu's report 2007 to the South Sudan Legislative Assembly. Indeed, the GOSS president ordered suspensions of both the minister of finance and his undersecretary and directed the minister of legal affairs to issue an immediate arrest warrant against them. The directives of the president were immediately implemented and both minister of finance and the undersecretary were arrested and placed in Central Equatoria Police custody. Mr. Ashrap Sayed Ahmed was also arrested. Surprisingly, a platoon of SPLA soldiers, some of whom were close relatives to the detained minister and undersecretary took the law in their own hands and went to the police station where they forcefully released them instantly. Thereafter they escorted them to their homes, where they remained protected by the said SPLA soldiers for some time. The owner of Al-Cardinal Company, on the other hand, bailed himself out with five million US dollars in cash. The story of the Al-Cardinal car deal remained a mystery in the minds of those who witnessed it. Both the GOSS president and his legal affairs minister were helpless, and they could not do anything with respect to that case relating to the accused minister of finance and his undersecretary as well as the Al-Cardinal owner, so he left everything to God to handle it. All men were freed, and even the president nominated the same alleged former minister of finance Arthur Akuen to the 2010 National Parliament representing his constituency, Aweil, Northern Bahr El Ghazal state. The former undersecretary became a business tycoon who owned several houses and plots, as well as other businesses in Juba town and various states in Greater Bahr El Ghazal.

Another corruption saga in the GOSS was the renovation of old and obsolete colonial buildings in all the ten states of South Sudan. The project had indeed drained most of the government resources to renovate those old buildings, which cost three times higher than the average cost per a new building. Most senior government officials, including ministers and top bras SPLA generals, were directly involved in the selection of contractors. Each was busy bringing his contractor to renovate his department's building or his allocated official residence with any price that suited him best, without going through the normal process. The ministries of Housing and Legal Affairs are the right bodies to go through, but most government officials at the top positions bypassed these two institutions knowingly for material benefits from such unlawful deals. The most noticeable in that well entrenched and coordinated corruption saga was the renovation of SSLA by a handpicked Chinese company with over US$6 million. The previous original cost for its construction by the Yugoslavian company that was subcontracted by the Regional Government (HEC) did not cost more than US$300,000. In the same way, the construction of all the ministerial complexes and residential quarters for fourteen ministers and their director generals did not cost more than $US3 million in 1976. The renovations of the Office of the President at the Ministerial Complex cost US$6 million. His Official Guest House J1 cost US$8.5 million. The president's daughter and her Ethiopian husband, as well as the wife of former Cabinet Affairs Minister Mr. Deng Alor Kuol, who is of Ethiopian origin, were awarded the contracts for renovating both J1 and the Office of the President for a total amount of US$14.5 million. These two premises would have not cost the GOSS more than US$5 million if new ones were to be erected in good face. Other corruption dealings were those of the Ministry of Education, where substantial amounts were allocated to the ministry by SSLA as a scholarship program in the neighboring countries of Kenya, Uganda, Ethiopia, Sudan, and even Egypt to provide scholarships for university and college students. Unfortunately, most of the real students did not benefit from the millions of dollars sent to all these countries through the Ministry of Education's representatives. Instead, the monies ended up being used for supporting families and children of some well-off personalities in the

GOSS and states, or being given to students in discriminative ways. Those students without close relatives in the Ministry of Education or connections at the highest level were not supported financially. Hundreds of scholarships were also offered to the GOSS by friendly countries for undergraduates and postgraduate studies, but such scholarships were distributed on nepotism basis. In the Ministry of Agriculture, several hundred tractors were purchased from India with the intention of upgrading and promoting the agricultural sector to increase food productivity throughout the ten states of South Sudan. Unfortunately, all the purchases were distributed to individuals who are well connected to government officials in the ministry, instead of distributing them to real farmers with technical knowhow. The road construction and Juba Airport had also cost the GOSS millions of dollars from unscrupulous contractors who were handpicked by the ministers concerned to construct both internal roads in Juba and Juba Airport. Prices were badly inflated and nothing much was done. Some of the companies were associated with the President and his cronies, who get contracts directly from the Office of the President without going through normal procedures.

In the Ministry of Health, corruption was very much entrenched from top to bottom. This involved medicines and medical equipment being purchased by the GOSS or donated by different donors for use by private clinics of doctors and clinical officers working the hospitals all over South Sudan. Without these purchases and donations, both outpatients and the ones admitted had to buy medicine for their treatments from pharmaceutical vendors; those who could not afford to buy medicines privately eventually died from treatable diseases like malaria and other curable ailments. Land grabbing was another major concern in the GOSS setup whereby some senior government officials and SPLA senior army officers used to take land from individuals or undemarcated lands by force. The Central Equatoria state officials and Bari community chiefs have also been involved deeply in selling land unlawfully, especially in Juba county, where the capital of South Sudan is situated. Several cases of land grabbing have been presented to the courts in Juba, but most of them did not result in settlements, because the court officials are either intimidated by land grabbers or bribed so that justice is denied. Other judges ended up being murdered by those who could not get their rights through legal means. It has become a very unfortunate situation attributed to weak institutions established by the GOSS in South Sudan that condoned such inhuman practices.

About 40 percent of the GOSS budget has been allocated to the ministry for SPLA and veteran affairs since 2006, and the SPLA received more than half a billion as its annual budget. However, oddly enough, the SPLA units in different parts of the country used to spend up to six months without getting their salaries. One wonders where the SPLA budget goes, yet the minister in charge of SPLA affairs has usually submitted a supplementary budget to Parliament before six months elapsed even though the allocated budget was meant for twelve months, like any other budgets worldwide. Over twenty thousand SPLA soldiers were deliberately demobilized from the army, and they were forced to return to their homes without any benefits after twenty-one years in liberation fighting. This group of SPLA demobilized soldiers was nicknamed "Not Confirmed," but during the war they actively participated in combat operations before the attainment of the CPA. The lucky ones were put under a special program: the Demobilization, Disarmament and Reintegration Programme (DDR), funded by UNDP in collaboration with the GOSS.

Several thousand ghost names in the SPLA and other organized forces; police, prison service, fire brigade, wildlife, national security, and civil service departments were routinely notified, but nobody bothered to screen them for the first three years after the establishment of the GOSS. Millions of SSP used to end up in the hands of some well-placed civil servants, senior officers, and their "godfathers" at the highest levels, who gave them all the necessary protection from prosecution. The Ministry of Legal Affairs and Constitutional Development had its own share of corruption practices by issuing licenses to thousands of companies, both national and international, without remitting the monies paid to the Ministry of Finance or the Ministry of Commerce, Trade and Industry as required. Top officials from the Ministry of Legal Affairs divided the monies collected from such licenses among themselves. The same thing occurred with the Custom Service and

Immigration Department, where monies were collected from businesses and individuals from different checkpoints at Uganda, Kenya, Ethiopia, DRC, and Sudan borders. Most of it was being divided by custom and immigration officials with their bosses in the headquarters in Juba or in the states concerned without going to the government treasury. The bank of South Sudan lavishly issued several millions of US dollars to individuals and fake businessmen and women who claimed to bring in food and other essential commodities from abroad or to foreign banks operating in the country. All NGOs have been operating freely since 2005, without any laws to regulate their operations in the country. The parliamentarians have been demanding a bill for NGOs to be tabled in the assembly for purposes of enacting them into a law but to no avail. The Ministry of Legal Affairs and Constitutional Development has been resisting the tabling of such a bill before the assembly because the department of registrar in the ministry had been the one collecting the monies for registrations of all charitable organizations and companies all over the country. Therefore, the individual beneficiaries from the ministry could not accept a bill that would regulate the activities of the NGOs in the country to be enacted into law because it would undermine their own personal gains. The decentralized system of government in South Sudan was badly misused by the power brokers—starting with the head of state, who possessed eight bulletproof cars that he had no reason at all to own in a poor region like South Sudan, which had not yet attained its independence from Sudan. Individual ministers and state governors used to own not less than four cars while 99 percent of the population lived below poverty lines, where well-functioning schools, hospitals, road networks, agricultural schemes, well-organized and trained SPLA soldiers and other law enforcement agents, clean drinking water, food security were not afforded by the government to its citizens. Most of the GOSS ministers could hardly be found in their assigned offices during working hours, as they spent most of their leisure time in foreign hotels in Juba town, playing cards with friends, or else on foreign trips where each got US$500 per diem allowances. The Interim Period, which started on July 9, 2005, and ended on July 9, 2011, therefore elapsed without much in terms of development, which was the main theme during the struggle. During the war the SPLM/SPLA claimed that once it achieved its ultimate objectives, the first thing it would do was to transform South Sudan into a vibrant and livable environment for its citizens. SSLA made several attempts by forming ad hoc committees to investigate the alleged corrupt practices within the GOSS through its Public Accounts Committee in collaboration with South Sudan Anti-Corruption Commission, but without success. Their combined findings were always discarded by either the Ministry of Legal Affairs, which acted as attorney general of the GOSS, or through the office of the president. The only corruption case that reached the attorney general's office and proceeded to the high court was that of Al-Cardinal Ltd., in which the owner of the company was sentenced but bailed himself out with U$5 million in cash, and the case has never been heard again. Mr. Asheraf Sayed Ahmed was still a free man doing his usual business smoothly in Juba.

The slogan of Dr. John Garang, "Take the towns to the people," had become a mere political slogan after his unfortunate demise. The current SPLM leadership under President Kiir had no plan to fulfill Dr. Garang's slogan, as his close associates had preoccupied his government all these years with squandering oil resources for personal use. In 2010 a general election was held throughout Sudan during which both President Omar El Bashir and First Vice President and President of the GOSS Lieutenant General Salva Kiir Mayardit were overwhelmingly elected as presidents. Their elections were to prepare ground for a referendum in South Sudan in one year's time. The elections were held between April 11, 2010, and April 15, 2010. President Salva Kiir, who was the sole SPLM candidate, got 93 percent of the total votes, and his main challenger, Dr. Lam Akol Ajawin, got 7 percent. The 2010 election was part of the general elections in the whole Sudan. In the SSLM, the SPLM got one hundred sixty seats, and the other ten were divided among different political parties. The SPLM had also retained its 28 percent from the National Assembly in Khartoum. Generally, the election was not fair because some independent candidates were either intimidated or the votes were rigged to SPLM's chosen candidates by polling officers and security officials who were monitoring the elections in South Sudan. The elections were meant for the Interim Period as part of the CPA implementation.

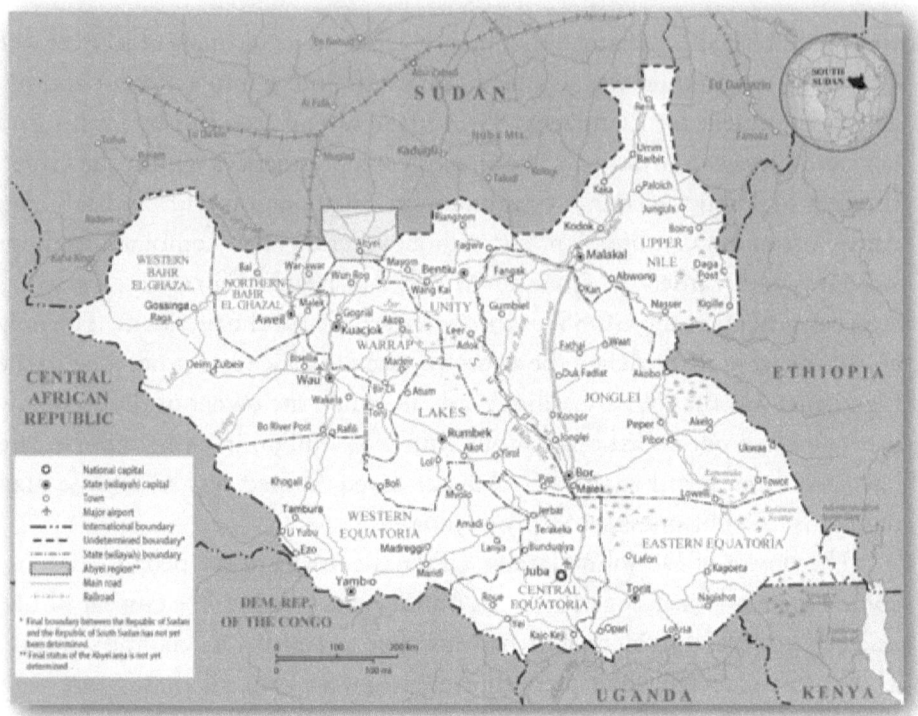

Map of the Republic of South Sudan after the independence in 2011

Independence of South Sudan

DURING THE SIGNING OF THE CPA in 2005, it was agreed that an Interim Period of six years would be observed, during which Sudan would remain united under President Omar Hassan El Bashir and South Sudan would be ruled by the GOSS under the leadership of President Salva Kiir Mayardit, who would also assume the position of first vice president of the republic. After the end of the Interim Period, an internationally supervised referendum would be held in the south to determine whether South Sudan should opt for being an independent state or remain part of Sudan. This referendum took place in South Sudan from January 9, 2011, to January 15, 2011. The referendum was the result of the 2005 Naivasha peace agreement known as the Comprehensive Peace Agreement, which was signed between the government of Sudan and the Sudan People's Liberation Movement/Army (SPLM/SPLA). A simultaneous referendum was supposed to be held in Abyei on whether to become part of South Sudan. Unfortunately, the Abyei referendum was postponed because of conflict over demarcation and residency rights between the Ngok Dinka and the Messiria Arab nomads, who also have claims over the territory. On February 7, 2011, the Referendum Commission published the final results, with 98.83 percent voting in favor of the independence of South Sudan and 1.17 percent voting for the unity of the country. Finally, on July 9, 2011, South Sudan was declared as an independent sovereign state, at which time 193 countries, including Sudan, recognized it. It automatically became a member of the United Nations. The declaration of independence ceremony was attended by huge numbers of participants from all over the ten states of Sudan. There were several heads of state and foreign dignitaries, including the Norwegian Crown Prince Haakon, who was there representing the Royal Kingdom of Norway. The Transitional Constitution of the Republic of South Sudan, 2011 was drafted by a Southern Sudan Constitutional Drafting Committee and came into force on the day of the independence of South Sudan after being signed by the president of the republic.

The Constitution replaced the existing 2005 Interim Constitution of Southern Sudan. The constitution establishes a presidential system of government headed by a president who is head of state, head of government, and the commander in chief of the armed forces. All these powers were vested on one man, and many people predicted that this would definitely entrench dictatorship in the nascent country, South Sudan. Following the declaration of independence, a new government was formed, at which time Salva Kiir appointed his longtime vice president, Dr. Riek Machar, and most of the cabinet members who were with him during the Interim Period administration from both GONU and the south. The South Sudan members from the National Assembly in Khartoum were brought to the National Assembly in Juba, a total of 332 MPs representing various political parties. The Council of States, or the Upper House, was established, with fifty MPs representing all the ten states of the Republic of South Sudan and each state represented by five members.

During the first week of April 2012, a border war broke out between the republics of Sudan and South Sudan over the Hegelig oil fields, which is claimed by the two countries. The South Sudan Army (SPLA) overran the Sudan Armed Forces garrison at Hegelig and controlled it before the UN threatened South Sudan with sanctions if the SPLM did not unconditionally withdraw from the territory. Then the SPLA forces were ordered by the president of South Sudan to immediately withdraw from the occupied Sudanese territory in order to avert United Nations sanctions against the newly born country. The government of South Sudan accused Khartoum of stealing crude oil worth several hundreds of million US dollars. In turn Khartoum threatened Juba with abruptly closing down the oil pipelines that carried South Sudan oil from Bentiu and Paloch oilfields to Port Sudan for shipment to international markets. The SPLA and SAF had fought in 2008 in Abyei, when the two parts were still under one Sudan, but that conflict was defused.

Thereafter, an Ethiopian contingent of a UN Interim Security Force for Abyei (UNISFA) of one battalion was mandated by the UN Security Council in New York to protect the Ngok Dinka residents in Abyei town and beyond. Most of the Abyei residents from Ngok Dinka have been moved to Agok, south of Abyei Bridge on Kiir River, which the Messiryia called Bhar el Arab. After the Hegelig border war, the government in Khartoum decided to obstruct the implementation of the CPA in the other marginalized areas of Blue Nile and Nuba Mountains. During that time, the SPLA Joint Integrated Units (JIUs) stationed there were attacked and eventually dislodged from their barracks by SAF forces. The two regions of Sudan that fought alongside the SPLA in the south and were granted special consideration in the CPA were forced back to war by Khartoum in 2012. They returned back to the liberation war in partnership with Darfurian rebel movements of JEM and Sudan Liberation Army (SLA) with full military and financial support from Juba and Kampala, respectively. The combined Sudanese rebel movements united their ranks under the Sudan Alliance Forces (SAF) while operating autonomously, with the sole objective of overthrowing the NCP-led government in Khartoum being spearheaded by Field Marshal Omar Hassan El Bashir. They are also morally supported internally in the country by disgruntled sectarian political parties such as National Umma Party of Sadiq El Mahdi, National Congress Party of Hassan El Turabi, and Unionist Democratic Party of Mohamed Osman El Mirghani. Since then, the fighting has been concentrated along Southern Darfur, Nuba Mountains, and Blue Nile states. Numerous peace talks have been conducted in Doha, Addis Ababa, Paris, and Frankfurt in order to end the conflict in the Sudan but to no avail. Massive displacements of several hundred thousand refugees into South Sudan, Chad, and Ethiopia have been going on all these years. In South Sudan alone, Yeta Refugee Camp in Unity state housed more than six thousand from Nuba Mountains, and Maban County in Upper Nile state has also accommodated over one hundred thousand refugees from Blue Nile state.

UPDF FORCES IN SOUTH SUDAN IN DECEMBER 2013

SPLM Internal Crisis

THE SPLM INTERNAL CRISIS IGNITED soon after the declaration of the independence of the Republic of South Sudan from Sudan on July 9, 2011. President Salva Kiir appeared more or less hostile to most of his SPLM senior colleagues whom he reappointed to his cabinet, including the vice president of the newly born South Sudan, Dr. Riek Machar Teny. The president developed negative attitudes toward certain members of his government after the passing of the Provisional Constitution of South Sudan by the National Assembly, signed into law on July 9, 2011. President Salva Kiir made sure that he silenced voices within his cabinet that had been vocal during the Interim Period and would want immediate reforms within the SPLM leadership. He started by stripping away some tasks that were constitutionally assigned to the vice president in order to create a situation of disharmony between them. When the vice president realized that the president had unfriendly motives toward him, he decided to declare his interest and intention to challenge him for the chairmanship of the SPLM in the upcoming Third National Convention of the SPLM, which was supposed to take place by February 2013.

The vice president was soon joined by comrade Pagan Amum, SPLM secretary general, and Madam Rebecca Nyandeng de Mabior, presidential advisor for gender and human rights, in his interest to challenge the president during the upcoming convention. The three of them were members of the Political Bureau of the SPLM—the highest organ in the party. President Salva Kiir had always resisted any democratic reforms and institutionalization of power in the SPLM for fear of losing his position to those spearheaded by his vice president and other senior colleagues from the SPLM Political Bureau. In turn, the president dismissed his entire cabinet, including the vice president on July 23, 2013, and replaced them mainly with uncommitted SPLM members or newly recruited members who had recently deserted the National Congress Party for the SPLM. This new group was part of the government of Sudan's collaborators during the war, and diehard SPLM members could not trust their loyalty to the party. The president also suspended the SPLM secretary general on false charges of corruption that the president had manufactured against him in order to tarnish his good reputation in the party. The president had, moreover, wrongfully dismissed the two constitutionally elected state governors of Unity state (Honorable Taban Deng Gai) and Lakes state (Honorable Engineer Chol Tong Mayay) on charges related to corruption and human rights violations in their respective states. The charges were categorically dismissed by the two former governors, who called them witch-hunts by the president and his close circles, who feared the transformation of the SPLM. Political wrangling apparently ensued between the government loyalists who supported the president and those who sided with former vice president Dr. Riek Machar. Some efforts were exerted by church leaders to reconcile them but to no avail. The president was adamant about refusing to accept any deal with his former colleagues from the SPLM Political Bureau whom he had dismissed unceremoniously from his cabinet.

Finally, on December 6, 2013, the former vice president and his supporters called a press conference at SPLM headquarters to inform the South Sudanese and the world at large about the emerging political differences within the SPLM leadership. In the press conference, the group called on SPLM Chairman Salva Kiir to convene the Political Bureau in order to set the agenda for the expected upcoming National Liberation Council. At that time, Dr. Riek Machar announced the public rally to be conducted by the group on December 14, 2013, at Dr. John Garang's Mausoleum. The SPLM supporters of the government had also booked December 14, 2013, as the official day for launching the National Liberation Council.

The two opposing SPLM groups were ready for confrontation because both of them were aiming for the same meetings on the same day using the same place at the same time. Some concerned Dinka elders and church leaders promptly alarmed by current SPLM show decided to intervene, and they appealed to the two SPLM groups to postpone their meetings in order to let the Dinka elders and church leaders reconcile them amicably. However, Dr. Machar, the team leader of the SPLM opposed to the SPLM loyalists, went ahead and released a statement to that effect. The NLC meeting therefore, went on as planned on Saturday morning, December 14, 2013. His Grace Paulino Lokudu Loro, the Catholic Archbishop of Juba, reiterated the appeal the bishops had made before and called for calm and harmony between the two SPLM opposing parties. In his opening speech, President Salva Kiir, SPLM chairman, downplayed the differences within the SPLM groups and instead accused his rival Dr. Riek Machar of undermining his leadership. Instead, he vehemently ignored the appeals made by the archbishop and Dinka community elders and deliberately referred to the 1991 split within the SPLM/SPLA as a reminder. He said this: "In the light of the recent development in which some comrades have come out to challenge my executive decisions, I must warn you that this behavior is tantamount to indiscipline, which will take us back to the days of the 1991 split."

The SPLM Chairman Salva Kiir Mayardit was ostensibly referring to Dr. Riek Machar, discrediting Dr. Machar's calls for democratic reforms within the SPLM to all NLC participants who attended the meeting. His statement infuriated Dr. Riek Machar, Madam Rebecca Nyandeng, Pagan Amum, and several senior SPLM members, so they decided to boycott the Sunday meeting. The said meeting was attended only by supporters of the chairman, as those of his deputy protested and marched out of the scheduled meeting.

On Sunday, December 15, 2013, as the NLC meeting was about to come to an end, President Salva Kiir apparently instructed the head of his personal aide, Major General Marial Ciennoung, the commander of Tiger Battalion, to leave the meeting venue in Nyakuron and return to his headquarters to disarm all the troops stationed there. General Marial followed the instruction from his boss and implemented the orders. However, after the disarmament was commenced successfully, he ordered all the Dinka elements to take their guns again from stores. When the Nuer elements heard that the Dinka elements of the SPLM were reissued their guns, quarrels began between Marial (a Dinka) and his deputy, Brigadier General James Kuach Gaak, who is a Nuer. Their arguments came to the close attention of some Nuer soldiers who happened to be nearby. Fighting immediately erupted between some Dinka soldiers who were guarding the armory and some Nuer soldiers, who broke in and armed themselves. This is how the fighting started in Juba at 10:00 p.m. GMT.

On Sunday night, the fighting was exclusively triggered by the orders from President Salva Kiir to General Marial to disarm the Nuer elements from the SPLA, who he suspected had sympathy for Dr. Riek Machar. General Marial Ciennoung shot his deputy, James Kuach Gaak, while the soldiers were still arguing. Brigadier James Kuach died a day later from the severe wounds he sustained from General Marial at Tiger Headquarters on December 15, 2013. In response to the unfortunate shooting of the Nuer officer James Kuach by his Dinka boss Brigadier Marial, Brigadier Peter Lim Bol and Col. Michael Guea Thaak reacted vigorously and bravely broke the store where the Nuer disarmed soldiers eventually equipped themselves. The fighting in Tiger headquarters started on the night of Sunday, December 15, 2015, and continued on Monday morning after the SPLA Chief of Staff General James Hoth Mai and his Sector II Commander General Charles Lam Chol—both from the Nuer tribe—apparently launched surprise and coordinated attacks against the Nuer elements who briefly captured and controlled the Presidential Guards headquarters in favor of the government. Both generals commanded their loyalist troops with the intention of crushing the mutinying Nuer soldiers from the SPLA Presidential Guards once and for all. I talked with both generals in the morning hours of December 16, 2013, before they launched their well-planned and coordinated attacks against the Nuer elements that controlled the Tiger headquarters.

The generals were advised not to wage war against their fellow Nuer while the situation was still confused, but they adamantly refused such advice and went ahead with their plan to recapture the Tiger military barracks and indeed they did it with heavy casualties on both sides. The fighting spread to different parts of the city of Juba, including the SPLA military headquarters, Bilpam, and New Side military barracks between the government loyalists and mutinying soldiers. When the government loyalists brought the crisis in Juba to an end on December 16, 2013, some Dinka elements from the Presidential Guards at Tiger and Lure military barracks, along with thousands of Dinka police and other organized forces, started terrorizing Nuer civilian residents at Gudella, Mia Sava, Mengateen, Aden, Guray, Khor William, Jebel Markets, Gumbo, and several other neighborhoods in Juba town.

This are some of the extracts from the Africa Union Report of Inquiry that being quoted from Radio Tamazuq 2015, in order for the readers of this book to understand such information was not directly originated from the author but from the African Union report.

The African Union Commission of Inquiry on South Sudan has released its final report concluding that "widespread and systematic" killings took place in Juba in December 2013, with violence later spreading elsewhere. The AU investigation found that the killings in Juba were carried out pursuant to a state policy and were coordinated and possibly also planned.

AU investigators found no evidence of a coup attempt as claimed by President Salva Kiir but instead concluded that a gunfight within the Presidential Guards was the immediate trigger for further violence in which "Dinka members of the Presidential guard and other security forces targeted Nuer soldiers and civilians... killing Nuer soldiers and civilians in and near their homes."

A number of Kiir's personal associates and presidential guard commanders are named in the report as operational sector commanders who led the operations that the AU Commission said resulted in mass killings in residential areas mid-December 2013 including Munuki 107, Khor William, New Site, Gudele One, Mangaten, Mia Saba, Custom and Nyakuron. Tens of thousands of members of the Nuer ethnic group fled to the UN Tongping base in the wake of these killings and still remain under UN protection today.

The AU report details numerous accounts of murders, rapes, torture and other atrocities including alleged cases of forced cannibalism perpetrated by members of the army and security forces. Articles 810, 811, 812, 813 and 814 of the report make the case that such acts were carried out with a degree of organization and planning.

In Article 810 the report notes that attacks against civilians in Juba "could have been planned," according to some of the Commission's informants. "Suggestions of evidence of planning are varied and the Commission has considered all the suggestions carefully weighing it with the totality of the information it has, and testimony it heard," the report notes.

Indications of planning and coordination include testimonies that irregular forces disguised as "street cleaners" allegedly scouted areas of Juba in the weeks before the massacres, as well as division of Juba into "four operational zones" and the setting up of roadblocks and checkpoints around the city.

"House to house searches were undertaken by security forces. During this operation male Nuers were targeted, identified, killed on the spot or gathered in one place and killed," states the Commission report.

The AU report identifies the four operational sector commanders as General Salva Mathok for Amarat neighborhood, General Bol Akot for Gudele and Mia Saba neighborhoods, General Garang Mabir for Mangaten and General Marial Chanuong for Khor William. Salva Mathok is a relative of Salva Kiir and Marial Chanuong is the head of Kiir's presidential guards. Bol Akot has been identified in previous reports as a "civilian" who led militia at the time of the massacres and whom Kiir later gave a senior rank in the army.

'THE VIOLENCE WAS ORGANIZED'

The AU report goes on to quote the Minister of Defense Kuol Manyang as saying that a militia loyal to Salva Kiir known as Rescue the President (Dut Ku Beny in Dinka) "killed most people here [in Juba] — from 15th to 18th." This refers to a force that other witnesses describe as Kiir's "personal army", which he allegedly recruited and based at his private farm at Luri near Juba.

Radio Tamazuj earlier this year interviewed ex-combatants of this militia recruited in Kiir's home region Bahr al Ghazal who confirmed that they participated in operations in Juba and also reported disciplinary and morale problems owing to poor training and consumption of alcohol.

"They were not part of the SPLA, they were not part of the police, they were not part of the National Security. It was a private army which Salva trained... The fighting in Giada was just to provoke. It was just only to be a signal for these guys to start their work," says one witness quoted in the AU report. "So immediately when this fighting started in the others, these guys were now deployed and they did the killing... So it was a deliberate, it was something planned."

Other testimonies in the report, however, point more to the role of organized forces in the killings rather than the so-called private army.

Article 812 of the Commission of Inquiry report concludes, "The evidence thus suggests that these crimes were committed pursuant to or in furtherance of a State policy. Indeed, the method under which these crimes were committed prove the 'widespread or systematic nature' of the attacks. The evidence also shows that it was an organized military operation that could not have been successful without concerted efforts from various actors in the military and government circles."

Professor Mahmood Mamdani, a Member of the AU Commission who authored a separate opinion on the Inquiry report stated, "The targeted violence was organized, not spontaneous. It was directed from a center."

Massacres at presidential palace and police station

According to the African Union report, there were at least two large massacres perpetrated in Juba, including one at the so-called 'J2 palace' and another at the Gudele Joint Operation Centre, a police station.

"The Commission was informed about an incident that took place at J2 palace (which is adjacent to the Presidential palace) on 16th December 2013 where about 90 Nuers and 21 soldiers were gathered by soldiers and executed with only 13 soldiers escaping with their lives. It was alleged that the 90 Nuers were civilians who were running away from the fighting that had erupted all over Juba."

"The 21 soldiers, the Commission heard, were Nuers who were part of the President's first ring of protection and had earlier on been disarmed by a senior military officer. It was alleged that the person who ordered the killing of the civilians and the disarmed soldiers was Lt. Colonel Lual Maroldit who was attached to the VIP close protection unit otherwise known as Tiger Battalion or Presidential Guard," adds the report.

Forensic evidence and witness testimony further pointed to "the targeted killing of about 134 Nuer men in Gudele joint operation centre" on 16 December. This massacre has previously been reported by the United Nations and other rights investigators.

War crimes in Bor and Malakal

The AU Commission of Inquiry says that war crimes and atrocities were also committed by rebel forces later in the war: "The Commission believes that war crimes were committed in Bor town through indiscriminate killings of civilians by the SPLA/IO and White Army forces allied to Dr. Riek Machar."

Atrocities were also reported to have been committed by Machar's forces or allied forces also in Malakal and outside Malakal in Baliet County where the AU Commission reported "much carnage." For example, the Commission cited a witness who said that SPLA-IO killed 10 hospital patients in Malakal in January. Female civilians who were sheltering in the hospital at the same time were also abducted by the rebels and have not been seen again.

"Gang rape was (and continues to be) a common feature of the atrocities committed during the on-going conflict in South Sudan. Women and men as witnesses and survivors have given statements with reference to rapes of women and girls by more than one person... There were reports by respondents on the wide use of objects such as stones, guns and sticks to rape women. In most instances, that was reported as a new and horrifying phenomenon."

"There are clear patterns of a vicious cycle of violence within violence developing," reads the AU report.

The African Union report was produced after research by investigators in 2014 but its release was repeatedly delayed by the AU Commission and AU Peace and Security Council for almost a year.

David Lieth Dador – Oslo 2015

David Lieth Dador was the only survivor of the 16 December 2013 Gudelle Police station massacre, where 400 unarmed Nuer men civilians were unfortunately massacred in one large hall by the Dinka sponsored militia loyal to President Kiir Mayardit. David and several hundreds of corpses were later collected from the hall and taken by trucks and their bodies were dumped in the forests. Those who collected the bodies did not check the bodies of all the dead so as to ensure that each of them had died instantly. He pretended to have died as well. After the bodies were off loaded and left in the forests for birds and animals to feed on, he regained consciousness and instantly managed to escape even though he sustained some gun shot wounds. He was the only witness to the Nuer Juba massacre that was conducted at Gudelle Police Station by the Dinka sponsored militia. He went directly to the UNMISS camp inside Juba with the help of a Good Samaritan. From there he was later smuggled out secretly by some of his close friends to Uganda, where he was taken to Sweden by UNHCR as a refugee in 2014. His wounds are still visible in his hands and other parts of the body. David was a fourth year student at Juba University, where he had been studying at the College of Geology and Mining. He is currently living in Norrbotten, Pajal Kommune, Sweden. His ordeal was as painful indeed as a true witness who memorized all that had been done to Nuer men only at Gudelle Police Station on 16 December 2013. The author took his picture during his brief visit to Oslo on the Eve of Christmas on 24 December 2015.

Over one hundred thousand Nuer IDPs residing at UNMISS camp in Bentiu town in very deplorable conditions

**Images of some of the Nuer civilians massacred by
Salva Kiir's forces in Juba in December 2013**

During this time, some twenty thousand Nuer civilians—mostly women, the elderly, children, and unarmed men—were summarily massacred in cold blood. The Nuer massacres occurred in large numbers in Juba from December 16, 2013, to December 19, 2013.

Memorial service conducted by the Nuer community in the United States to remember the more than twenty thousand unarmed Nuer civilians massacred by Kiir and his cohorts in Juba in December 2013

During that time, thousands of mutilated bodies were either buried in secret mass graves by their killers or dumped in the River Nile in order to conceal any evidence in the future. On December 16, 2013, President Salva Kiir called a press conference, during which he dressed in military uniform and told the press that a coup had been attempted by his former vice president, Dr. Riek Machar. He declared that Dr. Riek Machar had attempted a military coup against his government but that his loyalists had already crushed the coup plotters and the remnants were being pursued. In truth, there was no coup that linked the former vice president with the mutinying Nuer soldiers at the Tiger headquarters because the fighting that occurred from December 15, 2013, to December 16, 2013, was exclusively triggered by the president himself when he ordered the head of his Presidential Guards, General Marial Ciennoung, to disarm Nuer elements within his personal guards at Tiger headquarters.

The president himself had ordered the state governors of Warrap and Northern Bahr El Ghazal (Mrs. Nyandeng Malek and General Paul Malong Awan, respectively), to conscript at least fifteen thousand young men to be brought to Juba as his personal protection guards. The recruitments were done as he ordered, and the newly recruited soldiers were transported to Juba by trucks and camped at Lure military barracks—a few kilometers outside Juba. President Salva Kiir used this military barracks as his resting place on the weekends. Several thousand of President Kiir's cattle were also camped there as well. These are the soldiers who intensively carried out the murder of Nuer civilians in Juba. They carried out house-to-house searches to collect unarmed Nuer civilians and took them elsewhere to be murdered in various locations or they killed them instantly in their own residential quarters. Most of the government officials, members of NLC, members of parliament, students, senior officers of the army and other security organs, children, women, and the elderly were executed in cold blood. Some senior Dinka politicians and officers among them; General Salva Mathoth Gengdit, General Marial Noor Jok, General Anton Bol Madut, Brigadier General Marial Cinouong, General Paul Malong Awan, General Garang Mabil, Awut Deng Achuil, Martin Majut Yak, General Gergori who is the brother in-law of President Salva Kiir, Justice Ambrose Riing Thiik – Chairman of Jieng/Dinka Council of Elders and several others were behind the massacre of thousands of unarmed Nuer civilians in Juba. This was also documented in a leaked African Union Report of Inquiry on South Sudan in detail, where some of the same personalities mentioned appeared. The official residence of President Kiir known as J2 was indeed used by some of his close associates as a slaughter house along with the Gudelle Police station in Juba. Cannibalism was also practiced, where they forced their victims to eat themselves first before they murdered them. Men were also forced to perform sex before they were killed. Sharp objects were used in the private parts of women and girls after they were routinely raped and later killed by using such gruesome techniquesto torture their victims to death. This is the worst inhuman practice ever done in the modern world. Even during the Rwanda massacres such stories never surfaced at all. The African Union Report of Inquiry acknowledged the massacre of Nuer civilians in Juba and other towns but it failed to accept the genocide which was the real issue. What is the difference between massacring 20,000 unarmed civilians and committing a genocide of the same number? Would such a passive attitude and lack of transparency from the African Union be tolerated in the future by some African nations and they continue with their membership in the union? What is the difference between President Salva Kiir and Adolf Hitler of Germany who committed genocide against six million Jews in Europe during the Second World War? These questions need to be critically answered by the readers of this book and questions posed to the African Union for their soft position in not condemning the government of South Sudan for committing genocide against its own citizens wilfully.

Different police stations and some military barracks were used as execution places for Nuer victims by the Dinka militias (*Dutkubeny*) affiliated with the presidential guards. No Nuer was spared such an ordeal, including the Honorable Speaker Manasseh Magok Rundial, who narrowly escaped death at the hands of those who attempted to murder him. It was by God's grace that his life was saved by a certain Dinka MP who recognized him, but two of his nephews residing with him in the same house were summarily executed. The Honorable Speaker eventually managed to find his way to the UNMISS compound, where he stayed there under their protection before the situation subsided.

Some of the victims were taken to National Security Centres and executed, and their bodies were burned beyond human recognition with petrol. They were buried in several mass graves outside Juba or dumped in the River Nile. Over seventy thousand Nuer civilians and government officials took shelter at two UNMISS compounds at Jebel Kujur and Tongpiny. Some ministers, chairpersons of specialized committees in the National Assembly, heads of commission, and senior SPLA officers were among the Nuer IDPs residing at the UNMISS compounds in Juba. In the greater Upper Nile states of Jonglei, Unity, and Upper Nile the Nuer White Army and SPLA deserters from the Nuer tribe attacked SPLA Dinka soldiers, especially those who hailed from Warrap, Lakes, and Northern Bahr El Ghazal, as retaliation for the massacre of their community members and close relatives in Juba. In September 2013 President Salva Kiir had toured the four states of Greater Bahr El Ghazal—Lakes, Western Bahr El Ghazal, Warrap, and Northern Bahr El Ghazal—during which he made hate speeches by inciting Dinka to beware of Dr. Riek Machar, whom he accused of planning a coup against his government. In

Akon, his hometown, in a speech in Dinka, broadcast by SSTV, President Salva had this to say: "Look, this power I have belongs to you. You fought and died for it…now some people want to snatch it from me…will you accept it?" The people responded, "Aci ba gam," meaning "we will not accept."

During these tours, President Salva Kiir ordered General Paul Malong Awan, governor of Northern Bahr El Ghazal, to recruit three thousand youth to be trained and equipped, who later constituted his presidential guards. Recruitment of three thousand young men from Warrap and Northern Bahr El Ghazal states sent a signal to the rest of the South Sudanese communities that power belonged to the Dinka. Normally Salva Kiir's guards were supposed to be selected from the regular SPLA soldiers, constituted from different ethnicities instead of recruiting them from one community; South Sudan has sixty-four tribes in total. The president's safety is the responsibility of every South Sudanese because he is the leader of the entire nation.

The fabricated coup was merely a ploy for his rejection of the appeal made by Dinka elders and church leaders. Instead he issued orders to arrest or kill Dr. Riek Machar and his associates in order to close the chapter of dissent against his leadership. After Dr. Riek Machar escaped this onslaught and crossed the River Nile for his own safety with his dear wife Angelina Teny and several of his followers, most of the SPLM ministers and senior government officials who associated with Dr. Riek Machar were collected by the notorious National Security Service (NSS), which took them to ghost houses where they detained and tortured them. They were kept under solitary confinement for two months before they were finally released on January 30, 2014, and flown to Kenya under the escort of President Uhuru Kenyatta of Kenya. All of them were tried in court but found not guilty of the alleged coup that the government in Juba accused them of when they labeled them as coup collaborators in support of Riek Machar.

The press statement made by Dr. Riek Machar on December 6, 2013, is attached as Appendix IV. He made this statement before the fighting in Juba took place and morphed into genocide and the SPLA forces in Greater Upper Nile defected.

The Defection of the SPLA Forces in Greater Upper Nile

Dr. Riek Machar Teny with his field commanders
at Pagak SPLA general headquarters

The mighty Nuer White Army on a rescue mission

On December 23, 2013, Major General Peter Gatdet Yak, SPLA Division 8 commander, was the first SPLA senior officer to join the mutinying soldiers from Juba as a result of the massacre of several thousand unarmed Nuer civilians in Juba. He was based in Bor town, the capital of Jonglei state, when the genocide took place in Juba. General Peter Gatdet captured the SPLA division headquarters at Panpandiar and uprooted the government loyalists who attempted to quell down his rebellion. He eventually took over the entire state with the full support of the Nuer White Army, which came to his rescue, and that of the former vice president, Dr. Riek Machar, who sought sanctuary in the area controlled by General Gatdet. A former military paratrooper trained in the Sudan Military Academy in the mid 1970s, General Peter Gatdet fought in the Iran-Iraq war on behalf of the Iraqi army when former Sudanese President Jaafar Mohammed Nimeiri publicly supported former Iraqi dictator Saddam Hussein and sent thousands of his troops to Iraq in 1981.

General Peter Gatdet is a well-trained and brave general who fought several battles against successive regimes in Khartoum when he joined the rebellion movement in the South. He later came back to Sudan and joined the SPLM/SPLA movement in 1985, where he rose to the rank of alternate commander. After the December 2013 genocide in Juba, General Peter Gatdet and his forces would have captured Juba had it not been for the massive intervention of the Uganda People's Defence Force (UPDF), which fought on the side of the government of South Sudan.

The government had invited the UPDF two days after the Juba massacre took place. General Peter Gatdet and his troops were stopped from advancing onto Juba in Mangalla, Central Equatoria state, by UPDF and SPLM loyalist soldiers who overpowered them with helicopter gunships and military jets. Banned weapons of mass destruction, including cluster bombs, were used during the fighting in Jamaza, Mangalla, Sudan Safari, Kubri Makuach, Panpandiar, Malual Achot, Bor, and Mathiang areas. These areas were occupied by deserting SPLA soldiers and the White Army, mostly from the Lou and Gawaar clans of central Nuerland. They inflicted heavy casualties on both government and UPDF soldiers. It is estimated that between two and three thousand UPDF soldiers were killed during all the battles for control of the Juba-Bor road. Bor town exchanged hands more than twice, during which times the entire population of more than three hundred thousand fled either to the neighboring state of Lakes or proceeded to Juba, northern Kenya, and northern Uganda, where they sought refugee status. The town of Bor exchanged hands more than two times between the government and the SPLM/A–In Opposition (SPLM/A-IO) forces. Subsequently, the same fighting escalated to Bentiu, capital of Unity state, under command of General James Koang Chuol Ranley and his deputy, Brigadier General Makal Kuol. They managed to dislodge the SPLA government loyalists under overall Lt. General Jok Riak and Deputy Major General Santino Deng Wol on December 18, 2013, and eventually took over all the nine counties of Unity state. General James Koang is a veteran and well-trained officer who fought many battles during the Sudan civil war that ended after twenty-one years with the signing of the CPA in 2005. His forces were later dislodged from Bentiu and some counties, such as Mayom, Abiemnom, and Panriang, by government loyalists aided by thousands of mercenaries from UPDF, JEM, SPLA-N, SLA, and Bul Nuer militias under specific commands of General Bapiny Monytuil and his deputy Matthew Pul Jang. Bentiu and other counties' headquarters have been changing hands several times from the SPLM/A-IO on one hand and the government with its mercenary allies on the other since the outbreak of this war in December 2013. Several thousand unarmed civilians, mostly Nuer, got killed deliberately or in cross fire by the warring parties. Government institutions such as hospitals, schools, water facilities, churches, and mosques were not spared. The MSF hospital in Leer, which had been in operation for twenty-five years serving a population of more than one hundred thousand and the only Kalazaar referral center in the entire region, was unfortunately destroyed by the government forces and allied mercenaries in February 2014. They looted all the medicine and equipment from the Leer hospital and killed some of the staff, including Dr. Nhial Monykuany Bup—a physician trained and graduated from Helsinki University, Finland. Several hundred, mostly women, children, and elderly, were killed instantly by using the most gruesome techniques, such as throwing victims into burning houses alive. Also, castrating young Nuer boys was part of an extermination policy adopted by the Dinka-led government in Juba and its allied mercenaries. More than five hundred thousand civilians have so far abandoned their homesteads in the counties of Leer, Guit, Koch, Mayandit, Panyjier, Rubkona, and Mayom due to consistent insecurity. Several hundred thousands of their domestic livestock have been looted, completely leaving all the civilians hiding in forests and swamp areas virtually destitute and starving to death. The same government in Juba has also been uncooperative with some international NGOs and UN agencies that want to ferry relief assistance to the affected Nuer IDPs still hiding in the forests and swamp areas. Several hundreds of young girls and women have been abducted by their attackers and taken to Warrap and Northern Bahr El Gazel states with the help of their Bul Nuer sponsored militias under commands of Generals Bapiny Monytuil and Matthew Pul Jang.

In Upper Nile, the fighting started after the murder of some senior government officials from the state who attempted to escape to Nasir following the brutal massacre of thousands of their fellow Nuer in Juba in December 2013. These included a group of State Assembly members, senior state officials, and senior political officials. The fighting between the government loyalists and the White Army aided by some SPLA deserters started in Nasir and Ulang simultaneously on December 20, and it continued when the two towns briefly fell to the opposition forces. The fighting continued thereafter to Gelachel and eventually to Malakal on December 24. The fighting in the Upper Nile front has been under the over all command of General Gathoth Gatkuoth Hothnyang. The town of Malakal and other county headquarters—Panyikang, Baliet, Wedakona, and Akoka—have changed hands several times, driving out thousands of civilians from the Dinka and Shilluk tribes from their settlements and killing hundreds of others. In May 2014 the government forces launched coordinated attacks from Bor and Malakal, and they subsequently captured the towns of Ayod in Jonglei and Nasir in Upper Nile. At the same time the government forces briefly occupied Ulang town and Longichuk county's headquarters but were later dislodged by the forces of the opposition. The government forces are still in control of Nasir and Ayod towns, which have been deserted by the civil population since the government captured the towns nearly one and half years ago. Following the defection of General Johnson Olony to the forces of SPLM/A-IO headed by Dr. Riek Machar, government forces in Malakal and Wedakona, which they later recaptured, have become vulnerable. Therefore, the opposition forces have so far gained more ground militarily. Thus, the government has to choose between continuing with war that will not be favorable to them or accept a lasting peace in order to end the war in the country. The peace talks have been going on since January 2014, with the signing of the Cessasion of Hositilities (COHs) Agreement between the government of South Sudan headed by President Salva Kiir Mayardit and the SPLM/SPLA – IO Chairmanship of Dr. Riek Machar. The South Sudan peace talks have been under the mediation of

IGAD and its Troika partners for two years now. As of late, several countries have joined the IGAD mediation under the banner of IGAD Plus in which the two parties involved in the conflict have so far concluded a peace agreement known as IGAD Compromise Peace Agreement for Resolving the South Sudan Conflict, which was signed in Addis Ababa on the 17 August 2015, by SPLM/SPLA-IO Chairman and the SPLM Secretary General Pagan Amum who represented the SPLM Former Detainees. It was later signed separately by President Salva Kiir in Juba with IGAD Plus mediators on 26 August, 2015. But the implementation of this agreement remained to be seen because the government in Juba is not ready to implement it in spirit and letter. This is occurring while IGAD is still pressurizing both parties to implement it.

South Sudan's new peace deal in brief

The peace deal was signed by President Salva Kiir on Wednesday the 26 August 2015, in Juba and earlier by Dr. Riek Machar – leader of the SPLM/SPLA – IO with Pagan Amum – Leader of the SPLM Former Political Detainees on 17 August 2015 in Addis Ababa respectively. That agreement mandates the creation of a new power-sharing government in South Sudan and sets up transitional justice mechanisms, security measures, and reconciliation initiatives.

Here are a few highlights:

Transitional government

- Transitional Government of National Unity shall form within 90 days of signing. The period until then is called the "pre-transitional period."
- The new transitional government will be in office for 30 months (2.5 years).
- There will be elections 60 days (2 months) before the term ends.

CEASEFIRE AND SECURITY MEASURES

- Permanent ceasefire within 72 hours of signing, all allied militias will have to be disengaged.
- Withdrawal of all non South Sudanese forces from South Sudan within 45 days. -This refers primarily to the Ugandan army (UPDF).
- Immediate release of all Prisoners of War.
- All forces in the conflict areas will be assembled and cantoned within 30 days of the signing to enable screening, registration and/or disarmament. They will receive food, shelter and medical care.
- There will be a Joint Military Ceasefire Commission to oversee the cantonment.
- The warring armies will come under a 'Unified Command' within 18 months.
- A Strategic Defence and Security Review will be set up that includes participation of the warring parties, the political parties, and also churches, women's organizations, youth groups and academics. It will suggest within 150 days a plan for transformation of the security sector.

POWER-SHARING

- The majority of positions in the Council of Ministers of the new national government will remain in the hands of the current Kiir-led administration (53%). The armed opposition (SPLM/A-IO) will take 33%, 7% will be for other parties, and 7% for the SPLM "Former Detainees".
- Out of 30 ministers, 16 will be current supporters of Kiir, 10 will be from the Machar faction, 2 from the Former Detainees and 2 from other parties.
- The power sharing in the states of Jonglei, Unity and Upper Nile will be: 46% SPLM-Kiir, 40% SPLM-IO, 7% Former Detainees, 7% other political parties.

- The power-sharing in the executive branch of the other 7 states will be 85% for SPLM-Kiir and 15% for SPLA-IO.
- 7 ministers will be women.
- The parliament (National Legislative Assembly) will be expanded from 322 to 400 members. The incumbent members will remain in office. The added 68 members will be appointed by SPLM in Opposition (50), Former Detainees (1) and other political parties (17).
- All members unseated from the parliament following the crisis in December 2013 will be reinstated.
- The speaker will hail from Equatoria.

PRESIDENCY

- There will be a president, a first vice-president and a vice-president.
- The incumbent president (Kiir) will remain the president and he remains the Commander in Chief of the South Sudan National Defence Forces,
- The first vice president will be selected by SPLM in Opposition (led by Riek Machar), he will serve as the Commander in Chief of the Opposition forces in the first 90 days after signing until the armies of Kiir and Machar will be united. After that he will be acting commander in chief of the national defence forces only in the absence of the president.
- The president and the first vice-president have to agree on appointing state governors, military appointments and dismissals and appointments of the heads of independent commissions, for example, the Anti-Corruption Commission.
- The governors of Unity and Upper Nile will be appointed by the SPLA-IO and the governor of Jonglei will be appointed by Kiir.
- The Media Authority, an independent board for the media, as provided by law is not mentioned in the list of 18 independent government institutions to be established. Only the South Sudan Broadcasting Corporation is listed.

- The incumbent vice-president (James Wani Igga) will remain vice-president. He will mainly be involved in overseeing government national commissions
- and parastatals.
- In case of deadlock between the president and the vice-president a majority of 67% of the Council of Ministers is required to make a decision.
- The role of the SPLM remains unclear; the document hints at a 'unified ruling party', but the power-sharing ratios effectively treat the factions as distinct entities.

RECONSTRUCTION AND RECONCILIATION

- A joint monitoring and evaluation commission will be established within 15 days based in Juba with 6 members from the parties, 7 civil society members, 12 members from the neighbouring states, AU and IGAD and 7 international members including China, UK, US, Norway, UN and EU. The chairman will be appointed by IGAD.
- An international Special Reconstruction Fund (SRF) will be established with a start of yearly 100 million dollars deposited by the government.
- There will be a Compensation and Reparation Authority (CRA) for compensating victims.
- There will be a Commission for Truth, Reconciliation and Healing (CTRH). It will be mandated to establish an accurate historical record of human rights violations and receive applications from victims. It also should identify the perpetrators.
- The commission members will be appointed by the transitional government led by Salva Kiir, though with input from other bodies.

Justice

- A new Hybrid Court for South Sudan (HCSS) will be mandated to prosecute crimes including genocide, crimes against humanity, war crimes and other serious crimes like sexual violence.
- The court shall be established by the African Union. Most judges, prosecutors and defence counsels will come from African states other than South Sudan.
- No one shall be exempted from criminal responsibility on account of their official capacity as a government official, an elected official or claiming the defence of superior orders.

Conclusion

THE MAIN OBJECTIVE FOR THIS work is to evaluate and resolve the causes that interrupted the progress of the southern Sudanese national struggle from its inception. It is an attempt to expose the challenges that the Sudanese political leadership failed to deal with and which must be dealt with to realize the objectives of the historical struggle. The role of individual political actors in the struggle is traced, with speculation on the prospects for the settlement of the conflict. In other words, an attempt is made to answer questions such as-What are the obstacles? Who was responsible for creating those obstacles? And what might be the ultimate solution to resolve them? It is to be emphasized that the overriding obstacle often cited is that the SPLM/SPLA never followed well-defined political objectives.

Those who have been running it have been charged with putting their own personal interests above the interests of those they claimed to liberate. Most observers lamented that, since the inception of the SPLM/SPLA in 1983, its first victims were southerners who differed with the SPLM/SPLA leader Colonel John Garang on how to prosecute the war in the interest of the oppressed people of southern Sudan. Colonel John Garang persecuted Samuel Gai Tut, Benjamin Bol Akok, Joseph Oduho, Martin Majier Gai, Lokurnyang Lado, William Chuol Deng, and several other prominent southern Sudanese politicians. The SPLM/SPLA leadership executed all those personalities without adequate justifications to convince the southern people. President Nimeiri jailed such persons only for advocating separation of south Sudan from the north. The SPLM/SPLA leadership acts, however, have created mistrust and disunity among the southerners. The SPLM/SPLA, in fact, had contradictions in all its external relations.

To the Arab world, its leaders gave the impression that their movement's objective was to preserve the unity of Sudan under a secular system, a unity based on equality and justice for all Sudanese regardless of their color of skin or religious beliefs. For the black African states, they informed them that the SPLM/SPLA was fighting against Arab expansion toward the south of the Sahara. It therefore served as a useful human shield worth supporting against Arab/Islamic expansion. To the Western countries, the SPLM/SPLA was fighting against forced Islamization and Arabization of black African Christians in the southern part of the country. The SPLM/SPLA was engaged in seemingly endless "principle-shopping" business.

The SPLM/A leadership actions frustrated efforts toward south-south reunification so that some southerners chose to work with the NIF regime in Khartoum rather than continuing the struggle together with their own people. The civil war in Sudan that has been going on since the Akobo uprising in March 1975 gave birth to the formation of the Anya Nya II movement. Following the inception of the SPLM/SPLA in July 1983, the war intensified to being full-scale warfare. The warring parties in the Sudanese conflict were still unwilling to resolve their outstanding differences peacefully.

To make the already delicate situation more complicated, the National Islamic Front (NIF) regime in Khartoum had no desire to resolve the south-north conflict through peaceful and harmonious means. The regime believed in a military option rather than a political solution. As Dr. Abdalla Turabi—the real wheel behind the NIF regime in Khartoum before he fell off—put it clearly in one of his statements in the Sudanese media, "the NIF regime had only two friends: oil and Allah." Hence, the NIF's interest in the south was the land and its resources and not its population. The north continued to implement a policy of forced Islamization and Arabization after 1990 and succeeded in this process by exploiting the state of disunity and confusion among southerners.

The NIF government also embarked on the displacement of southern Sudanese ethnic groups located in the oil fields along the south-north boundaries in northern and western Upper Nile region. The plan was to settle the Bagara and Rizeigat Arab tribal groups along the areas of Renk and Bentiu. Lack of unity among the southern Sudanese people, which was caused by internal splits and rivalry, became more complicated than the north-south conflict itself because tribalism engulfed it all. South-south internal reconciliation requires that all efforts and resources be exerted to realize peace in South Sudan. The chronological narrative of the South Sudan struggle has been laid out in this volume, *The Rise and Fall of SPLM/SPLA Leadership*, to pave the way for more volumes that will deal with the issues dividing South Sudanese. The objective is to attain sustainable peace in South Sudan and the actual liberation intended by the first mutineers of Torit, who incited the first Sudanese civil war on August 18, 1955. This war led to the formation of the Anya Nya liberation movement and paved the way for the SPLM/SPLA.

Hon. Samuel Gai Tut—Leader of Anya Nya II

THIS BOOK IS EXPLICITLY DEDICATED to Honorable Samuel Gai Tut, the leader of the South Sudan liberation movement Anya Nya II. The late Honorable Samuel Gai Tut was born in the 1940s, at Kurmayom village, Waat Payam, Nyirol County, in south Sudan. At school age, he began primary school at Wanglel and later attended Atar Intermediate School in Jonglei. In 1961 the late Samuel Gai entered Rumbek Secondary School, where he completed first and second year. In 1963, before beginning his third year at Rumbek Secondary School, Samuel Gai quit school and joined the South Sudan

Liberation Movement (SSLM), better known as Anya Nya. While in the Anya Nya movement, he rose to the rank of commander and conducted most of his operations like other Anya Nya field commanders in the Upper Nile province of present-day South Sudan.

The late Samuel Gai was an accomplished, brave, true, and nationalistic leader who fought successive Arab occupying forces in southern Sudan during the 1960s and the early 1970s. During the Addis Ababa negotiations and subsequent agreement in 1972, he objected to the agreement, labeling it as a sellout. The late Samuel Gai accused his boss, Major General Joseph Lagu, of compromising the overall interest of south Sudanese people in return for his own material gains from Arab rulers in the north. Like some of his colleagues who rejected the Addis Ababa Agreement from the initial stage, the late Samuel Gai was eventually convinced by his other colleagues to accept the accord, which he did with hesitation. Being a skillful guerrilla fighter, he knew very well that the host country Ethiopia from where his forces operated was already in favor of the agreement. Consequently, if he decided to continue with the struggle singlehandedly without any external support, his forces would have had difficulty in maintaining their logistics. So he and his forces succumbed to the agreement but his position was already known by President Jaafar Nimeiri and General Joseph Lagu, who headed the Anya Nya forces in the south.

This was why the late Samuel Gai was demoted to the rank of Lieutenant Colonel and put under strict supervision by the Sudan security force, lest he instigate an uprising in southern Sudan. Lieutenant Colonel Samuel Gai was retired early from the Sudan Armed Forces in 1974. This occurred two years after the conclusion of the Addis Ababa Agreement because he objected to the amalgamation of the ex-Anya Nya fighters with the north Sudanese Arab soldiers, which led to open quarrels with his boss, Major General Joseph Lagu, the commanding officer of the Sudan Armed Forces stationed in the southern Sudan region of Juba. As the head of the Sudan Armed Forces in the south, Major General Lagu recommended the early retirements of Lieutenant Colonel Samuel Gai along with his closest friend, Captain William Abdalla Chuol Deng, and immediately integrated them into civil service. Retired

Lieutenant Colonel Gai Tut then became an executive director in local government. In 1975, following the Akobo Mutiny by ex-Anya Nya forces under First Lieutenant Vincent Kuany Latjor (which resulted in the death of Lieutenant Colonel Abel Kol Ater, who was commanding the garrison), Samuel Gai was briefly detained by the Sudan Intelligence Service because they accused him of being part of the mutiny.

After his release in 1978, Lieutenant Colonel Samuel Gai joined politics and contested a seat in the elections in the southern region. During that time, he captured his Waat constituency seat and was elected to the People's Regional Assembly. From there he was appointed minister of wildlife conservation and tourism in the government headed by Retired Major General Joseph Lagu. Samuel Gai held this position and portfolio during the governments of major generals Joseph Lagu and Gismala Abdalla Rasas in 1978 and 1981, respectively. He was twice unopposed and elected to the southern Sudan Regional Assembly in 1978 and 1982.

In May 1983 Samuel Gai left his residence in Malakal and went to his village at Turok, Kurmayom, on his way to Ethiopia to join the southern Sudan rebellion movement. There he met the late Colonel John Garang de Mabior at the Anya Nya II center at Marol, from which they were later flown to Addis Ababa using a helicopter provided by the Ethiopian government. In July 1983 the prominent south Sudanese figures met at Itang Refugee Camp and formed the Sudan People's Liberation Movement/Army (SPLM/SPLA) under the overall chairmanship of veteran politician Akuot Atem de Mayen.

This move was immediately objected to, however, by some south Sudanese army officers and politicians who advocated for the late Colonel Dr. John Garang to become the chairman instead of Akuot Atem. This is how differences originated among the south Sudanese leaders and led to a split between the two factions of SPLM/SPLA led by Colonel John Garang on one hand and Anya Nya II headed by Akuot Atem and Samuel Gai Tut respectively. The late Samuel Gai Tut was unfortunately killed in action by SPLA forces stationed at Adura/Thiajak on March 28, 1984, at 10.00 a.m. Sudan local time. Unfortunately, Gai Tut met his untimely death at the hands of his fellow southerners in spite of the fact that he had dedicated his life for their cause. He had sustained more than seven gunshot wounds during the Anya Nya war in the 1960s, including losing a finger on his right hand, which was injured by an enemy's bullet. His death and the deaths of countless other national heroes whose fates are not remembered by our present leaders are very sad indeed.

Therefore, I am advocating for the name of the late Colonel Samuel Gai Tut to be put on the list of our national heroes and heroines whenever we commemorate them. I want to remind the readers of this book that the reason I took this opportunity to write the biography of the late Samuel Gai Tut is that I was physically there when the fight at Adura/Thiajak occurred. I was deeply saddened by the number of people who were killed that day. More than two hundred people were, sadly, killed by their own people instead of by the very enemy we all took up arms against. Southerners must learn to tolerate their differences and forgive themselves as one people with a common destiny. We have already achieved our ultimate goal—the independence of the Republic of South Sudan, which our forefathers, fathers, and the present generation fought for. Now it is time to remember our national heroes and heroines and embark on developmental activities that will unite us all instead of looking at ourselves as enemies.

Appreciations are due to all other south Sudanese fallen heroes and heroines who purposely sacrificed their precious lives for the cause of their oppressed people throughout the national struggles. The reason Samuel Gai is so important in this book is his willingness to stand for the liberation of South Sudan like others before him. Unfortunately, he lost his life at the hands of the wrong enemy—the SPLM/SPLA movement of Dr. John Garang de Mabior, who maliciously resisted the call for the liberation of an independent South Sudan state in favor of a united, secular, new Sudan, which he later abandoned. The dreams of Samuel Gai and his colleagues who perished along with him, including Joseph Oduho, Benjamin Bol Akok, Akuot Atem de Mayen, William Chuol Deng, Martin Majier Gai, Lokurnyang Ladu, and numerous others, were later realized through a call for an internationally supervised referendum in South Sudan. This was advocated for by the Nasir Faction of the SPLM/SPLA led by Dr. Riek Machar Teny, Dr. Lam Akol Ajawin and Gordon Koang Chol on August 28, 1991, following the split within the SPLM/SPLA movement and with the subsequent signing of the CPA in 2005 between the SPLM/SPLA and the Sudan government, which recognized the rights of the people of South Sudan.

The independence of South Sudan, which was attained on July 9, 2011, came as a result of long and bitter struggles that cost the lives of nearly three million people from Anya Nya I, Anya Nya II, and SPLM/SPLA liberation wars against successive Arab regimes in Khartoum. I personally took the death of Samuel Gai and others as a challenge to the south-south internal unity. I was there when Samuel Gai was killed in Adura—a small town situated along the Ethiopia/Sudan border on March 28, 1984, at the hands of SPLA forces who were specifically instructed to kill him. Samuel Gai was a tough Anya Nya freedom fighter, trained by Israeli agents during the first civil war that ended in 1972 with the signing of the Addis Ababa Accord, during which he was given the rank of lieutenant colonel.

In 1974 Samuel Gai was unceremoniously dismissed from the Sudan Armed Force by President Jaafar Mohammed Nimeiri and later detained following the Akobo uprising of 1975. After his release from detention, Samuel Gai was appointed executive director in the local government by the High Executive Council of Southern Sudan under the leadership of Abel Alier—a body that was formed in 1972 following the Addis Ababa Accord. By 1978 Samuel Gai was elected unopposed to the People's Regional Assembly as a Member of Parliament by his constituency stronghold of Waat rural area. Thereafter, he was appointed by Joseph Lagu to minister of wildlife, conservation and tourism. In 1983 Samuel Gai apparently defected from the government of Sudan and joined the Anya Nya II movement. Together with several thousand south Sudanese, he eventually formed the SPLM/SPLA under Akuot Atem de Mayen's chairmanship.

As mentioned before, Colonel Dr. John Garang and his group vehemently rejected the nomination of Akuot Atem as the chairman of the newly formed movement, and he nominated himself instead. Samuel Gai was a true liberator, a father, a unifier, and nationalist south Sudanese leader who will always be remembered by generations in South Sudan's history for his immense contributions and for being an advocate of South Sudan's independence. His death was kept strictly secret for nearly two years by his ardent supporters, and it widely divided the people of southern Sudan along Dinka and Nuer ethnic lines for decades.

Appendix I: Participants in Addis Ababa Peace Talks of 1972

For the Government of the Democratic Republic of the Sudan:

1. Abel Alier Wal-Kuai
   Vice President and Minister of State for Southern Affairs
2. Dr. Mansour Khalid
   Minister for Foreign Affairs
3. Dr. Jaafar Mohammed Ali Bakhiet
   Minister for Local Government
4. Major General PSC Mohammed El Baghir Ahmed
   Minister of Interior
5. Abdel Rahman Abdalla
   Minister for Public Service and Administrative Reform
6. Brigadier PSC Mirghani Suleiman
7. Colonel Kamal Abusher

For the South Sudan Liberation Movement:

1. Ezboni Mondiri Gwonza
   Leader of the Delegation
2. Dr. Lawrence Wol Wol
   Secretary of the Delegation
3. E. Mading de Garang
   Spokesman of the Delegation

4. Colonel Frederick Brian Maggot
   Special Military Representative
5. Oliver Batali Albino
   Member
6. Anjelo Voga Morjan
   Member
7. Rev. Paul Puot
   Member
8. Job Adier de Jok
   Member

Witnesses:

1. Nyabiyelul Kifle
   Representative of His Imperial Majesty, the Emperor of Ethiopia
2. Leopoldo J. Niilus
   Representative of the World Council of Churches
3. Kodwo E. Ankrah
   Representative of the World Council of Churches
4. Rev. Canon Burges Carr
   General Secretary, All Africa Conference of Churches
5. Samuel Athi Bwogo
   Representative of Sudan Council of Churches
   Attestation:
   I attest that these signatures are genuine and true:
   Rev. Canon Burges Carr, moderator.

These were the list of witnesses who witnessed the signing of the Addis Ababa Accord which was concluded in the Ethiopia capital Addis Ababa on 27 February 1972, under auspecies of His Majesty Emperor Haile Salesse of Ethiopia.

Appendix II: List of SPLM/SPLA Political Detainees and Those Executed

THE LIST OF SPLM/SPLA POLITICAL detainees and those executed according to the Nasir Declaration follows.

1. Joseph Oduho—killed at Kongor by SPLA in 1993.
2. Martin Majier Gai—executed by SPLA in 1993 while in detention.
3. Commander Kerubino Kuanyin Bol—escaped to Uganda in 1992.
4. Commander Arok Thon Arok—escaped to Uganda in 1992.
5. Commander John Kulang Puot—escaped to Uganda in 1992.
6. Dr. Amon Mon Wantok—escaped to Kenya in 1992.
7. A/Commander Alfred Lado Gore—escaped to Kenya in 1992.
8. A/Commander Kuac Makuei—escaped to Kenya in 1993.
9. A/Commander Victor Bol Ayolnhom—died while in detention.
10. A/Commander Martin Makur Aleyou—executed by SPLA in 1993.
11. A/Commander Chol Deng Alaak—escaped to Kenya in 1992.
12. A/Commander Philip Chol Biowei—released by SPLA in 1992.
13. A/Commander Wilson Kur Chol—released by SPLA in 1992.
14. A/Commander Maker Deng Malou—released by SPLA in 1992.
15. A/Commander Faustino Atem Gualdit—escaped to Uganda in 1992.
16. Captain George Maker Benjamin Bil—escaped to Kenya in 1992.
17. Captain Malath Joseph Lueth—executed by SPLA in 1992.

18. Captain Tut Lony Baboth—executed by SPLA in 1992.
19. Dr. Oguo Luigi Adwok—executed by SPLA in 1991.
20. Dr. Carlo Madut—executed by SPLA in 1994.

Appendix III: List of SSDF Commanders That Remained With SAF and Later Rejoined the SPLA

HERE IS THE LIST OF SSDF commanders that remained with SAF and later rejoined the SPLA following the signing of Juba declaration on January 8, 2006, between GOSS President Salva Kiir Mayardit and SSDF leader General Paulino Matip Nhial.

Major General Paulino Matip Nhial (chief of staff, SSDF)
Major General Gordon Koang Chol (deputy chief of staff, SSDF)
Major General Vincent Kuany Latjor
Major General Clement Wani Konga
Major General Gabriel Gatwech Chan (Tang Ginye)
Major General Simon Gatwech Dual
Major General Tom Al Nur
Major General Ismael Konyi
Major General Kawach Makuei
Major General Magar Aciek
Major General Abdul Bagi Ayiiy
Major General Duit Yiech
Major General James Mabor Dhol
Major General John Both Teny
Major General Timoth Taban Juoc
Major General Gathoth Gatkuoth
Major General Peter Gadet Yakah

Major General Saddam Chayuot Nyang
Major General Tahip Garluak
Major General Papiny Montuiel Ojang
Major General Bipan Machar
Major General Leah Dieu
Major General Yohannes Yoal Bath
Wutnyang Gatkek
Professor David de Chand
Brigadier Biel Torkech Rambang
Brigadier Gawar Manyoak
Brigadier Chuol Gakah Yier
Brigadier Duoth Lam Juuk
Brigadier William Reath Gai
Brigadier Dor Manjuor
Brigadier John Gile Yual
Brigadier Henry Lam Juoc
Brigadier Kueth Simon etc.

Appendix IV: Press Statement Made by Dr. Riek Machar on December 6, 2013

PRESS STATEMENT
Revolutionary comrades, members of the SPLM—
Our esteemed people of South Sudan—
Distinguished Members of the Press—

We, the members of the SPLM Political Bureau, National Liberation Council, and SPLM leaders have called this press conference to enlighten our people on the internal crisis that has engulfed the SPLM leadership and paralyzed its functions in the government and in our society. The crisis started immediately after the tragic death of the SPLM historical and eternal leader Dr. John Garang de Mabior and manifested itself in the following:

- *The anti-Garang elements inside and outside the SPLM encircled comrade Salva Kiir Mayardit's leadership of the SPLM and the government of Southern Sudan [2005–2007]. This phenomenon compromised SPLM positions vis-à-vis the NCP in the CPA implementation, and in many incidences General Salva Kiir retreated from positions negotiated earlier by Dr. John Garang. These elements, using their relationship with General Salva Kiir, targeted and ostracized certain SPLM leaders and cadres they nicknamed "Garang orphans/boys," creating schisms and precipitating open quarrels within the SPLM ranks;*

- *The shift in decision-making process from SPLM national organs to regional and ethnic lobbies around the SPLM chairman when it came to appointments to positions in government; that membership of the SPLM and one's participation in the revolutionary struggle became irrelevant. The SPLM is NOT a ruling party. In practice, decisions are essentially made by one person, and in most cases directed by regional and ethnic lobbies and close business associates surrounding the SPLM chairman;*
- *The efforts to transform the SPLM from a liberation movement into a mass based political party have totally been frustrated by the chairman. General Salva ignored the grassroots views and demands garnered between July and August 2012 for the SPLM reorganization. The Political Bureau, the only organ that met nonetheless it had been difficult to translate its resolutions into plans of action in the Executive or legislations in the National Assembly, because of lack of collective leadership and the paralysis of the General Secretariat;*
- *There is no formal communication between the party organs at the national level and those in the States, County, Payam, and Boma levels. The government drives the SPLM rather than the other way round. The SPLM chairman now uses his executive powers as president of the republic, relying on his presidential ADVISORS, to manage the SPLM and the country.*

The crisis reached boiling point in March 2013 when General Salva Kiir canceled the meeting of the National Liberation Council; issued a presidential decree withdrawing the delegated powers from his vice president and first deputy chairman. Other decrees followed, including the dismissal on false grounds of the Governors of Lakes and Unity states; the dismissal and appointment of a new cabinet and the suspension of the SPLM Secretary General. We want to assure our people that these were personal decisions by General Salva Kiir since neither the PB nor the National Liberation Council (NLC) deliberated on these decisions, which have far-reaching implications for the SPLM and the country. The SPLM chairman has completely immobilized the party, abandoned collective leadership, and jettisoned all democratic pretensions to decision making. The SPLM is no longer the ruling party. The leader of South Sudan Democratic Forum heads the SPLM Government Cabinet, and recent infiltrators/converts from the NCP now lead the National Legislative Assembly and the Council of States respectively. The chairman did not care to appoint second or third tier SPLM leaders and cadres to occupy these positions if he had trouble with the first tier leaders. In the army, General Salva Kiir Mayardit has demobilized the seasoned SPLA commanders and made them redundant. This action amounts to erasing the historical legacy of the SPLM, suggesting that comrade Salva Kiir is on track to form his personal army, in the guise of Presidential Guards. General Salva Kiir intends to form his own political party linked to the NCP and has nothing to do with the historic struggle of our people. As a result, the chairman unconstitutionally dissolved key SPLM organs, namely the Political Bureau and the National Liberation Council and the National and States Secretariat on account that their mandates had expired in May 2013. He has already instructed the state governors (instead of the State SPLM Secretariats) to appoint their preferred delegates to the SPLM 3rd National Convention scheduled for February 2014. The intention is to sideline and prevent SPLM historical leaders and cadres categorized as "potential competitors" from participation in the Convention. This is very dangerous move and is likely to plunge the party and the country into the abyss.

We want to bring to the attention of the masses of our people that General Salva Kiir has surrendered the SPLM power to opportunists and foreign agents. These actions undermine the hard-won independence and sovereignty of the Republic of South Sudan.

The government of South Sudan is misleading the public that it is servicing the 4.5 billion USD debt. It is not known where these monies were loaned from and on what they were spent, as the country has been *under austerity regime since April 2012. This is definitely a question of corruption that must be addressed together with the dura saga, the shoddy road contracts, and the issue of seventy-five letters of defamation of SPLM historical leaders and cadres.*

The deep-seated divisions within the SPLM leadership, exacerbated by dictatorial tendencies of the SPLM chairman, and the dysfunctional SPLM structures from national to local levels are likely to create instability in the party and in the country. For these reasons, and out of our sincere concern about future of our people, we the SPLM members of the Political Bureau and the Leadership of the party are obliged to inform the public about the true state of affairs in the SPLM and how General Salva Kiir is driving our beloved Republic of South Sudan into chaos and disorder.

In order to resolve this crisis, we call on the SPLM chairman to convene the Political Bureau to set the agenda for the National Liberation Council so as to correct the deviation from the SPLM vision and direction. And address the present challenges within the SPLM with the view of revitalizing and restoring the SPLM to the driving seat. The SPLM should hold the steering wheel of the two historical processes of nation building and state building.
Long live the struggle of our people
Glory and honor to our martyrs
Long live South Sudan
Long live SPLM—Viva SPLM viva
Juba, December 6, 2013

Glossary

ALIER WAL-KUAI, ABEL—FORMER VICE PRESIDENT to Jaafar Mohammed Nimeiri from 1971 to 1983 and president of the High Executive Council (HEC) in the Southern Region, Juba. He held the position of president of HEC twice from 1972 to 1978 and again from 1980 to 1981. He is a well-known lawyer and a prominent politician.

Atem de Mayan, Akuot—former member of the regional parliament and regional minister of public service and manpower from 1978 to 1979 and a veteran of the Anya Nya movement from 1963. He joined the Anya Nya II movement in 1983 and was elected chairman of the joint Anya Nya II and SPLM/SPLA in July 1983. Following a disagreement among the south Sudanese rebels over the issue of leadership, Atem and Anya Nya II rebels left Ethiopia and returned to Sudan, where he continued to head the movement until his death in 1985.

Abboud, General Ibrahim—former army general who seized power from an elected civilian prime minister, Abdalla Bey Khalil, on November 17, 1958, only three years after Sudan got its independence from Great Britain. He was known for his forced Islamization and Arabization of the black African people of south Sudan. Abboud's government was overthrown by a popular uprising on October 24, 1964.

Anya Nya I—a secessionist movement formed in the early 1960s by south Sudanese military and civilian intellectuals with an ultimate goal of achieving an independent South Sudan separate from the north Sudanese–Arabized new colonialists. Anya Nya I fought guerrilla warfare until 1972, when an agreement was signed in Addis Ababa, Ethiopia, on February 27, 1972, which concluded the seventeen-year civil war in the Sudan.

Anya Nya II—a South Sudanese liberation movement formed by ex-Anya Nya I soldiers who mutinied in the town of Akobo on March 5, 1975, after they had defied orders to transfer them to north Sudan. Their goal was to fight for an independent South Sudan. The Anya Nya II movement carried on the struggle for seven years before the SPLA was created in 1983 by a group of prominent south Sudanese politicians and former army soldiers who mutinied in May 1983 at Bor, Pochalla, Pibor, Ayod, and Wankei.

Vincent Kuany Latjor was the Anya Nya II chairman and Gordon Koang Chol his deputy. Following a 1983 disagreement among south Sudanese in Ethiopia over the issue of leadership, the Anya Nya II leadership was changed, and Akuot Atem was chosen to head the movement, with Samuel Gai Tut as his deputy and William Chuol Deng as chief of staff. The Anya Nya II fighters withdrew to Sudan after combined Ethiopian soldiers and supporters of Colonel John Garang attacked their operational headquarters at Bilpam in October 1983. Subsequently, following intensified wars between the Anya Nya II and the SPLA forces, the former elected leaders were brutally killed by the SPLA in March 1984 and July 1985. Following the death of all three principal Anya Nya II leaders and while Vincent Kuany remained in prison inside Ethiopia, Gordon Koang took over the Anya Nya II leadership until the two groups finally reconciled their differences and united again in 1987–1988 under Colonel John Garang's leadership of the SPLM/SPLA. The other Anya Nya II splinter groups, which were opposing unity with SPLA under John Garang, remained in opposition. Four Anya Nya II commanders led those groups: Paulino Matip Nhial, William Reath Gai, Tang Ginya, and Gordon Koang Banypiny. These four leaders finally joined the SPLA Nasir Faction following the split within the SPLA on August 28, 1991.

Abdalla Turabi, Dr. Hassan—leader of the National Islamic Front (NIF), the ruling Islamic fundamentalist party in Sudan, which was renamed as National Congress Party in 1999. Turabi was a former lecturer at Khartoum University, Faculty of Law. He is the chairman of NIF and self-proclaimed spiritual leader of Islamists in the Sudan. He occupies the position of the speaker of the National Assembly and the post of secretary general of the National Congress ruling party. On December 12, 1999, President Bashir deposed him and detained him for a long period after he was accused of undermining the president. He remained in opposition as chairman of the National Congress Party (NCP).

Akol Ajawin, Dr. Lam—former lecturer at Khartoum University, Faculty of Engineering. Dr. Akol completed his postgraduate studies in the United Kingdom, where he earned a PhD in chemical engineering. He joined the SPLA in 1986. Having completed his military training at Bonga Training Centre, he was assigned to northern Upper Nile as zonal commander. He broke away from the SPLA under Colonel John Garang with Dr. Riek Machar and Commander Gordon Koang Chol on August 28, 1991, and formed the SPLA Nasir Faction. In 1993 he and Riek Machar, William Nyuon, Kerubino Kuanyin, Gordon Koang, Arok Thon, and Joseph Oduho met at Kongor in south Sudan and formed the SPLA-United. At the Akobo Convention in 1994, the SPLA-United was dissolved and its name changed to South Sudan Independence Movement/Army (SSIM/A) under the chairmanship of Dr. Riek Machar. Dr. Lam Akol remained the leader of a splinter group, SPLA-United. Toward the end of September 1997, he pledged his full support to the April 21, 1997, Peace Agreement and finally signed the agreement in Fashoda, South Sudan, with the Sudanese government delegation. He held several ministerial positions, including that of foreign affairs. In the 2010 Sudan general elections, Dr. Lam Akol contested for the post of president of GOSS, challenging the incumbent President Kiir, but he was defeated. He is the chairman of SPLM—DC and the main opposition leader in the national assembly in South Sudan.

Akuon, Joseph Otew—was deputy to General Joseph Lagu, leader of Southern Sudan Liberation Movement (SSLM), the political wing of the Anya Nya I movement. A tough guerrilla fighter, he was trained in Israel during the first Sudanese civil war. He was killed by north Sudanese Arab troops in 1971 at Khor Ploos—about ten kilometers from Malakal. Akuon died a few months before the signing of the Addis Ababa Accord, which granted southern Sudan local autonomy within the framework of a united socialist Sudan.

His death was regarded by most of his colleagues and supporters as a great setback for the Anya Nya I movement.

Awet Akot, Daniel—member of the SPLA Politico-Military High Command (PMHC) and zonal commander for northern Bahr El Ghazal region from 1987. Awet was accused of liquidating some of his SPLA colleagues from the Nuer ethnic group who were under his command in Bahr El Ghazal following the split within the SPLA leadership in 1991. Following the CPA, he held several important positions, including that of governor of Lakes state and minister of interior. He served as the deputy speaker of the South Sudan National Assembly.

Bol, Samuel Aru—Prominent South Sudanese politician. He served as vice president of the High Executive Council and Minister of Administration, Police and Prison during 1978–1979 under the presidency of General Joseph Lagu. He also held the post of deputy prime minister of Sudan during the Transitional Military Council (TMC), which overthrew President Nimeiri in April 1985. Bol was deputy chairman of the Union of Sudan African Parties (USAP) and one of the seven south Sudanese leaders who signed the April 21, 1997, Peace Agreement with President Omar Hassan El Bashir. He died of natural causes while in Khartoum.

Bol Akok, Benjamin—former deputy speaker of the People's Regional Assembly, member of Parliament, and minister of agriculture and natural resources in the regional government of southern Sudan in 1978. Bol was first SPLM/SPLA spokesman in the UK from 1983 to 1984. On his trip to the Ethiopian capital Addis Ababa in 1984, Bol was arrested and murdered by SPLA agents, apparently in collaboration with Ethiopian security, for unknown reasons.

Chol, Gordon Koang—former Anya Nya II leader and a veteran Anya Nya I soldier during the first Sudanese civil war. In 1972 he and a few of his colleagues refused to recognize the Addis Ababa Agreement. He remained in Ethiopia as a refugee until he eventually joined the mutinied soldiers from Akobo in 1975 and formed the Anya Nya II movement. In October 1983 combined Ethiopian soldiers and Colonel John Garang's SPLA supporters attacked his headquarters at Bilpam. He and his forces evacuated Ethiopia and returned to Sudan, where he handed over the leadership of Anya Nya II to Akuot Atem de Mayan, who was previously and officially elected as chairman of the joint SPLA and Anya Nya II movements. Chol assumed the chairmanship of Anya Nya II following the death of Akuot Atem de Mayan, Samuel Gai Tut, and William Chuol Deng in 1985 and remained in opposition against the SPLA. After discreet negotiations, he joined the SPLA ranks with his supporters in 1987–1988. Gordon Koang Chol was one of the three SPLA senior commanders who broke away from Colonel John Garang in 1991 and formed the Nasir Faction of the SPLA, which was sometime later renamed SSIM/A. After the signing of the CPA in 2005, General Gordon Koang Chol and some of his followers refused to join the government of South Sudan under the leadership of General Salva Kiir Mayardit and thus remained in opposition, supported by Khartoum, under the SSDF splinter leadership.

Chuol Deng, William—veteran Anya Nya I guerrilla fighter. After the Addis Ababa Agreement in February 1972, he was absorbed into the Sudanese Armed Forces with the rank of captain. In 1974 he was dismissed from the army together with Colonel Samuel Gai Tut when they opposed the proposal to transfer south Sudanese soldiers to north Sudan. He was also implicated in the Akobo uprising of 1975, during which he was arrested. After his release from jail, he served as administrator in Malakal town. He left Sudan during 1983 and joined the Anya Nya II movement. Following the formation of the SPLA, he was elected deputy chief of staff to Colonel Garang, who was elected at the time as the chief of staff of the new movement under Akuot Atem de Mayan's leadership. In August 1983, Chuol and other Anya Nya II leaders left Ethiopia and returned to Sudan. He continued as chief of staff and later took over the leadership of the movement following the death of Samuel Gai Tut and Akuot de Mayan. SPLA forces killed him on July 5, 1985.

Ding Wol, Lual—former member of the People's Regional Assembly at Juba. He joined the SPLA movement in early 1985. In 1988 Ding was promoted to the membership of the so-called PMHC, where he became Colonel John Garang's personal advisor. He held such positions as advisor to both John Garang and the GOSS under the leadership of Salva Kiir. He served as member of the National Legislative Assembly as an MP and was a renowned politician.

Gual, Peter Gatkuoth—former vice president of the High Executive Council and regional minister of finance and economic planning. Gual held other political positions both in the south and in the central government, including commissioner of Upper Nile province, minister of industry and mining, caretaker president of the HEC following the resignation of General Joseph Lagu in 1979, and minister of transport in the central government in 1985. Gual passed away in London in January 1992.

Gai, David Dak Biey—former first secretary at the Sudanese Embassy in Tanzania in 1980. He left his job in 1981 and joined the Anya Nya II movement, where he became its secretary general. In 1982 Gai was kidnapped with other Anya Nya II political leaders in Nairobi, Kenya, and sent to Sudan by Sudanese agents in collaboration with Kenyan security. Gai and his colleagues were in coffin boxes after having been injected with a sleeping medicine and deported back to Sudan. Gai was released after the fall of President Nimeiri. He joined the SPLA in 1985; he participated actively in SPLA military operations in the Equatoria and Bahr El Ghazal regions. In 1987 he and Daniel Koat Matthews successfully brought the SPLA and Anya Nya II together. He died in January 1990 in Addis Ababa, Ethiopia.

Hassan Bashir, Lieutenant General Omar—president of Sudan since June 1989. General El Bashir came to power through a bloodless military coup, which he waged on June 30, 1989. He overthrew the elected civilian prime minister, Sadiq El Mahdi. President Bashir is a member of the National Islamic Front (NIF), headed by the well-known self-proclaimed spiritual Islamist leader Dr. Hassan Abdalla Turabi. El Bashir had been fighting the SPLA forces in southern Sudan before he took power from Sadiq El Mahdi. He served as commander of Mayom garrison in western Upper Nile region for four years before the garrison of Mayom was finally overrun by SPLA forces under Commander Riek Machar. El Bashir signed the Khartoum Peace Agreement with his erstwhile enemy, Riek Machar, with the aim of bringing the ongoing civil strife in southern Sudan to an end. His government negotiated the peace agreement and signed the CPA with the SPLM/SPLA under Dr. John Garang in 2005 in Nairobi, Kenya.

Emperor Haile Selassie—The ruler of Ethiopia from 1930 and the architect of the Addis Ababa Agreement, which brought peace in Sudan after seventeen years of civil war between north and south Sudan. He was murdered by military coup leaders under the chairmanship of Colonel Mengistu Haile Mariam in 1974.

Muortart Mayen, Gordon—trained police officer who later joined politics and became a minister in the Sudan before joining the Anya Nya liberation movement in the 1960s. He was elected president of Nile Provisional Government. He denounced the Addis Ababa Agreement as a sellout. Gordon moved to the UK and remained a position leader in the Sudan. He joined the Anya Nya II during its formation but later declined. Following the signing of the CPA, he was nominated as member of parliament representing his constituency in Lakes state. He died in 2009.

Sir El Khatim, El Khalifa—former director general of Sudan. Following the overthrow of the Sudan military dictator, General Ibrahim Abboud, in 1964 through a popular uprising, Sir El Khatim was installed as caretaker president of the Republic of Sudan pending general elections, which later brought Prime Minister Sadiq El Mahdi to power in 1966.

Haile Mariam, Mengistu—former ruler of Ethiopia from 1974 to 1991. He came to power through a military coup that overthrew the Emperor Haile Selassie in 1974. Haile Mariam received support since 1975 from Eastern socialist bloc countries, from which he solicited military support against the secessionist and liberation movements in northern Ethiopia. Colonel Mengistu supported the SPLM/SPLA Movement from 1983 until combined EPRDF and EPLF opposition forces finally overthrew his Marxist regime on May 25, 1991.

Igga, James Wani—freedom fighter and politician. Igga is a trained economist from Egypt who joined the SPLA in 1984. He was one of the fifteen strongest SPLA Military High Command under Colonel John Garang. Igga held several positions in the movement, including that of secretary general of the SPLM. He had been the speaker of the South Sudan Legislation

Assembly twice, before and after the independence of the Republic of South Sudan. He is the vice president of the Republic of South Sudan.

Jaden, Aggrey—prominent politician and the first south Sudanese to graduate from Khartoum University, in 1950. Jaden was one of the four south Sudanese who were allocated four positions from the eight hundred positions left by the British colonial administration to be filled by Sudanese following the declaration of independence of the Sudan on January 1, 1956. He fled to exile in 1958 and formed the Sudan Africa National Union (SANU) together with Joseph Oduho and William Deng Nhial. Jaden was one of the south Sudanese politicians who denounced the Addis Ababa Agreement of 1972, calling it a sellout. Therefore, he remained in exile until 1978, when he returned to Sudan. He died in Juba in 1987.

Joak, John Luk—prominent lawyer and politician. He was elected to the Regional Assembly from 1978 to 1981. He left Sudan in the early 1980s to go to the UK for postgraduate studies. In 1983 John Luk became a member of the SPLM Central Committee in the UK, acting at the same time as spokesman of the movement. Following the split within the SPLA in August 1991, he and some of his colleagues joined the Nasir Faction, where he retained his position as spokesman. On August 14, 1995, he and some SSIM/A senior commanders broke away from Commander Riek Machar and formed their own splinter faction with the support of the SPLA leader Colonel John Garang. Commander William Nyuon Bany led the new breakaway group, SSIM (II). Following the death of William Nyuon Bany in January 1996, John Luk assumed the leadership of the group, and he and his supporters finally rejoined SPLA Mainstream in 1996. Colonel John Garang appointed him his secretary for culture and information, a post he was relieved from two years later. After the signing of the CPA, he held several ministerial positions in the SPLM-led government. He also served as minister of justice and a member in the National Assembly. Following the outbreak of the current civil war, John Luk and ten other colleagues were briefly detained by the government of Salva Kiir and accused of masterminding a failed coup d'etat that was claimed by the government to have been orchestrated by Dr. Riek Machar, former vice president of South Sudan. However, he was later released along with his detained colleagues and taken to Kenya by the Kenyan President Uhuru Kenyatta. He remained in opposition against the government in Juba under the SPLM-FD.

Nhial, William Deng—prominent politician who joined the South Sudan struggle in the 1960s and formed Sudan Africa National Union (SANU) along with his colleagues Aggrey Jaden and Joseph Oduho in east Africa. In 1964 internal disagreements over the leadership of SANU arose in which William Deng returned to Sudan and continued as opposition leader under SANU. He was murdered by Sudan armed forces on May 5, 1968, while conducting an election campaign in his home area Tonj, Bahr El Ghazal province.

Khalid, Dr. Mansour—former Sudanese foreign minister under President Nimeiri and one of the architects of the Addis Ababa Accord of 1972. He resigned from his position and went to exile in the United States and later to Europe, where he worked with the United Nations Environmental Programme. Khalid joined the SPLA in 1984 and became political advisor to Dr. John Garang. After the CPA, he was appointed presidential advisor in the government of National Unity. He is a prominent Sudan politician and a writer.

Kuanyin Bol, Major Kerubino—former army major and leader of the Bor Mutiny on May 15, 1983. Upon his arrival in Ethiopia he declared his support to Colonel John Garang, who appointed him his deputy. Following a disagreement with Garang, Kuanyin was detained from 1988 to 1992. He escaped to Uganda along with Arok Thon Arok and later formed the SPLA-United together with Riek Machar, William Nyuon, Lam Akol, Joseph Oduho, Arok Thon, Peter Abdelrahman Sule, Atem Gualdit, Gordon Koang Chol, and others in March 1993. He was appointed deputy to Commander Riek Machar. However, a year later he broke away again and established his own organization. Kuanyin was the leader of the SPLA-BGG, one of the six south Sudanese groups that signed the Khartoum Peace Agreement with the Sudanese government on April 21, 1997. He redefected to the SPLA faction of Colonel John Garang on December 28, 1997, but again broke away from Garang's group and sought refuge at Mankien in the Bentiu area under the protection of General Paulino Matip Nhial, where he met his death at the hands of Matip's mutinied soldiers who defected to the SPLA on September 10, 1999.

Kiir Mayardit, Salva—former captain in the Sudanese Intelligence Service. Mayardit left Sudan in May 1983 along with Colonel Garang and others and went to Ethiopia. When Colonel Garang became the leader of the SPLM/SPLA in July 1983, Mayardit was appointed SPLA deputy chief of staff for security and operations. After the August 1991 split in the ranks of the movement, Mayardit became Colonel Garang's number two in command and assumed the overall leadership of the SPLM/SPLA following the death of John Garang in a helicopter crash on July 30, 2005. He became first vice president of the Republic of Sudan and president of the Government of South Sudan (GOSS). After South Sudan gained its independence from Sudan on July 9, 2011, General Salva Kiir was confirmed president of the newly born Republic of South Sudan. He retained the position of SPLM chairmanship. In July 2013 he dissolved his entire cabinet and apparently sacked his long-time vice president, Dr. Riek Machar. However, in December 2013 President Kiir instigated the conflict within the SPLM party that resulted to the Juba massacre of over twenty thousand unarmed Nuer civilians by his tribal militias known as Dutkubeny and Gelweng, numbering fifteen thousand Dinka youth, which he trained, armed, and deployed at his farm at Lure—about ten kilometers from Juba town—before the outbreak of fighting in Juba.

Lagu Yanga, Retired Major General Joseph—former leader of Southern Sudan Liberation Movement (SSLM), better known as Anya Nya. In February 1972 he signed the Addis Ababa Accord with President Nimeiri, which ended the seventeen-year civil war in the Sudan. President Nimeiri appointed Joseph Lagu as major general in the Sudanese Armed Forces. After his retirement from the army, he joined active politics and was elected by his supporters to the Regional Assembly in 1978 as president of the High Executive Council. In January 1980 he resigned from his position after the opposition group in the Regional Assembly accused him of corruption. In 1981 he instigated the redivision of the south into three fragile regions. In 1983 President Nimeiri appointed him as his second vice president. Until late 1999 General Lagu was working under the NIF government as roving ambassador. Following the signing of the CPA in 2005, General Lagu shifted his support to the SPLM-led government in South Sudan and President Kiir appointed him as one of his presidential advisors.

Lado, Lakurnyang—former law student at Cairo University in Khartoum and human rights activist. Before joining Anya Nya II in the middle of 1982, Lado was the leader of the Front for the Liberation of Southern Sudan; a youth-dominated political organization that was in operation throughout southern Sudan from 1981 to 1983. In 1984 SPLA soldiers caught him in his village at Pibor district. Lado was taken to Ethiopia and executed at the SPLA military training center at Bonga in September 1984. He never supported the SPLM/SPLA policy of a united new Sudan. Lado was a diehard South Sudan separation advocate from his school days. This was his only crime that led to his execution by the SPLM/SPLA leadership.

Lugi Adwok, Dr. Ogwo—worked with ICRC in South Sudan before the split within the SPLA in August 1991. After the split, SPLA agents of Colonel John Garang at Loki, northern Kenya, kidnapped and secretly smuggled him into south Sudan, where he was summarily executed. He was accused of supporting the breakaway group of the SPLA Nasir Faction.

Matthews, Daniel Koat—veteran Anya Nya I freedom fighter and former regional minister of youth and sports in 1978 and regional minister of industry and mining in 1982. Matthews was the first governor of Upper Nile region after the redivision of the southern part of Sudan into three regions in June 1983. After the fall of Nimeiri in 1985, he joined the SPLA movement in 1986 and was commissioned as captain. Matthews actively played an important role in reconciling the SPLA and Anya Nya II in 1987. He chose self-imposed exile in Sweden. Daniel Koat Matthews is one of the prominent South Sudanese politicians. He returned to South Sudan after the signing of the CPA but left again following the outbreak of the current civil war in South Sudan and is currently living in Nairobi, Kenya.

Malwal Madut, Bona—former minister of culture and information in the central government under President Nimeiri in the 1970s. He also held some important ministerial positions in the regional government in the south, including finance and economic planning and industry and mining during Abel Alier's second term in office from 1980 to 1982. While living in his self-imposed exile in the UK, Madut in 1990 established a newsletter known as "The Sudan Democratic Gazette." He is a member of the Asmara-based north Sudanese–dominated opposition group National Democratic Alliance (NDA). Following the signing of the CPA and subsequent declaration of the independence of the Republic of South Sudan, Madut remained in his self-exile in the UK. He is a renowned South Sudanese politician and writer.

Majier Gai, Martin—a veteran south Sudanese politician, he was regional minister of coordination and legal affairs from 1980 to 1982 and a prominent lawyer. Majier joined the SPLA in 1983 and served as the movement's secretary for legal affairs. He wrote the draft of the famous SPLM Manifesto. After he differed with Colonel Garang politically, the SPLA leader ordered Majier's detention in early 1988. While in detention Majier was murdered by SPLA agents in 1993.

Machar Teny-Dhurgon, Dr. Riek—former lecturer at Khartoum University, Faculty of Engineering. Machar earned a PhD in Mechanical Engineering at Bradford University, UK. He joined the SPLA during its inception in 1983 and served as SPLA zonal commander for the whole western Upper Nile region. Dr. Machar defected from the SPLA mainstream under Colonel John Garang on August 28, 1991, together with Dr. Lam Akol Ajawin and Commander Gordon Koang Chol. Together with other SPLA senior commanders, Machar formed the SPLA Nasir Faction under his leadership. The SPLA Nasir Faction was renamed SPLM/SPLA-United following the defection of Commander William Nyuon Bany on September 27, 1992, from the SPLA mainstream. SPLM/SPLA-United later changed to South Sudan Independence Movement/Army (SSIM/SSIA), after the Akobo Convention in October 1994. On April 10, 1996, Machar and Kerubino Kuanyin Bol, leader of the SPLA/BGG, signed a Political Charter with an aim to end the war in south Sudan. On April 21, 1997, Dr. Machar and five other factional leaders signed the Peace Agreement with the Sudan government of General Omar El Bashir.

Among those who signed the Peace Agreement were Commander Kerubino Kuanyin Bol of the SPLM/SPLA Bahr El Ghazal Group, Dr. Theophilous Ochang Luti of the Equatoria Defence Force, Commander Arok Thon Arok of Bor Citizens Alliance, Samuel Aru Bol of Union of Sudan African Parties (USAP), and Commander Kawach Makwei of South Sudan Independence Group. The SPLA/SPLM under Colonel John Garang refused to participate in the agreement. In January 2000 Machar redefected to south Sudan's bush and formed his own organization, known as Sudan People's Democratic Movement (SPDF/A). In January 2002 Machar and John Garang signed the merger that brought the two factions of the SPLA under the unified leadership of John Garang. Machar was made second deputy of the SPLM/SPLA. Following the death of John Garang in July 2005, Machar was appointed deputy chairman of the SPLM and vice president of the GOSS by President Salva Kiir Mayardit. He retained the same post of vice president of the Republic of South Sudan until July 2013, when he was unceremoniously removed from his position by President Salva Kiir Mayardit. In December 2013 he and his colleagues from the SPLM Political Bureau had attempted to challenge President Kiir when he announced his interest to run in the next general elections against the incumbent president with the SPLM party ticket. Dr. Riek Machar and some of his colleagues, including his wife, Madam Angelina Teny, escaped death following the fighting in the Tiger Headquarters in Juba, in which about thirty-five of his personal aides were unfortunately massacred in his own official residential quarter by government soldiers. His house was completely demolished by tanks and heavy weapons when the government soldiers killed all the residents found inside the vice president's complex. Since then he has formed a resistance movement known as SPLM/A-IO, which is waging a protracted war against the tyrant regime of Salva Kiir in Juba.

de Mabior, John Garang—during the first Sudanese civil war in the 1960s, he fled to east Africa, where he completed his undergraduate education at Dar es Salaam University in Tanzania before going to the United States for further studies in 1968. He returned to Sudan in 1972, following the Addis Ababa Agreement, and was absorbed into Anya Nya I with the rank of captain. He served in the army at the Bor garrison before leaving Sudan again in 1977–1978 for postgraduate studies in the United States. He returned to Sudan in 1982 and served in the Sudanese Armed Forces with the rank of colonel and lectured on a part-time basis in the University of Khartoum's Faculty of Agriculture. While in the army, he earned a PhD in rural economy from Iowa State University. In May 1983 he was dispatched by President Nimeiri to negotiate with mutinying soldiers at his hometown of Bor. Instead of returning to Khartoum, having failed to convince the mutinying soldiers and the commanding officers, Colonel Garang followed the rebel soldiers who were on their way to Ethiopia. While at Itang Refugee Camp, Dr. Garang, in collaboration with the Ethiopian government, usurped the movement's leadership from his uncle Akuot Atem de Mayan, who was overwhelmingly elected by South Sudanese rebels as the head of their movement. Colonel Garang remained head of the SPLM/SPLA mainstream faction, a movement that continuously disintegrated into several factions afterward. Colonel Garang signed the CPA with President Omar El Bashir to end the ongoing war in the Sudan. On July 9, 2005, he was appointed by Presider El Bashir as his first vice president and president of the Government of South Sudan (GOSS). He died in a helicopter crash on his way back from Uganda on July 30, 2005.

Madut, Dr. Carlo—former SPLM's SRRA health coordinator. Following the split within the SPLA movement, Madut joined the breakaway group, the Nasir Faction, where he became the director of its humanitarian wing RASS. In 1994 he resigned from his RASS position and went to Uganda, where his family was living at a refugee camp. Carlo was kidnapped by the SPLA agents from the camp in northern Uganda and taken to south Sudan, where he was executed.

Makur Aleyou, Martin—former Sudanese Army colonel who joined the SPLA in 1983 and became the zonal commander of northern Bahr El Ghazal region. He was detained in 1985 until Colonel Garang's security agents murdered him in detention in 1993 together with Judge Martin Majier and Colonel Martin Majbour.

Al Mahdi, Sadiq Abdulrahman—leader of the Umma Party and a great grandson of Mohammed Ahmed ibn Abdalla, who proclaimed himself Mahdi (literally savior). At the age of twenty-nine, Sadiq became prime minister, serving between 1966 and 1967 and again from 1986 to 1989. In June 1989 General Omar Hassan El Bashir, in collaboration with the NIF, overthrew Mahdi's second civilian regime. In 1997 he escaped from Sudan and joined the National Democratic Alliance—a coalition of different opposition groups in the Sudan including the SPLA faction of Dr. John Garang opposing El Bashir's government. The NDA's objective was to overthrow Bashir's government and replace it with a secular one. He is a prominent Sudanese politician in opposition to the government of General El Bashir in Khartoum.

Nimeiri, Jaafar Mohammed—was enrolled into the Sudanese Military Academy in the 1950s. While serving in the army, Colonel Nimeiri staged a bloodless military coup, supported by the Sudanese Communist Party, on May 25, 1969. He overthrew a coalition civilian government led by Mohammed Ahmed Maghoub. In 1971 Major Hashim Al Atta, Major Farouq Hamdalla, and Colonel Babikir El Nur staged a Communist coup against President Nimeiri. Following his divorce from the Communist Party, Nimeiri abandoned its agenda and adopted a pan-Arabist program. A year after the Communist coup, Nimeiri concluded the Addis Ababa Agreement with the south Sudanese rebels, which granted the south regional autonomy within the framework of a united socialist Sudan. In 1983 he abrogated the Addis Ababa Accord and at the same time proclaimed Islamic sharia law in Sudan on September 24, 1983. Nimeiri's defense minister, General Abdul Rahman Sawar El Dahab, removed him from power through a military coup on April 6, 1985, while his boss was on an official visit in the United States. Nimeiri spent nearly fourteen years in Egypt, where he took refuge following his overthrow and returned to Sudan on May 22, 1999. He died in Khartoum thereafter.

Nyuon Bany, Major William—a tough guerrilla fighter who joined Any Nya I in the beginning of the 1960s. In 1972 Nyuon was absorbed into the Sudanese Armed Forces with the rank of captain. He was later promoted to the rank of major. During his service in the army, Nyuon was in charge of military operations against Anya Nya II guerrillas in the south. In June 1983 he led the mutiny at Ayod and joined other south Sudanese in Ethiopia. Colonel

Garang appointed him his chief of staff, and he assumed the position of deputy chairmanship of the SPLM following the detention of Kerubino Kuanyin Bol in 1988. Nyuon led the SPLA mainstream delegation to the Abuja Peace Talks with the Sudan government in May 1992. Commander William Nyuon broke away from the SPLA faction of Colonel John Garang on September 27, 1992, and formed his own independent group, which he christened SPLA Forces of Unity. In March 1993 Nyuon and other south Sudanese opposition groups formed the SPLA-United at Kongor on March 26, 1993. On August 14, 1995, while in Nairobi, he and some SSIM/A commanders declared the overthrow of Dr. Riek Machar from the SSIM/A leadership, with Nyuon as the new chairman and commander in chief of the movement. With support from the SPLA mainstream leader, Commander William Nyuon was flown to Kongor, the birthplace of John Garang. From there he attacked and briefly occupied the town of Ayod from Commander Riek Machar's forces. A few weeks later, he was driven out from Ayod to Kongor, and in early January 1996, he came back and reoccupied Ayod, driving the forces of Riek Machar from the town. He was finally killed at Ayod on January 15, 1996.

Ngor Machiek, Lieutenant Colonel Francis—former Sudanese Army officer and a founding member of the SPLA in 1983. Commander Ngor was one of the first SPLA commanders sent by Colonel Garang in 1985 to fight against Gajaak Nuer civilians at Jakou area. Commander Ngor was killed while fighting the Nuer civilians at Manjangdit near Malual Gahoth.

Nyachiluk, Nyachigak—one of the university students who left Sudan along with Lakurnyang Lado late in 1982 for Ethiopia with the intention of joining Anya Nya II, already stationed there. Nyachiluk defected from Anya Nya II in 1983 and joined the SPLA, where he was promoted to the rank of alternate commander after he treacherously captured his former colleague Lakurnyang Lado from a village located in his home area, Pibor. Nyachiluk took Lado to Ethiopia, where his boss Colonel John Garang executed him in September 1984 at Bonga Training Centre. Nyachigak was eventually killed in Kapoeta in January 1985 by Sudanese government troops.

Oduho, Joseph—one of the South Sudanese nationalist leaders, a teacher by profession, first elected to the National Assembly in Khartoum in 1958.

He went into exile during the 1960s, when he and other south Sudanese intellectuals formed the Sudan African National Union (SANU). Oduho was a founding member of Anya Nya, and he was elected chairman of the SANU, the political wing of the Anya Nya movement. Following the Addis Ababa Agreement of February 1972, he went back to Sudan and joined in politics. He held various positions in the regional government, including minister of public service and manpower. In 1983 he went to Ethiopia and formed the SPLA with other south Sudanese leaders. He served as SPLM foreign affairs secretary. In 1988 he disagreed with Colonel Garang, whom he accused of running the movement in a dictatorial way. He was in detention from 1988 until he finally escaped to Uganda through the help of some SPLA deserters in 1992. In March 1993 he traveled to Kongor, where he met other factional leaders and formed the SPLA-United under the chairmanship of Dr. Riek Machar. While still in Kongor on March 27, 1993, he was killed by SPLA forces of Colonel John Garang who attacked the town of Panyigor.

Obur Ayang, Matthew—former speaker of the People's Regional Assembly and minister of education and guidance in the regional government from 1978 to 1980. In 1983 President Nimeiri detained Obur and others because they opposed the redivision of southern Sudan into three regions. Following his release from detention at the notorious Kober state prison in 1984, Obur escaped to Ethiopia with the intention of joining the SPLA. Known for his radical views, Obur disagreed with Colonel John Garang. He criticized the latter for encouraging disunity among south Sudanese people. In early 1985 he left Ethiopia for Kenya and finally went to Sudan after the fall of President Nimeiri in April 1985. He died in a South African hospital in 2011, and his body was brought back to South Sudan and buried in his hometown, Malakal.

Osman El Mirghani, Mohammed—leader of the Democratic Unionist Party (DUP), a coalition partner of Umma Party during the civilian administration under Prime Minister Sadiq El Mahdi, 1986–1989. El Mirghani's party signed a memorandum of understanding with the SPLA in November 1988 that became known as the SPLA/DUP Accord. He joined the opposition forces after the military coup that brought Omar El Bashir to power and formed the National Democratic Alliance (NDA) under his chairmanship. He lived in Khartoum as an opposition leader to President Omar El Bashir's government.

Sudan People's Liberation Movement and Sudan People's Liberation Army (SPLM/SPLA)—formed by a group of prominent south Sudanese politicians and former soldiers who mutinied at Bor, Pochalla, Pibor, and Ayod in 1983. The SPLM/SPLA was created in July 1983 with the goal of establishing a "United Secular New Sudan" based on equality, freedom, and social justice. Akuot Atem de Mayan was elected its chairman. Other important positions were distributed as follows: Samuel Gai Tut to head the defense, Joseph Oduho for foreign affairs, Colonel John Garang as chief of staff, and Martin Majier Gai for legal affairs. But Colonel Garang refused to abide by the results of the election. He assumed the position of chairmanship with the help of Colonel Mengistu Haile Mariam, the ruler of Ethiopia. After August 1991 the movement disintegrated into several factions, some of which signed a peace agreement with the Sudanese government. In 2005 the SPLM/SPLA under the overall leadership of Colonel John Garang signed the Comprehensive Peace Agreement (CPA) with Khartoum in order to bring the war in Sudan to an end. During the interim period and after the independence of the Republic of South Sudan from Sudan on July 9, 2011, the SPLM/SPLA remained the ruling party in the country.

Tut, Samuel Gai—a veteran Anya Nya I commander during the 1960s and prominent south Sudanese politician. Following the Addis Ababa Agreement in 1972, Gai was absorbed into the Sudanese Armed Forces with the rank of lieutenant colonel. Two years later President Nimeiri dismissed Gai from the army after he disagreed with his boss, Major General Joseph Lagu, when he objected to the transfer of south Sudanese soldiers to north Sudan. In 1978 he was elected in his constituency, Waat, as a member of the People's Regional Assembly in Juba. Gai served as minister of wildlife conservation and tourism twice. In 1983 he left Sudan and joined the Anya Nya II movement in Ethiopia. SPLA forces at Adura, Ethiopia, brutally killed him on March 28, 1984.

Tutlam, Dr. Timothy Tongyik—a medical doctor by profession, Tutlam completed his higher education and university while in exile and remained in Ethiopia following the Addis Ababa Accord. He continued practicing his medical career in various locations in Ethiopia, while at the same time being active in south Sudanese politics. He joined the SPLA movement in 1988, following the unification of the SPLM/SPLA and Anya Nya II movements under the unified leadership of Dr. John Garang de Mabior. Following the SPLA split in 1991, Dr. Timothy narrowly escaped death from John Garang's loyalists while treating war wounded and civilians at Ashwa Clinic at Magwei County, CES, and fled to Uganda with the help of some local people from that county. Dr. Timothy was elected governor of Upper Nile state after the signing of the April 21, 1997, Khartoum Peace Agreement. He died in a misterous plane crash in Nasir along with the Sudan Vice President General Zubier Mohammed Salah, Arok Thon Arok and several others on 12 February 1998.

Thon Arok, Arok—served as major in the Sudanese Armed Forces, intelligence unit. He left Sudan in 1983 and joined other south Sudanese who fled to Ethiopia. Arok was appointed the SPLA deputy chief of staff for administration and logistics, but SPLM/SPLA leader Colonel John Garang arrested him in 1987 on charges that he had attempted to overthrow him from the SPLA leadership. Major Arok Thon escaped together with Kerubino Kuanyin from SPLA detention in 1992, with the help of Commander William Nyuon Bany following his defection from the SPLA, and crossed the border into Uganda. Arok was one of the six south Sudanese leaders who signed the Khartoum Peace Agreement with the Sudanese government of Omar El Bashir on April 21, 1997, as a result of which he was promoted to the military rank of brigadier. He died in a plane crash in Nasir on February 12, 1998.

Tang, Joseph Kiir—former sergeant major in the Sudanese Armed Forces and one of the ringleaders of the mutinying soldiers at Bor. Tang took over the command after Battalion 105 commanding officer Major Kerubino Kuanyin was seriously wounded during the fighting. Upon his arrival in Ethiopia, Tang placed all Battalion 105 military hardware at Anya Nya II headquarters at Bilpam, instead of taking them up to the refugee camp at Itang where Major Kerubino and others were. Colonel Garang's loyalists executed Tang upon Colonel Garang's orders following the attack on the Anya Nya II camp in October 1983, because the guns that he personally stored at the Anya Nya

II camp where taken or used by them during the fighting against the SPLA and Ethiopian forces.

Yac Arop, Dr. Justin—a gynecologist and a former regional minister of health and social welfare. Yac joined the SPLA in 1984 and became its first secretary general for humanitarian affairs (SRRA). He was one of Colonel John Garang's close advisors. Dr. Yac held numerous ministerial positions in the regional government and the GOSS. He died in a plane crash on May 2, 1998, along with the SPLA minister of defence and veteran affairs, Lieutenant General Dominic Dim Deng.

Gore, Lt. General Alfred Ladu—former SPLA commander, MP, and minister of environment and natural resources. He narrowly escaped death from Salva Kiir's security agents in Juba as he walked on foot from Juba to Panyjiar, Unity state, with over three thousand SPLA soldiers who retreated from Juba following combined attacks on their positions held by the UPDF and government forces. He is currently the deputy chairman and deputy commander in chief of the SPLM/A-IO under the leadership of Dr. Riek Machar. He is a renowned and outspoken politician known throughout the country.

A SELECT BIBLIOGRAPHY

Albino, Oliver Batali. *The Sudan: A Southern Viewpoint*. London: Oxford University Press/Institute of Race Relations, 1970.

Alier, Abel. *Too Many Agreements Dishonoured; Southern Sudan*. Reading, UK: Ithaca Press. It was published in January 1990.

Collins, Robert O. *Shadows in the Grass: British in the Southern Sudan, 1898–1956*. New Haven and London: Yale University Press, 1983.

Comprehensive Peace Agreement (CPA): A collective of several protocols signed between the Government of Sudan and the SPLM on January 9, 2005, Nairobi, Kenya. It was disseminated to all SPLM/A members in Rumbek in February 2005.

First, Ruth. *Power in Africa*. New York: Pantheon Books, 1970.

Hoile, David. *Sudan, Propaganda and Distortion: Allegations of Slavery-Related Practices; An Open Letter to Baroness Cox and Christian Solidarity International*. London: The Sudan Foundation, 1997.

Interim National Constitution of the Republic of the Sudan & Interim Constitution of Southern Sudan; Ratified in 2005, in Khartoum and Juba, Sudan. It was distributed to all members of Southern Sudan Legislative Assembly in 2005.

Johnson, Douglas H. *African Issues; The Root Causes of Sudan's Civil Wars*. 2003, in UK.

Khalid, Mansour. *Nimeiri and the May Revolution of Dis-May*. London: KPI Limited, 1985.

O'Balance, Edgar. *The Secret War in the Sudan 1955–1972*. Plymouth: Latimer Trend & Company Ltd., 1977.

Southern Sudan Vision, issue No. 5, May 15, 1992. Published by the Department of Information and Culture, the Interim National Executive Committee of the SPLM, Nairobi, Kenya.

Spectrum, May/June 1991. Published bimonthly by News Bureau International, PO Box 87 Ellingsrudåsen, 1006 Oslo 10, Norway.

SPLM. *Sudan Today: A Collection of Talks Given at the Africa Centre, London, March 1985*. London: SPLM London office, 1985.

The Sudan Peace Agreement: The Republic Palace, Khartoum, April 21, 1997. It was later circulated in different news media.

About the Author

Daniel Wuor Joak

Hon. Daniel Joak was born on January 1, 1962, at Nyangore Payam, Ulang County, Upper Nile state in southern Sudan; he is the son of John Jock (Joak) Kong and Mary Chol Duoth. He grew up at Nyangore Payam during the first Sudanese civil war, which started with the Torit uprising on August 18, 1955, between successive Khartoum regimes and the South Sudan Liberation Movement, better known as the Anya Nya movement. This civil war ended with the signing of the Addis Ababa Agreement in 1972, which granted the people of southern Sudan local autonomy within a framework of a united Sudan. Following the Addis Ababa Agreement, Daniel Wuor attended primary school at Ulang Primary and thereafter finished his intermediate and part of secondary school in Juba and Nasir, respectively. In 1984 he joined the south Sudan liberation struggle in Ethiopia but did not participate in the front line because of internal disagreement within the two south Sudan liberation movements, the Anya Nya II and SPLM/SPLA. Toward the end of 1984, Daniel Wuor was taken to Kenya by UNHCR on transit and, in July 1985, to Norway for resettlement as a refugee. Daniel Wuor had both his secondary school and higher education in Norway, where he studied business administration and international marketing at the Norwegian School of Economics and Business Administration (NHH). He was also a political activist while in Norway. In 2002 he left Norway for Kenya, where he established a relief organization known as ACHA, which became a renowned national NGO in south Sudan during the war, assisting the needy people in Ulang County with basic humanitarian needs. When the Comprehensive Peace Agreement was concluded in January 2005, Daniel Wuor was nominated by the SPLM as an MP representing Ulang constituency in the South Sudan Legislative Assembly (SSLA). In 2013, he became the state minister of education, science, and technology in Upper Nile state. After war broke out in South Sudan in 2013, Daniel Wuor returned to Norway, where his family has been residing since, and he has continued with his political activism as before.

www.ingramcontent.com/pod-product-compliance
Lightning Source LLC
Chambersburg PA
CBHW031413290426
44110CB00011B/358